Peter Lombard observed that sacraments signify and sanctify. John Calvin similarly described sacraments as both signs and means of grace. Baptists are often regarded as theological outliers who reject this remarkable Protestant-Catholic *consensus fidelium*. Yet significant theological voices under the standard of "Baptist sacramentalism" have begun to challenge this popular assumption. Until recently it might have been thought that this retrieval movement was limited to a small group of English and Americans. This important study by Sergii Sannikov makes a compelling case that Baptist sacramentalism is not a Western theological phenomenon but deeply resonates with the faith and practice of Baptists in Eastern Europe. It deserves serious study by Baptists and non-Baptists alike.

Curtis W. Freeman, PhD
Research Professor of Theology and Baptist Studies,
Ruth D. Duncan Director of the Baptist House of Studies,
Duke Divinity School, North Carolina, USA

In this original and well-crafted book, the author breaks new ground by placing a sacramental theology in the context of Eastern European Baptist church life. While covering some familiar issues that have characterized recent writing on the renewal of Baptist sacramentality, he deals with them in a fresh way from his location in a church life which has been typically suspicious of sacramental language. Showing a masterly scholarly acquaintance with the wider historical Christian tradition, and with skillful awareness of the diversity of his own heritage in both East and West, he develops a compelling theology of divine presence, action and, encounter in the sacraments. This book is not only essential reading for fellow Baptists, but of great significance for ecumenical conversation.

Paul S. Fiddes, PhD
Professor of Systematic Theology,
University of Oxford, UK
Principal Emeritus and Senior Research Fellow,
Regent's Park College, Oxford, UK

Signs of the Presence

Signs of the Presence

Toward an Eastern European Baptist Sacramentalism

Sergii Sannikov

Translator

Rostislav Tkachenko

© 2025 Sergii Sannikov

Published 2025 by Langham Global Library
An imprint of Langham Publishing
www.langhampublishing.org

Langham Publishing and its imprints are a ministry of Langham Partnership

Langham Partnership
PO Box 296, Carlisle, Cumbria, CA3 9WZ, UK
www.langham.org

ISBNs:
978-1-78641-165-5 Print
978-1-78641-257-7 ePub
978-1-78641-258-4 PDF

Sergii Sannikov has asserted his right under the Copyright, Designs and Patents Act, 1988 to be identified as the Author of this work.

All rights reserved. No part of this publication may be reproduced, stored in a retrieval system or transmitted, in any form or by any means, electronic, mechanical, photocopying, recording or otherwise, without the prior written permission of the publisher or the Copyright Licensing Agency.

Requests to reuse content from Langham Publishing are processed through PLSclear. Please visit www.plsclear.com to complete your request.

Unless otherwise marked Scripture quotations are taken from the Holy Bible, New International Version®, NIV®. Copyright © 1973, 1978, 1984, 2011 by Biblica, Inc.™ Used by permission of Zondervan.

Scripture quotations marked (NRSV) are taken from the New Revised Standard Version Bible, copyright © 1989 National Council of the Churches of Christ in the United States of America. Used by permission. All rights reserved.

Scripture quotations marked (ESV) are taken from The Holy Bible, English Standard Version®(ESV®), copyright © 2001 by Crossway, a publishing ministry of Good News Publishers. Used by permission. All rights reserved.

British Library Cataloguing-in-Publication Data
A catalogue record for this book is available from the British Library

ISBN: 978-1-78641-165-5

Cover & Book Design: projectluz.com

Translated from the Ukranian by Rostislav Tkachenko

Langham Partnership actively supports theological dialogue and an author's right to publish but does not necessarily endorse the views and opinions set forth here or in works referenced within this publication, nor can we guarantee technical and grammatical correctness. Langham Partnership does not accept any responsibility or liability to persons or property as a consequence of the reading, use or interpretation of its published content.

Contents

Foreword ix
Introduction 1

1   A General Introduction to Baptist Sacramentalism 3
      General Signs of Presence 12
      Special Signs called Sacraments. 13
      The Church's Sacraments 15

2   The Theology of Baptism. 25
      A Convention or Reality? Baptism as a Symbol 35
      The Door to the Church: Baptism as Initiation. 39
      The Seal of the Covenant: Baptism as a Promise. 43
      Death and Resurrection: Baptism as Union with Christ 47
      A Sign of Grace: Baptism as a Means of Grace 54
      Proclaiming the Word: Baptism as a Confession of Faith 60
      Humble Receiving: Baptism as an Act of Obedience 65
      Baptism as Encounter. 70

3   The Eucharistic Theology 75
      The Lord's Supper in the Eastern European Context 82
      The Lord's Supper as Remembrance. 102
      The Lord's Supper as Proclamation of Christ's Death. 108
      The Lord's Supper as the Partaking of the Body and Blood of Christ . . . 112
      Symbol or Sign?. 120
      The Lord's Supper as Communion 125
      The Lord's Supper as Thanksgiving. 129
      The Lord's Supper as Sanctification. 133
      The Lord's Supper as a Foretaste of What Is to Come 143

4   Other Sacraments. 161
      Blessing. 169
      Sacrifice and Testimony. 172
      Ordination to Ministry. 175
      Post-Initiation 182
      Healings 184

| 5 | Practical Aspects of Church Ordinances | 203 |

    1. The Word 207
    2. Music 207
    3. Prayer 208
    4. Repentance 209
    5. Rituals 209
    6. Koinonia 210
    7. Contemplation 210
    Validity and Efficacy 212
    The Sacred and the Profane 217
    The Contingent Nature of the Encounter 224
    The Lord's Supper and the Pandemic 233
    The Lord's Supper and the War 235

Conclusion 239

Bibliography 241

Foreword

It is quite likely that, like myself, many of this book's readers could hardly imagine the conditions under which Sergii Sannikov has written this monograph. In an email sent as the manuscript neared completion, he shared, "Odesa is still being bombed regularly, but God is protecting us, and I am still serving in the church and seminary."[1] This is an important book, not just because what Sannikov has endured while writing it, but because of its contribution to the revival of sacramental thought among Baptists. Years of scholarly and pastoral service to Baptist churches and believers in Ukraine have positioned him, in a way few others are, to introduce and examine the sacramental thought of Eastern European Baptists. In so doing, he has added needed, original insight to the study of sacramental thought and practice among Baptists. In this space, I would like to call attention to three significant, related contributions Sannikov provides.

First, there should be no serious debate whether the "sacramental recovery" of recent decades among Baptists primarily in the United Kingdom and North America is in fact a recovery. It is indeed a recovery, not an innovation against the backdrop of a uniformly non- or anti-sacramental past, and certainly not deviation from such a past. One may debate whether holding sacramental views is a good thing for Baptists or not. Yet arguments against it cannot proceed by claiming the warrant of history. One need only read the early sources, the confessions and catechisms, the treatises and hymns, to discover abundant evidence, not just of sacramental terminology, but of sacramental imagination and thought. It is impossible to deny this with intellectual integrity. Even early Baptists' critiques of the sacramental ideas and practices of other churches, of sacraments and sacramental ideas *simpliciter*, are never complete and outright rejections. Their critique was for the sake of more faithful understanding of God's work in the church, and hence for a more faithful embodiment of the church.

The same intellectual integrity necessitates, however, that one must acknowledge that to say these true things about early Baptists does not say everything necessary and certainly does not end the argument outright. As

---

1. Sergii Sannikov, personal communication, July 12, 2025.

is well documented, Baptist thought on both sides of the Atlantic underwent significant changes in the centuries after the seventeenth century foundings of various Baptist movements. Though for different reasons, Baptists in North America and in the United Kingdom alike experienced a waning of sacramental awareness, not to mention sacramental thought, particularly in the early decades of the nineteenth century. In the United Kingdom, sacramental sensibility among Baptists was truncated. In North America, it was almost entirely lost.

Thus, by the time the Baptist movement took hold on the European continent, it had come to lack robust commitment to sacramentality. The Baptist life that grew in Ukrainian soil was more pietist than sacramentalist. The sacramental heritage of the seventeenth century was all but unknown. Sannikov does not attempt to evade this. Rather he turns to the lived experience of Baptists in Eastern Europe. As seems to be the case with all Baptists, there was variation among the Slavic Baptists. Yet he provides a thick description of their practice, showing clear evidence that there has been for them an experience of God's presence in baptism and the Lord's Supper, in Scripture and life together in Baptist community, and experience exceeding the categories by which these rites have been named and described. Thus, he formulates a theology adequate to the experience, and indeed for the sake of deepening that experience in contemporary practice.

In doing this, Sannikov's second contribution becomes evident. He brings Western and Eastern Baptist thought into creative and mutually critical dialogue, naming along the way important similarities and differences in their history and thought. In addition, he explores perennial questions of Baptist sacramental thought in ways that enables his readers to grasp how these questions may differ in an Eastern context: the relation of faith and baptism, what it means rightly to discern the body in the Lord's Supper, whether the bread should be leavened or unleavened. He offers richly textured discussions of the sacraments and time, and of questions of sacramental validity and efficacy, questions rarely asked by Baptists in the West.

There is a third contribution. Sannikov names clearly what is at the heart of Baptist sacramental theology: encounter with God. This rings deeply true to the theology of the early Baptists. It is the reality of encounter with Christ, not questions of substance and modes of presence or absence as in Catholic, Lutheran, Calvinist, and Zwinglian theology, that is essential to sacramental thought in a Baptist context, whether Western or Eastern. In this, though he never names explicitly, Sannikov explores at length what is at stake in holding baptism and the Supper to be sacraments of the encounter of Christ and the church. "Matter matters," he says at one point, critiquing Baptist tendencies at times to slip from thinking in spiritual modes to nearly gnostic ones. We might consider the stark words of the Lutheran theologian, Robert Jenson, that a disembodied presence cannot bless, but only curse.[2] This is an important word for Baptists who gather around the Bath and the Table in the midst of a world in which curse is keenly felt. And in this light, we must again acknowledge that we owe Sergii Sannikov a great debt of thanks for what he teaches us here. May the Christ who comes near in sacramental realities bless Sergii, and the sisters and brothers with whom he gathers in unimaginable conditions.

Philip E. Thompson, PhD
Kairos University/Sioux Falls Seminary

---

2. Robert W. Jenson, "The Church and the Sacraments," in *The Cambridge Companion to Christian Doctrine*, ed. Colin E. Gunton, (Cambridge University Press, 1997), 211, https://doi.org/10.1017/CCOL0521471184.013.

Introduction

The global crisis and the quest for a new world order have moved the world from the unstable state of postmodernity into a new era. We are witnessing a surge of new religiosity and a growing interest in mysticism and the sacred, albeit in a completely different form from that of the classical Middle Ages. This interest seems to reveal a deep-seated longing for a real, living communion with God, coupled with a suspicious attitude toward official, traditional forms of religion. The demand for an authentic experience of the divine presence is growing in historical churches, evangelical communities, and secular milieu.

This trend calls for a deep and holistic conception of sacramentality and sacramentalism. To address this challenge, I have undertaken a year-long study of Eastern European Baptist theology and church practices from a sacramental perspective, resulting in a three-volume series of books under the general title *The Signs of Presence*.[1] The present book is an abridged, condensed summary of these three volumes whose purpose is to introduce the English-speaking academic community to an avidly developing Eastern European evangelical theology and its liturgical praxis.

In this book, I seek to show that sacramentalism was always present in early Baptist thought and continues to feature in the liturgical life of Eastern European Baptist churches[2] despite their declared anti-sacramentalism. It seems important to restore the sacramental dimension of church rituals to Baptist theology and balance its rationalism with a vision of mystery and mystical divine presence. Equally significant is the need to eliminate the gnostic split between the material and the spiritual by restoring a biblical understanding of the world's integrity and God's redemptive work upon the soul and the body.

The study attempts to present a holistic theological picture of the principal church rituals. It is not based on denying other non-Baptist views but on a

---

1. Volume 1: *Znaki Prisutstviya: Vodnoye Kreshcheniye (The Signs of Presence: Water Baptism)* (Kyiv: Dukh i Litera, 2019); volume 2: *Znaki Prisutstviya: Vecherya Gospodnya (The Signs of Presence: The Lord's Supper)* (Kyiv: Dukh i Litera, 2023); volume 3: *Znaki Prisutstviya: Rukopolozheniye i Drugiye Tserkovnyie Ritualy (The Signs of Presence: Ordination and Other Church Rituals)* (Kyiv: Dukh i Litera, forthcoming).

2. The term Eastern European Baptists is used here to refer to a large group of related Evangelical Baptist movements living geographically in Eastern Europe, dominated by Eastern Orthodoxy and the former Russian Empire.

positive analysis of water baptism, the Lord's Supper, ordination, and other church ordinances. The work examines the distinctive features of Eastern European Baptist liturgy in its current state, as well as the biblical basis for, and the historical understanding of, Baptist church sacraments, all set against the backdrop of the wider Christian tradition.

The book is divided into five sections. The first chapter provides a general introduction to Baptist sacramentology; the second analyzes the theology of baptism; the third examines the theology of the Eucharist; and the fourth considers other church sacraments (ordination, proclamation of the word, etc.). The fifth and last chapter reflects on the practical aspects of administering the ordinances in the Eastern European context.

This large-scale project of studying sacramental theology in the Eastern European region was made possible thanks to the financial and organizational support of the Eastern European Institute of Theology. This book came into being due to the initiative and unrelenting support of its director, Dr. Roman Soloviy, for which I warmly thank him. I would also like to express my gratitude to Taras Dyatlik, Dr. Yuriy Chornomorets, and Dr. Oleksandr Geychenko, who have supported this project for many years and provided their advice and helpful comments. Special thanks to the translator Rostislav Tkachenko and Luke Lewis, Director of Publishing at Langham Publishing. I sincerely appreciate the effort of the Langham Partnership's management, who have encouraged and contributed to the development of theology in the global world and sponsored the publication of this book. I would also like to acknowledge the very important and outstanding contribution of our dear friend Dr. Anthony Cross, who passed away before seeing this book. He was the one who inspired me to undertake this project. I also extend my heartfelt thanks to Dr. Phillip Thompson and Dr. Curtis Freeman, who made many valuable comments to ensure that the ideas in this book are understandable to English-speaking readers.

Finally, the biggest thanks go to the Lord, who blessed and helped me to write this book while I was in Odesa during two years of Russian aggression amidst the frequent howling of air raid sirens and missile blasts. The fact that this book has been completed is a true sign of his presence and grace.

Sergii Sannikov
Odesa (Ukraine), March 2024

1

A General Introduction to Baptist Sacramentalism

Baptist Sacramentalism – Oxymoron or Valid Notion?

It is common knowledge that Baptists tend to be anti-sacramental. This is why the name "Baptist sacramentalism" is often perceived as a contradiction in terms, an oxymoron or a misrepresentation of true Baptist identity. Alternatively, in a milder form, it is regarded as a contextualization that Baptist theology undergoes when influenced by an Eastern Orthodox or Catholic environment.[1]

Viktor Schlonkin writes, "For us Baptists, Baptism and Holy Communion are symbols that point to a new life in God."[2] Most Baptists in the United States would agree that Baptism and the Lord's Supper are mere symbols unrelated to Christ's actions in the present. The latest official statement of the largest Baptist association in the United States, the Southern Baptist Convention (SBC), which has more than twelve million members, says water baptism "is an act of obedience symbolizing the believer's faith in a crucified, buried, and risen Savior, the believer's death to sin, the burial of the old life, and the resurrection to walk in newness of life in Christ Jesus."[3] The same doctrinal statement describes the Lord's Supper in symbolic, anti-sacramental language: "The Lord's Supper is a symbolic act of obedience whereby members of the church, through partaking of the bread and the fruit of the vine, memorialize

---

1. This is how Constantine Prokhorov explains real Baptist sacramentalism in his book: Prokhorov, *Russian Baptists and Orthodoxy*.

2. Schlonkin, "Tainstva Yevangel'skikh khristian-baptistov" ("The Sacraments of Evangelical Christians-Baptists").

3. SBC, "The Baptist Faith and Message."

the death of the Redeemer and anticipate His second coming."[4] Here is how the American researcher Christopher Bryan Moody encapsulates this tendency in his doctoral dissertation focusing on the rejection of Baptist sacramentalism in America: "According to many Southern Baptist thinkers, any slight sacramental overtone would serve to promote something heretical without fail. In other words, to alter the functional theology of the ordinances is to promote the erosion of the foundational truths of Protestant dogma, such as *sola gratia*, *sola fide*, and *solus Christus*."[5]

Thus, it seems clear that the Baptist tradition completely rejects sacramental language, and any use of it, at best, is perplexing and, more commonly, generates anger and irritation. However, Christopher J. Ellis, a well-known theologian and minister of the British Baptist Union, narrates an experiment he conducted with his Baptist friends who feared the word sacrament. He simply asked them to tell him what God was doing in baptism. "The answers I receive are often close to what I would call a 'high theology' of the sacraments, yet often from people who would be shocked to hear such a libellous suggestion."[6] The situation is somewhat similar with Eastern European Baptists. While articulating the formal-symbolic character of the church sacraments and proclaiming at the level of doctrine the real absence of Christ and any spiritual phenomena in baptism and the Lord's Supper, Eastern European Baptists' liturgical practices exhibit the opposite views.

While claiming that baptism and Holy Communion are solely commemorative of actual events that occurred in the past, the Eastern European Baptistic tradition practices fasting and stern spiritual preparation prior to baptism. Also, during the ritual itself, a special prayer is offered, usually with raised hands. As Constantine Prokhorov has convincingly shown, the eucharistic practices of the Evangelical Baptist during the Soviet period were characterized by a typically sacramental attitude to the bread and cup of the Supper. This tendency was discernable in such features as "penitential prayers, singing in a minor key, frequently accompanied with tears, and a preaching about the suffering Christ."[7] The way Holy Communion was celebrated further reinforced this perception:

> As the cover was slowly and solemnly taken off the Bread and Cup, there was [a] special common prayer by the presbyter and all the

---

4. SBC, "The Baptist Faith and Message."
5. Moody, "American Baptismal Sacramentalism?," 187.
6. Ellis, "Embodied Grace: Exploring the Sacraments," 3.
7. Prokhorov, *Russian Baptists and Orthodoxy*, 160.

congregation (as the "royal priesthood"), calling down the divine grace on the "great holy" Bread and Cup. The bread and wine were always received standing with the pious tradition of immediately picking up any accidentally dropped bread crumbs from the floor. A common Russian Baptist description of the Lord's Supper was the "Breaking of Bread." There was also, however, stress on the "Cup", and a widespread belief that communicants must drink deeply from the Cup, not just sip from it. . . . [Also,] when bread and wine [were] taken to the homes of the sick members, the view was that it was better to take this from the bread broken and the wine used at the church.[8]

Such behavior speaks more to mainstream Baptist views than theological treatises do. It is easy to trace this sacramental attitude in Eastern European Baptist hymnography, in the contents of sermons given before baptism, etc.[9]

Although official Baptist documents used to insist that the Eucharist was only a symbol of the Lord's body and blood[10] and that baptism was merely the fulfillment of Christ's commandment, it is well known that the church, not the academy, shapes theology. *Lex orandi, lex credendi*, that is, church practice precedes theological reflection. As James McClendon Jr. argues in his now classic work, it is the *convictions* that a congregation holds that create a true Baptist theology.[11] Therefore, Baptist theology is rooted in and emerges from the practice of congregational life rather than from some theorizing.

The *sacramental turn* began to take shape in Baptist theology from the mid-twentieth century onward. This recent development came to be known as "Baptist Sacramentalism." It does not employ the apophatic language of confrontation with the historic churches. Instead, it engages in a careful and profound analysis of the biblical and theological foundations of the church's ordinances and the nature of the church itself. This movement began in Britain in the writings of scholars such as H. Wheeler Robinson, George Beasley-

---

8. Prokhorov, *Russian Baptists and Orthodoxy*, 160–61.

9. For example, during water baptism, Baptists most often sing, "All ye that were baptized into Christ, into Christ ye have been clothed," or "The flowing stream shall not reveal my holy secret to a man." *Pesn' Vozrozhdeniya 2800 (Song of Revival 2800)* No. 415 and 408, respectively.

10. The official *Dogmatics of the Evangelical Christians-Baptists* published in 1970 says the following concerning the Lord's Supper: "Baptists believe that the bread and wine are visible signs, symbols of the broken body of Christ and His shed blood." Bychkov and Mitskevich, *Dogmatika (Dogmatics)*, 190.

11. McClendon Jr., *Ethics: Systematic Theology 1.*.

Murray, Neville Clark, and others.[12] The beginning of the third millennium has witnessed the arrival of the second wave of this movement, associated with the names of Paul S. Fiddes, Anthony R. Cross, John Colwell, and others.[13] A chain of publications entitled *Baptist Sacramentalism*, *Baptist Sacramentalism 2*, and *Baptist Sacramentalism 3*,[14] all edited by Anthony Cross and Philip Thompson, became the unifying platform for this strand of theological thought. The leading publisher distributing books on Baptist sacramentalism was initially the British Paternoster Press and, later, Wipf and Stock Publishers. In addition, several special issues of academic Baptist periodicals have addressed the topic of sacramental interpretation of Baptist liturgics.[15]

Baptistic sacramental theology found its advocates in the North American continent in Stanley Fowler, Philip E. Thompson, Steven R. Harmon, Curtis W. Freeman, Mark Medley, Elizabeth Newman, Mikael Broadway, and many others.[16] Scott W. Bullard calls them *New Baptist Sacramentalists*,[17] although admitting that this is a misnomer since all the representatives of this movement insist that they are restoring the old, indigenous Baptist theology, not creating a new one.

It was, however, McClendon Jr. who provided the overall theological foundation for Baptist sacramentalism. His comprehensive three-volume *Systematic Theology (Ethics, Doctrine, Witness)*[18] draws on the resources of the broad Christian tradition and calls for an enhanced role for baptism and the Lord's Supper. He emphasizes that these ordinances are not mere symbols but commemorative signs. Naturally, this trend has drawn criticism, especially from officials of the Southern Baptist Convention and some Baptist schools.[19]

---

12. Robinson, "The Nature and Character," 411–20; Beasley-Murray, *Baptism in the New Testament*; Clark, *An Approach to the Theology*.

13. Fiddes, *Reflections on the Water*; Cross, *Recovering the Evangelical Sacrament*; Colwell, *Promise and Presence*.

14. Cross and Thompson, eds., *Baptist Sacramentalism 1*; Cross and Thompson, *Baptist Sacramentalism 2*; Cross and Thompson, *Baptist Sacramentalism 3*.

15. Thompson, "Baptists and Liturgy."

16. Fowler, *More Than a Symbol*; Thompson, "Sacraments and Religious Liberty," 36–54; Harmon, *Towards Baptist Catholicity*; Freeman, *Contesting Catholicity*.

17. Bullard, "James William McClendon Jr.," 267.

18. McClendon Jr., *Ethics: Systematic Theology 1*; McClendon Jr., *Doctrine: Systematic Theology 2*; McClendon Jr., *Witness: Systematic Theology 3*.

19. See, for example, a critique of Baptist Sacramentalism in Harsch, "Were the First Baptists Sacramentalists?," 25–44.

Definition of Terms

Over the last thirty to fifty years, sacramental theology has been a field of theological studies that attempts to understand the economy of divine mysteries (1 Cor 4:1), that is, to answer the question: How is the divine present in the secular, the holy in the profane, and the transcendent in the immanent?

Baptist sacramental theology operates with a few basic terms: *mystery*, *sacrament*, and *ordinance*. The Latin word *sacramentum* and the corresponding Greek word μυστηρίων both refer to mystery, that is, something mysterious, or sacred. In the beginning, the lexical meanings of these two words were slightly different. But over time, any distinction between the word sacrament, which emphasizes the significative character of the phenomenon, and the word mystery, which emphasizes concealment and enigma, disappeared, and these two terms began to be used as complete synonyms.

The semantic content of the word sacrament means a sign that does not merely point to something else, as a column of smoke points to a fire, but which *acts*, accomplishing something mysterious and leaving a certain trace. In other words, it is a performative, effective sign. A road sign simply shows the way, but the burning bush that Moses saw in the desert did much more than that. It both pointed to God and manifested Him, changing the whole future life of Moses. It was a mysterious sacramental sign of God's presence.

Baptist theologian Fiddes believes that "sacraments are pieces of matter that God takes and uses as special places of encounter with Himself."[20] The Orthodox liturgist Nicholas Afanasiev, looking at the sacraments from the framework of his Eucharistic ecclesiology, claims that all actions performed in the church are sacraments.[21] The Dominican, Edward Schillebeeckx, believes that a sacrament, in the broadest sense, is the sacramental presence of God on earth, awaiting a human response, even if there is no such response.[22] Louis-Marie Chauvet adds that "sacraments [are] the most powerful expression of a faith that exists only 'at the mercy of the body.' . . . What is most spiritual always takes place in the most corporeal."[23] These, and similar definitions abound.[24] To sum up, we can say that it is more appropriate to describe the processes

---

20. Fiddes, *Reflections on the Water*, 47.
21. Afanasiev, "Tainstva i Taynodeystviya (*Sacramenta et Sacramentalia*)," 17–34.
22. Schillebeeckx, *Christ the Sacrament*, 133.
23. Chauvet, *The Sacraments: The Word*, xii.
24. For instance, Joseph Ratzinger writes: "What is a sacrament? The question is very far-reaching; the scope of it changes depending upon whether the question is posed in terms of the history of religion or theologically, and within theology it makes a difference whether one approaches the question historically or dogmatically, for in different periods of Chris-

occurring at the moment of the divine presence in terms of communication and encounter rather than in the instrumental language of transmission when something is being imparted to someone. In the broadest sense of the word, a sacrament is *an event of encounter*, in particular, *an encounter between man and God through Jesus Christ*.

Encounter is not an ordinary, casual get-together with a predictable outcome but an unexpected and happy rendezvous, that changes the people who meet each other. The encounter involves facing something new, something unforeseen. Even if the encounters happen regularly and become recurrent, they can still refresh and renew each person participating. At least, this is what any real encounter with the living Christ does. Every subsequent encounter may outwardly look the same as the previous one. Still, in reality, it delivers an unexpected experience, having something mysterious about it and being unlike any past encounter. Every next meeting with Christ is, in a way, a first experience. And if a sacrament, such as the Eucharist, becomes an ordinary, customary ritual, the encounter disappears; all that remains is an empty clone, a shell of an encounter, though an outsider may not notice any difference.

The encounter presupposes meeting each other face to face, or even colliding with each other. It takes place when one, figuratively speaking, "bumps into" something or someone, unlike a "normal" meeting where all participants are there with each other, but no collision occurs. A meeting has occurred, and the participants have left, passed by, yet unnoticed by each other. In a genuine encounter, however, the participants recognize each other, come to understand each other's intentions, and accept one another.

An encounter is a meeting of loving hearts, not business partners. Therefore, the purpose of such a meeting is not to solve problems but to have intimate fellowship. This is why such meetings are always refreshing and ever new; one never gets tired of them nor gets bored as long as there is a fellowship of love. Of course, one should not expect that sacraments will necessarily change the situation, although this sometimes happens. A sacrament changes the participant and removes their questions but does not always answer them.

An encounter is a meeting that always has a mysterious and unpredictable element to it. The collision of two material objects can be predicted with almost absolute accuracy, whereas the meeting of two or more persons retains an element of unpredictability. A fortiori, the meeting of man with God is

---

tian history the word 'sacrament' meant different things." Ratzinger, *Joseph Ratzinger Collected Works*, 179–80.

always unpredictable. In the encounter with Christ, man receives what he never expected, or could have foreseen.

In a broad sense, from the participant's point of view, the sacrament is an encounter with the mysterious Christ. In a technical sense, the sacrament stands as the *inscrutable mediating presence of the sacred in the profane* in a particular place and under specific conditions. In this sense, the sacrament is a phenomenon that represents the cross-boundary processes that occur when contact between the spiritual and the material takes place. Still, this encounter happens not directly but through the mediation of certain material signs. It is precisely the presence of material mediators that distinguishes sacrament from mystical and numinous experience.

The first Confessions of Faith that date from the earliest Amsterdam period of the Baptist Church history (1609–1611) use the term "sacrament" when speaking of baptism and the Lord's Supper. This is the case with the "Short Confession of Faith in XX articles, by John Smyth, of 1609," Article 13, and "A Short Confession of Faith, 1610," Article 28. But in the subsequent, later Confession, entitled "A Declaration of Faith of English People Remaining at Amsterdam, 1611," Article 11, the term "holy ordinances" is used for the first time in reference to sacred ecclesial acts.[25] Thus, the term "ordinance" as referring to certain church activities appeared very early in Baptist history and, as Anthony Cross has shown in his book *Baptism and the Baptists*, based on extensive historical material, it was used interchangeably with the term "sacrament" from the seventeenth century on until the thirties of the twentieth century.

Cross notes that at the level of everyday consciousness, Baptist congregations did not make any special distinction between these terms. However, Baptist texts, especially those coming from the nineteenth century, use the term "ordinance" exclusively. A similar situation can be observed in the first decades of the Baptist movement in the Eastern European lands. Early Baptist's confessions of faith do mention "sacrament,"[26] but without giving it a sacramental meaning prevalent in the Eastern Orthodox Church. Nevertheless, the confessions translated from Western sources or heavily influenced by Western European theology spoke only of "ordinance."[27]

Technically speaking, the word "ordinance" is more biblical than "sacrament," which may have been why Baptists have preferred the former term. Thus, the Old Testament introduces the notion of "a lasting ordinance" (Exod

---

25. Lumpkin, *Baptist Confessions of Faith*, 101, 109, 120.
26. Zhabotinskiy, "Prosheniye Ivana Ryaboshapki (Ivan Ryaboshapka's plea)," 142.
27. Sannikov, ed., *Istoriya Baptizma (The History of Baptist Movement)*, 426–27.

12:14, NIV, and similar passages) when speaking of God-appointed feasts, sacrifices, and moral commandments. In fact, all the ethical and ceremonial requirements the Scripture identifies as the Lord's commands are his "ordinances." By helping a beggar, clothing the poor, or offering prayers, Christians fulfill the Lord's decrees. This broad view is quite biblical but not really historical. Usually, the term "ordinances" describes only public acts the church performs in the form of traditional rites. Most often, it refers to baptism and the Lord's Supper as the two main ordinances of the Lord, but sometimes, the term is applied to other ecclesial acts as well.

John Mark Hicks's remark captures the terminological ambiguity well:

> As ordinances we perform the story, proclaim the gospel, and [make a] commitment ourselves to following the story of Jesus; as sacraments God performs what God has promised in the gospel, incorporates us into [the] story of Jesus, and actualizes new creation in our lives.[28]

Indeed, the notion of the ordinance is primarily anthropological as it focuses on the doers of the commandments: "Repent and be baptized, every one of you" (Acts 2:38) and "do this, whenever you drink it, in remembrance of me" (1 Cor 11:25). In other words, it focuses on what people should do, not on what God does, and presupposes obedience first and foremost. In contrast, the concept of sacrament primarily points to what God is doing when the sacred act is performed.

The meaning of the term "sacrament" has a distinctive feature: it is not so much about obedient fulfillment as it is about something happening at this particular moment. This is what distinguishes a sacrament from an ordinance in the first place. But interestingly, the final documents of the Catholic-Baptist Interchurch Dialogue refer to ecclesiastical sacraments as "ordinances/sacraments." Paragraph 77 of the 2006–2010 report says:

> The terms "sacrament" and "ordinance" express both God's own gift of love (agape) and faith-filled human response. The sacrament/ordinance becomes the point of intersection between a divine commitment and a human commitment, where the priority belongs to God's salvific act.[29]

---

28. Hicks, "Ordinance or Sacrament," 206.

29. Commission on Doctrine and Christian Unity BWA, "The Word of God," 37. The Baptist-Catholic dialogue is also available in print and through ATLA under the title "Baptist and Catholics Together: The Word of God in the Life of the Church" in *The American Baptist Quarterly* 31, no. 1 (Spring 2012).

In other words, the authors of this document articulate a holistic viewpoint that does not oppose sacraments and ordinances but links them.

The Divine Presence and Its Signs

The divine presence is literally "diffused" around us, permeating the world. It manifested itself in the act of creation ("Through him all things were made," John 1:3). It always works to sustain the life of all living things ("For in him we live and move and have our being," Acts 17:28). Without his loving hand (Psalm 145:16), the world would have perished long ago from entropic processes. It is no accident that in the New Testament, Christ is more than once called Κύριος παντοκράτωρ, the Lord Almighty (2 Cor 6:18; Rev 1:8; 4:8).

The divine presence in the material world is a special kind of mystery that cannot, in principle, be disclosed, unlike the secrets of nature, which people gradually unveil as science advances. This presence is sacramental and would be utterly unknowable since the godhead is, by nature, totally different from us. Yet, this mystery becomes partially accessible through the dialectical tension of revelation on one side and the cognitive capacity of humanity on the other. Sacramental theology emerges and develops in this intersection of divine gift and human endeavor. It focuses on material signs as traces of the invisible presence but rises above them into the realm of mystical experience, trying to comprehend the essence of the cross-boundary processes when the spiritual and material come into contact with each other.

The whole world should be regarded as a sacrament of creation, a garden God cultivates and loves, and a sacrament in Alexander Schmemann's words.[30] However, such a pan-sacramental approach promises little for the theological analysis of ecclesial sacramental acts. As John Colwell notes, "to presume the sacramentality of all creation is to undermine the sacramentality of specific signs within creation. When all is deemed to signify nothing remains significant. Pan-sacramentalism emasculates sacramentality."[31] Put differently, when every existing thing we see around us is treated as an inscrutable sign of the mystery of God's creation, the special relationship between Christ and his church and the unique personal relationship of the Lord with each of his followers vanishes. Therefore, a careful study of the church's sacramental life and theology requires delineating the signs that have certain *specific* attributes of the divine presence.

---

30. Schmemann, "Mir kak Tainstvo (The World as Sacrament)," 33.
31. Colwell, *Promise and Presence*, 55.

The sign of the divine presence always fulfills a dual function: it points to God on the one hand and manifests his presence on the other. The binary character of the sign allows it not to be identified with the signified, but to embody the presence of God that transcends being or his act in being. The ecclesial signs of the divine presence fulfill yet another function – they somehow connect the reality of the godhead with the reality of being. In other words, the special sign of the divine presence is performative. It is like the cloud of God's glory in the desert, which both pointed to the most high, and manifested his presence. Yet, it remains essentially mysterious, connecting the unconnectable, combining the incompatible: divine super-being and material substance. Therefore, such a sign is always a sacrament, that is, a mystery.

The signs of God's presence can be categorized and hierarchized as follows.

General Signs of Presence

General signs include, first and foremost, all of God's creation, which points to the creator and manifests his wisdom and creative power (Psalm 19:1). The creation itself and the laws governing it are signs of God's love. As the pinnacle of God's creation, a human being is an even greater sign of this love. He is capable of comprehending this world on both micro- and macro-levels; he can reach the spiritual world and be in communion with the creator; alternatively, he can sink to the very bottom of spiritual reality by choosing the path of rebellion.

Another common sign that testifies to God is the history of humankind. Economic factors or production relations alone cannot account for its sudden turns and vagaries. Where does the passionarity[32] that captures entire nations and inspires charismatic leaders to carry out coups and reshape the world map come from? Who controls scientific discoveries and technologies? Who appoints kings, presidents, and other leaders? History is not the work of Freemasons, the secret government, or the Zionists. There is the one who stands above it all and directs world affairs according to the course of events he foretold through his servants, the prophets. Every historical phenomenon bears a mark of God's presence.

No lesser signs of the presence are man's encounters with the most high. These include more than just personal experiences of intimate contact with the spiritual world, which one can barely describe because there are no appropri-

---

32. Lev Gumilev introduced the concept of "passionarity." It means the activity for expansion of a certain ethnic group, and especially for its leaders, at a certain point in time.

ate words to capture this kind of encounter. These encounters may take the form of a non-accidental accident, an answer to an unspoken request, or an unexpected fulfillment of a passionate desire for the impossible. This kind of experience may even seem an extraordinary coincidence that happens just when it is needed! People may call it fate or chance, but in reality, it is a sign of the divine presence.

These groups of general signs of the presence share a handful of features. Their double purpose is to point out and manifest. They are open to all people and the entire spiritual world, but only those who are aware of these signs, that is, who keep their eyes and hearts open, can discern them. For others, these signs are not signs at all but are perceived as facts, unexplainable coincidences, or simple this-worldly life events. Sometimes, they are not perceived at all.

Special Signs called Sacraments

First of all, they include Christ, who is the primordial sacrament. He is a sacrament, as Leonard Vander Zee writes, primarily on account of his incarnation.[33] Being God fully and absolutely, Jesus accomplished kenosis as divine self-humiliation by becoming human (Phil. 2:6–8). Therefore, by virtue of his double nature, Christ is the mediator between God and men, belonging to the two worlds while remaining a mystery (sacrament) himself.

The Lord became the original sacrament because also through him, all things acquired their being (John 1:3), and he is rightly called their very beginning, the *arché*. The apostle John spells this out very clearly by saying that in the beginning, there was the Word, *logos* (ἐν ἀρχῇ ἦν ὁ λόγος). The logos is not only the one through whom God the Father creates but also the one who constitutes the beginning itself.

There are some other reasons why Jesus is a sacrament, in addition to the fact of the incarnation and the mystery of creation. His sacramentality has to do with the atonement. By redeeming the world from sin, he accomplished the most mysterious and incomprehensible work in the universe's history. As the creator of all things visible and invisible, Christ alone had the supreme right to take creation into himself to free it from sin. Jesus incorporated into himself not only individuality and personhood, but also humanity as such – the very human nature, their essence, their "ousia" (οὐσία). This is why he was able to take away people's sins (1 Pet 2:24) and become the cumulative sin in place of all humankind (2 Cor 5:21) and the last Adam (1 Cor 15:45),

---

33. Vander Zee, *Christ, Baptism and the Lord's Supper*, 45–46.

the progenitor of the new people of God. Christ, therefore, becomes a sacrament through the mystery of creation, the mystery of the incarnation, and the mystery of redemption.

The church occupies the second place after Christ in this category of sacraments. It is the mystery that points to and reveals the Savior and that, just like him, has a double divine-human nature. On the one hand, the church is a spiritual entity, a mystical organism; on the other hand, it is a pretty material organization. It is created by Christ, comes from him, and is oriented to him. Yet, at the same time, it is a sign and instrument of service to people. In a sense, the church is the tool through which Jesus accomplishes the world's salvation. Herein lies its double nature and its mystery.

The invisible universal church reveals itself to the world only through the assembly of God's children. Even if it does not perfectly represent the body of Christ, the community functions as a mediator. It creates the space for an encounter with God, enabling this encounter through the language of its tradition, certain gestures, practices, aesthetic environment, preaching, music, and so on. Therefore, the church itself becomes a sacrament.

There is also the third special sacrament, the Bible. The word of God has the power to change hearts, regenerate sinners, and guide people to the path of truth. It is possible because of its divine-human nature since the Bible has dual authorship. It is not a text God literally dictated, with men acting as writing tools or passive secretaries, but a co-authored divine and human composition (2 Pet 1:21), yielding a divinely inspired text. Figuratively speaking, God "exhaled" truth and "breathed" it into the biblical text through the people he chose for this ministry (2 Tim 3:16).

Because of the Bible's dual nature, it objectively contains the power to change people. However, this power is not in the letter but in the Spirit, not in academic exegesis but in transformational preaching. To unleash this power and give it the opportunity for transformative action, and, secondly, to freely agree to accept and entrust oneself to this power – this is what we are supposed to do. These are the conditions that make the word of God into a subjectively efficacious transformative sacrament.

The fourth sacrament within the category of special signs of God's presence might be identified with the born-again Christian through whom Christ manifests Himself and works in this world. Jesus makes this person's heart his dwelling place (John 14:23), and, as a result, this man or woman becomes a child of God who has a twofold, divine-human nature. This is the great mystery contained in the simple words, "you are in Christ Jesus" (1 Cor 1:30) and "Christ Jesus is in you" (2 Cor 13:5), and it is because of it that the regenerate person becomes the sacrament of God. The apostle Paul describes it in the following words: "God has chosen to make known among the Gentiles the glorious riches of this mystery, which is Christ in you, the hope of glory" (Col 1:27). In other words, the apostle makes it clear that the Christian in whom Christ dwells becomes himself a sacrament of the Holy Spirit, a sacrament of faith, and, we might conclude by way of summarizing, a "sacrament of Christ."

The Church's Sacraments

They function as instruments that help to fulfill the mystery of grace, which "even angels long to look into" (1 Pet 1:12). That is to say that they are the acts through which the construction of Christ's church is carried out. They are called sacraments because they are incomprehensible, very much like the mystery of God himself. Outwardly, they are the events of a community's life that make the encounter of man with God possible inside the church's environment. The two essential system-forming sacraments are, of course, *water baptism*, which builds up the church, and the *Lord's Supper*, which nourishes and gathers the church together. There is also an additional[34] sacrament, *ordination*, which authenticates church membership and appoints ministers to the congregation.

All these sacraments have an external, material signifying component that helps the human spirit to connect with the spirit of God. Therefore, they function as a bridge of faith, linking the disciples with their really present master. Church sacraments also have additional, unique characteristics that differentiate them from the general and special sacraments. They differ in their (1) source, (2) form of institution, and (3) locus of enactment.

First, these are the signs *Christ instituted* for his church. They did not exist in the primordial creation, though they were undoubtedly part of God's design. Second, these ecclesial signs are remarkably *repeatable* and *performative* in nature. They are not performed on a one-time basis but regularly, with a particular frequency. Furthermore, they are efficacious signs, producing something in and for those who participate in them. In particular, they may change the participant's status, condition, values, etc.

Third, ecclesial sacraments have a complex *individual-and-communal* nature. They "address" each participant individually but only in the context

---

34. Some scholars include among the sacraments the *preaching of the Word* that mysteriously transforms people, as well as communal *praise and worship* insofar as they serve both one's neighbors and, quite directly, God, incomprehensibly uniting the earthly praise and the glorious choirs of heaven. This is in many ways a valid observation, and I will say more about it in chapter 4.

of the ecclesial community. Celebrating and participating in these sacraments requires more than one's personal faith. Rather, it should be a shared faith that is confirmed by common experiences and a common tradition. Without the community's faith, the individual loses the criteria against which she can verify the truth of her personal faith and, consequently, is at a complete loss, becoming susceptible to random choices and unverified beliefs. Conversely, standing as it were on the "shoulders" of their community's tradition, the individual believer happily exploits all of its achievements and takes into account all of its errors. As the Christian philosopher Eric Charles Rust notes, "the Christian sacraments both point to and involve us in an experience of the living Christ as he comes to us in the body of believers which is his Church."[35] We can see Christ in every born-again brother and sister, and in their unity, we can clearly discern the body of Christ. At the same time, Christ meets each one of us individually, not destroying our personal qualities but forming in us the values and the vision of the kingdom of God that the whole community of believers unanimously shares.

The Reality of Christ's Presence in the Sacraments

For many evangelical Christians, the notion of Christ's real presence in baptism, the Lord's Supper, or other church rites seems to be a purely Catholic or Eastern Orthodox concept. As the American researcher Newman notes, the modern Baptist movement is characterized by "the location of salvation in the individual, the emphasis of the Lord's Supper as symbolic rather than real and the elevation of the spiritual over the physical are convictions that reinforce each another."[36] The separation between the spiritual and the material with a focus on the spiritual certainly leads to a denial of Christ's real presence. Thus, the question arises: Is Christ present in baptism and the Lord's Supper, or is he really absent? And if he is present, in what way? This complex question is arguably one of the most pressing and debated issues in Baptist sacramental thinking, especially in their eucharistic theology.

According to the understanding shared by the historic churches (Roman Catholicism and Eastern Orthodoxy), Christ is physically present in the Eucharist, with his body and blood subsisting in the form of bread and wine. The real presence is interpreted as the material and substantial (objective, physical) presence. To explain the discrepancy between experience and doctrine,

---

35. Rust, "Theology of the Lord's Supper," 36.
36. Newman, "The Lord's Supper," 217.

theologians began to separate the accidents and substance of the eucharistic meal. They formulated the view that outwardly, the bread and wine remain bread and wine, but their essence is replaced by the essence of Christ's body and blood. However, it is impossible to admit the existence of unchanged accidents that persist after the essence has changed because the hypostasis as a set of specific accidents is by definition connected with a particular essence (substance), so that any change in the essence inevitably entails a change of its accidents. A phenomenon like this is not found anywhere in nature and can only be explained in terms of a miracle, but there are no apparent signs of a miracle in this case. All the gospel miracles were evident to the participants and observers. Still, finding reliable experiential evidence for the miraculous substitution of the body and blood of Christ for the bread and wine during the Lord's Supper is difficult. Consequently, an appeal to a miracle, in this case, is merely based on a theological construct, which seems to be a weak argument to support a belief in it.

The opposite, so-called Zwinglian view, which the majority of evangelical groups profess, is that Christ is present in the Lord's Supper, just like in other sacraments, only spiritually or mentally, that is, in participants' memories or mental images, but not in his flesh. In other words, the real presence is understood as a real absence ("an empty table," as Elizabeth Newman puts it[37]). According to Paul Fiddes, early Baptist authors relentlessly emphasized that Christ, who had flesh and soul, now remained in heaven at the right hand of the father, waiting to return to earth. He quotes the famous Baptist author Benjamin Keach and his *Tropologia*: "His body cannot be in two places at one and the same time."[38] But Fiddes goes on to rightly point out that the "form of the argument does seem to place human rationality above divine mysteries . . . and open up the vital theological question of the way that Christ can be present at all in the church."[39]

To reconcile Christ's promise to be with his disciples on earth (Matt 28:20) and his presence in heaven, Baptist theologians tend to explain Christ's real presence in spiritual terms as resulting from the Holy Spirit's presence. Usually, in this spiritualistic approach, it is assumed that either the Holy Spirit takes the participant in the sacrament into heaven to sweet communion with Christ, or Christ in the Holy Spirit is present with the disciples everywhere, and in particular at baptism or the Lord's Supper.

---

37. Newman, "The Lord's Supper," 217.
38. Fiddes, *Tracks and Traces*, 161.
39. Fiddes, 162.

Freeman, drawing on the research by Carlyl Marney[40] and Warren Carr,[41] states that "to recover a sacramental faith and practice address the basic question of how to speak meaningfully of Jesus Christ as living and present in the gathering community. The answer, as narrated in the second chapter of Acts, is that *Jesus Christ is present in the church through the Holy Spirit.*"[42] Then, continuing in this line of reasoning, Freeman suggests that the most obvious sign pointing to the risen Christ's real presence is the word that is read, studied, and proclaimed in the community. He says, "The ministry of the Word thus re-present[s] the living Lord, so that, as Christ is made audibly present through the Word, Christ becomes visibly present in his body as Word creates life anew."[43] Thus, from the perspective of many Baptist theologians, the ministry of the Holy Spirit through the ministry of the word proves the reality of Christ's presence in the sacraments.[44]

However, the explanation of the Lord's real presence as the presence of the Holy Spirit, the word, or the gift does not capture the specificity of the indwelling of the second person of the Trinity, who is certainly active through all of these manifestations but is not reducible to them. Christ cannot be fully identified with the Holy Spirit, the word, or the gift, although such an identification avoids the theological quandary of Christ's omnipresence at any point in space. As John Calvin aptly put it: "Moreover, I am not satisfied with those persons who, recognizing that we have some communion with Christ when they would show what it is, make us partakers of the Spirit only, omitting mention of flesh and blood."[45] Indeed, the presence of Christ, who has a divine-human and not only spiritual nature, needs to be explained more precisely and specifically because the presence of the Holy Spirit is not hypostatically the presence of Christ, although essentially, they are one. When appearing to the disciples after the resurrection, Christ said that he was flesh and not spirit (Luke 24:39). Therefore, the common and standard answer that Jesus is present in the Lord's Supper through the Holy Spirit is undoubtedly correct but insufficient.

If one wants to speak about Christ's real presence, first, it is necessary to understand the concept of reality. Obviously, it is impossible to reduce reality to the existence of physical objects. At present, there is an array of studies

---

40. Austin Study Group, *Report on the Table of the Lord*.
41. Carr, *Baptism: Conscience and Clue*, 12–15.
42. Freeman, *Contesting Catholicity*, 312.
43. Freeman, *Contesting Catholicity*, 313.
44. See also Yates, "Role of the Holy Spirit," 350–59.
45. Calvin, *Institutes of the Christian Religion*, 1366–77.

that explore different types or dimensions of reality, and many articles and monographs have been published on this particular topic.[46] Reality was the central concept of Semyon Frank's philosophy. Different forms of reality have been vigorously scrutinized by Jean Baudrillard, Jacques Lacan, Slavoj Žižek, and other researchers in their works. It is clear that besides the corporeal reality given in our sensations, there are many other types of reality: the reality of scientific theories and ideas, virtual reality, and other realities which we know only through our consciousness, but which are not registered either by human senses or by technical devices. Moreover, even empirical, material reality becomes a reality for the knower only through their awareness. For example, the space-time continuum exists objectively, but it is hardly one's "reality" unless they are aware of it.

An important form of reality is signified or symbolic reality, the reality of signs. It is the reality that integrates physical reality and its significations into one whole. Take the example of banknotes or monetary units of the internet. Their physical reality is entirely different from the reality that their denomination signifies. Another example is the reality of the authority that a certain political leader or chief wields – you can neither deny its existence nor detect it by any device. As Semyon Frank wrote: "Hitler's sadism, insane power-lust, and megalomania were for mankind recently, unfortunately, an empirical reality no less objective and much more formidable and powerful than a hurricane or an earthquake."[47] The bloody war in Ukraine has once again confirmed this sad observation.

God's omnipresence is also real, though not physically tangible. One can potentially explain it in many different ways. Most often, omnipresence is interpreted as his presence through divine knowledge or power. Still, a better explanation of Christ's omnipresence would be through the idea of a unique mode of existence of Jesus's new body, which is described in terms of *entension*, i.e., the ability to penetrate everything everywhere at once and, thus, seemingly be at all points in the universe. This unique property of Christ is not limited to the fact that he was able to pass through a closed door and appear to his disciples (John 20: 19, 26). In the broad sense of the word, as Hud Hudson notes, "to entend is to be wholly and entirely located at some non-point-sized region (in the case of omnipresence, at the maximally inclusive region) and to be wholly located at each of that region's proper subregions (in the case of

---

46. See an overview in: Pazina, *Tipy Real'nosti (The types of reality)*..
47. Frank, *Reality and Man: An Essay*, 2.

omnipresence, at every other region there is)."[48] In other words, *to entend* is to be really – not symbolically or metaphorically – at every possible location. An example of this presence through entention is *space-time*, which exists in the universe but is not localized at any particular place.

After the resurrection, the body of the God-man Jesus, possessing the ability of ubiquitous entension, can not only pass through closed doors but also be present everywhere, including in every single sacrament, without becoming a material entity but remaining the risen Savior. At certain moments, Christ can reveal a particular image accessible to human contemplation, as if *becoming himself condensed*. This was the case with John on the island of Patmos (Rev 1:12–17), who saw the risen Christ. The Lord, who permeated the whole universe, manifested himself at a certain moment and in a certain place in an image similar to that of the Son of Man. It was also the case in other theophanic appearances (for instance, 1 Corinthians 15:5–8). However, Jesus Christ's localized theophanies do not limit his ability to permeate the entire universe. In other words, the divine-human body of Jesus, having the property of entention after the resurrection, can be present everywhere, including every numerically distinct sacrament, without getting materialized but remaining the risen Savior. This is why the apostle Paul said, he "is not far from any one of us. For in him we live and move and have our being" (Acts 17:27–28).

In theological jargon, the equivalent of entention is Greek *perichoresis* and its Latin counterpart *circumencessio*, both of which mean interpenetration. This theological term is commonly used in Christology to describe the intra-trinitarian relationships within the godhead, in which each person, while remaining himself, at the same time fully and completely permeates and indwells the other person. As Karl Barth put it, the hypostases of the godhead "mutually condition and permeate one another so completely that one is always in the other two and the other two in the one."[49] Thus, each hypostasis remains distinct, but together, they constitute an inseparable wholeness, mutually permeating each other. The perichoretic concept of entention allows one to maintain the distinction between the persons of the Trinity while showing their individual relationships with the world and, simultaneously, emphasize their common life wherein each of them lives in the other.

The perichoretic entention makes it possible not only for the Holy Spirit but also for Christ himself to be really present in each individual sacrament.

---

48. Hudson, "Omnipresence," 209.
49. Barth, *Church Dogmatics*, 370.

It is, in fact, an application of the old expression, "Christ is in you, and you are in Christ."

Christ is personally present in every sacrament and makes himself known through his word, preaching, and other liturgical elements, but not all participants in the sacrament discover him. He often goes unrecognized by a traveler on the road to Emmaus simply because the Christian has little prior knowledge and experience of him, or does not expect, let alone anticipate, to encounter Jesus during the sacrament. Many evangelicals are so sure that Christ is *not* present at the time of baptism or in the Lord's Supper that an encounter with him cannot occur for them, even though he is there, waiting for them. The doctrinal tenets that claim that the sacramental act is only a symbol impoverish the encounter and preclude an experience of meeting with the living Lord.

One should also keep in mind that any personal encounter is essentially an encounter with a signified reality, not with a complete objective reality. The objective presence of a person in front of me does not mean that she is really present. Presence becomes real only through awareness. In an ontological sense, the *other* can be really present in my sight or my knowledge (if there is no visual contact). They are separated from all other individuals, their presence has specific physical boundaries, and I can recognize and distinguish them from other members of society. Still, in a personal sense, they can be excluded from my life, and I may consciously ignore them. This often happens even within our social bubbles. Lack of attention, indifference, and carelessness in relationships frequently signal one's personal absence despite their actual physical presence.

It happens that people deliberately deny someone's presence, "He doesn't exist for me; he is blotted out of my life." This person still exists in objective reality, but in my subjective reality, they may be completely or partially absent. It is not enough for the other to reveal his presence to me in some way, distancing himself from his absence. I should also direct my consciousness toward him and turn him into an object of presence. Furthermore, his absence and presence are in dynamic tension. The other's presence can dominate his absence and vice versa. My attitude to the other might change, and so will the dynamics of his presence/absence in my life. Donald Gray explains it well:

> Even in the most intimate of relationships there is a holding back, an inadequacy of giving, a falling short of response to the other. In short our personal self-communication to the other is always fragmentary and partial. We may be physically present and personally absent; indeed we may be personally present and absent at

the same time in contradiction to our own deepest intentions but without any necessary contradiction in experience or thought.[50]

Another critical aspect of the other's real presence is that when meeting and communicating with an interlocutor, a person usually abstracts, removes, and does not notice many of his absolutely real attributes, both good and bad. For example, one may know well about the interlocutor that he is highly irritable or, on the contrary, overly apathetic; he may have personal attachments to some things, unpleasant habits, medical issues, etc. When we meet him in person, we do not – even cannot – notice all of this. Even at this specific moment when I meet a real person, I always create a certain virtual image, a sign of the interlocutor, and communication takes place with this sign. But this signified image is not something fictitious. It is perceived as reality and *is* reality, though incomplete reality. Žižek correctly observes that people never reach out to the genuine reality of the interlocutor.[51] In fact, communication takes place only with the interlocutor's image each of us tends to create in our minds. This image never embraces the fullness of the other's reality. In the encounter with Christ during the sacrament, the Christian also encounters a signified reality that divine revelation, prior personal and collective religious experience, and the liturgical setting of the sacrament have created for her. It is an absolutely real personal encounter. It takes place in reality. Yet, it is not an encounter with the whole Christ but with his signified reality insofar as he is revealed to the participant.

The real Christ who attends the sacramental encounter event comes from the future. The Christ of memory comes from the past, so there is no full presence in this case. The notion of the signified reality – the sign's reality – allows us to see the Christ who comes from the eschatological future. During any sacrament, there is, as it were, a condensation of his omnipresent entention, which creates the effect of "already but not yet." Christ is already really and fully here, and at the same time, he is not yet here definitively and completely. This understanding points to his necessary presence in the sacrament and, to no lesser extent, emphasizes his equally necessary absence. It is important to say and remember that Christ's presence and absence occur simultaneously. For example, if we assume that Jesus is already present in the flesh during Holy Communion, as historical churches think, why wait for his revelation in the flesh on the Lord's Day? In fact, both the Eucharist and baptism constitute an

---

50. Gray, "Real Absence: A Note," 22.
51. Wright, *Slavoj Žižek: The Reality of the Virtual*, documentary, 2004.

encounter with the really present Christ, who is at the same time really absent. He is here, but he is not completely here yet. No matter how often he appears during the sacrament, he is yet to come. In other words, the eschatological tension between Christ's sacramental presence and absence makes it possible to look forward to Christ's second coming while at the same time working enthusiastically to build his kingdom here and now.

Hence, Christ is undoubtedly present in every sacramental event in a real way. Still, his presence is to be understood not as a material presence but as a personal presence through perichoretic penetration. As George Worgul has accurately described it,

> this is not a physical presence resembling a thing in a place; this is not a purely mental presence as a remembrance of a past and completed event; this is not an exhaustive presence which can fix, possess or control the divine; this is not a magical presence which can conjure up the divine through special words or actions.[52]

He goes on to point out positive affirmations about God's sacramental presence:

> This is a presence of a mystery which is inexhaustible. This is the presence of the one and only triune God. This is the presence of God in freedom as a gift. This is a real presence, that is, an encounter with God present through word, minister, gathered community, and sacramental symbol. This is an interpersonal presence, a true meeting of persons and a true exchange of selves.[53]

Since Christ's real presence always operates in the *presence-absence* dichotomy, he cannot be mastered, he cannot be subdued, and he cannot be possessed as one possesses a thing, or grasped as one apprehends a phenomenon. It is he who masters a person, who grasps and subdues him, and who owns him. Therefore, no rituals and ceremonies, even the most appropriate ones, can hold him. Nevertheless, Jesus promised to reveal himself in particular material acts without being bound by them but freely consenting to be present through them. In this sense, the sacraments are the unmistakable signs of Christ's presence, his mark, trait, or trace, that he leaves in the hearts of his disciples when he meets them at the moment of the sacramental event in response to their faith.

---

52. Worgul, "Root Metaphors and Sacramental Presence," 194–95.
53. Worgul, 195.

2

The Theology of Baptism[1]

The Theology of Baptism in Baptist History

Early Baptist writings that addressed the topic of baptism were typically written with a polemical purpose. They criticized paedobaptism, the teaching that justified infant baptism, and focused on the manner and practices of baptism, discussing the status of the baptized person's faith, the symbolism of the baptismal acts (for example, the importance of complete immersion), or the imagery of the whole ritual (particularly, the symbolic identification with and immersion "into" Christ). But there was little theological reflection on the act of baptism itself. Here is a germane observation that H. Wheeler Robinson, a researcher of Baptist baptismal theology, has made: "A common fault of many addresses on baptism by Baptists is that they are too negative, that they are often more concerned with showing, what New Testament baptism is not, rather than what it is."[2] This means that the early Baptist theology of baptism, which was formed in polemics with that of the historic churches, was essentially apophatic.

In their book on the water baptism debate,[3] Stanley Porter and Anthony Cross note that the period from the seventeenth to the mid-twentieth century saw no serious theological works exploring the meaning and content of baptism.[4] Still, the situation began to change dramatically with the publication of

---

1. This chapter is an expanded version of the author's Chapter 12: Cross and Thompson. *Baptist Sacramentalism 3*. Used with permission.

2. Robinson, "The Place of Baptism," 209.

3. Porter and Cross, *Dimensions of Baptism*, 33–39; Also see Payne, "Baptism in Recent Discussion," 15–24; Also see Bridge and Phypers, *The Water that Divides*.

4. This is also evident in the bibliography Cross provides, presenting publications in chronological order. Until the mid-twentieth century, serious books on water baptism appeared very

Emil Brunner's lectures in 1938 and Karl Barth's lectures in 1943,[5] where both of them argued for infant baptism. In response to this, many new publications proliferated. Of particular significance was the public debate that took place between the famous biblical scholars Joachim Jeremias and Kurt Aland in the late fifties and mid-sixties over the origin and practice of infant baptism.[6] This debate spawned a new stream of books, articles, and monographs. Some Baptist theologians produced a number of noteworthy books: among them, George Beasley-Murray's *Baptism in the New Testament*, Neville Clark's *An Approach to the Theology of the Sacraments*, and Alec Gilmore's *Christian Baptism*.[7] These Baptist scholars began to reclaim and revitalize the distinctively Baptist view of water baptism as a necessary element in the unified and multidimensional process of salvation, thus becoming the forerunners of contemporary Baptist sacramentalism. Particular mention should be made of James Dunn's important book written in the late 1960s, *The Baptism in the Holy Spirit*,[8] and Reginald Ernest Oscar White's *The Biblical Doctrine of Initiation*,[9] published in 1960 but still very relevant.

Besides, this period witnessed many critical works defending the Zwinglian tradition of understanding baptism, firmly established and rather widespread among Baptists since the nineteenth century. The new understanding of baptism caused a particularly acute reaction in North America. William Powell Tuck, a prominent Baptist minister in the United States, wrote in *Our Baptist Tradition*: "We do not believe in baptismal regeneration. We believe that baptism is a sign or a symbol that the person who is being baptized is already regenerated."[10] In Great Britain, a sharp critic of the new understanding of baptism was David Gay, who published *Baptist Sacramentalism: A Warning to Baptists*.[11]

Near the end of the twentieth century and beginning of the twenty-first century, there was renewed interest in the theology of water baptism. The

---

rarely, but since the 1940s, there has been an avalanche of books, articles, and dissertations on the subject.

5. I refer to: Brunner *The Divine-Human Encounter*, and Barth, *The Teaching of the Church*.

6. Jeremias, *Infant Baptism in the First Four Centuries*; Aland, *Did the Early Church Baptize Infants?*; Jeremias, *The Origins of Infant Baptism*.

7. Beasley-Murray, *Baptism in the New Testament*; Clark, *An Approach to the Theology*; Gilmore, *Christian Baptism*.

8. Dunn, *The Baptism in the Holy Spirit*; see also Atkinson, *Baptism in the Spirit*.

9. White, *The Biblical Doctrine of Initiation*.

10. Tuck, *Our Baptist Tradition*, 11.

11. Gay, *Baptist Sacramentalism*.

Baptist community in both North America and Europe has seen extensive and serious academic work done on the subject recently. Eminent and influential British scholars such as Paul Fiddes, Brian Haynes, Neville Clarke, Christopher Ellis, Richard Kidd, and Anthony Cross have contributed to a renewed interest in and a deeper and more sustained development of the theology of baptism. Anthony Cross's work in this area is especially notable. He not only published many articles and books about baptism itself, but also edited a series of programmatic volumes under the rather telling title: *Baptist Sacramentalism*.[12] Paul Fiddes's books and articles dealing with this topic were no less important.[13] A parallel development was emerging at the same time in North America. Numerous enthusiasts began making a case for, and advancing a more nuanced conceptualization of water baptism. These included Fowler and his *More Than a Symbol*,[14] Philip Thompson and others with their "Re-Envisioning Baptist Identity,"[15] and Brandon Jones.[16] Other notable North American Baptist theologians who defend the sacramentalist position in regard to the theology of baptism include Clark Pinnock, Stanley Grenz, Timothy George, Stephen Harmon, and Curtis Freeman.

The Eastern European Baptist tradition did not witness any particular debate over the doctrine of water baptism until the 1990s. However, since the beginning of the Baptist movement in this part of the world, there have been two groups with a somewhat different theology of sacraments. The Evangelical Christians ("Prokhanovtsy" named after their leader Ivan Prokhanov),[17] with their headquarters in St. Petersburg, tended to repeat the Victorian British Baptists' language and insisted that baptism was only a symbol of already-accomplished salvation. At the same time, the Baptists of the Caucasus, who

---

12. Cross and Thompson, eds., *Baptist Sacramentalism*; Cross and Thompson, eds., *Baptist Sacramentalism 2*; Cross and Thompson, eds., *Baptist Sacramentalism 3*; Cross, *Recovering the Evangelical Sacrament*; See also: Cross, *Baptism and the Baptists*.

13. Fiddes, *Reflections on the Water*; Fiddes, "Baptism and the Process," 48–65; Fiddes, *Tracks and Traces: Baptist Identity*.

14. Fowler, *More Than a Symbol*; See also: Fowler, *Rethinking Baptism*.

15. Broadway et al., "Re-Envisioning Baptist Identity," 303–10.

16. Jones, *Waters of Promise*.

17. Evangelical Christian history began soon after Lord Radstock's (1833–1913) arrival in St. Petersburg (Russia) in 1874. History of this movement is closely tied to the personage of Ivan Prokhanov (1869–1935), who joined the Evangelical Christians and headed the movement from 1908 to 1928.

had emerged from the Molokan background,[18] took a more thoughtful position regarding the essence of water baptism and leaned toward a more sacramental view. For example, Vasily Vasilievich Ivanov-Klyshnikov, a major figure in the history of the Baptist movement in the Caucasus, sheds light on the early days of this movement and recalls the story of early debates over the meaning of baptism.[19] He reports how he had to pursue a double strategy: on the one hand, to defend the importance of baptism against the Molokan elders, who were known to reject this ritual categorically and, on the other hand, to emphasize its secondary character in disputes with Eastern Orthodox missionaries, arguing that only those who believed should be baptized. These two different perspectives on baptism in Eastern Europe coexisted quite peacefully almost until the end of the twentieth century.

Serious debates about the meaning of water baptism began in the late 1990s, when many pamphlets and books, originally written in the North American Baptist tradition and now translated for Eastern European audiences, started circulating in post-Soviet countries. When these texts are analyzed it becomes clear that most authors writing on this subject are mainly concerned with showing that baptism does not save. Thus, Harold G. Rawlings writes in *Basic Baptist Beliefs*: "Baptism is an outer *manifestation* or a *symbol* of salvation; it neither saves nor even conduces salvation (1 Pet 3:21; 1 Cor 1:17)" (italics in original).[20] Interestingly, the author quotes as his proof text a passage from 1 Peter, which says unequivocally that baptism "saves you by the resurrection of Jesus Christ." This is a typical example of reading a New Testament text through the lens of confessional bias.

Many official Eastern European Baptist documents contain the same idea, though in a milder form. For example, the *Brief Catechism of the Russian Baptist Union* reads (paragraph 3.9.2): "Does water baptism confer salvation? A person obtains salvation at the moment of repentance, and water baptism testifies to salvation already accomplished."[21] Statements like this are clearly targeted at defenders of infant baptism, but the problem with this discussion is

---

18. The Molokans are an East European spiritual Christian group. Semyon Uklein (1733–1809) is considered to be the founder of the Molokans. In general, they held the written Bible in the highest regard, rejected the institutionalized formalism of Orthodoxy in favor of more emphasis on "Original Christianity" as they understood it. The Molokans emphasized spirituality and such sacramental practices as water baptism interpreted only as signs and symbols.

19. Ivanov-Klyshnikov, *Izbrannye Stat'i i Propovedi (Selected Essays and Sermons)*.

20. Rawlings, *Basic Baptist Beliefs*, 244.

21. Ivanov, *Veruyem: Katekhizis dlya Tserkvey Yevangel'skikh Khristian-Baptistov (We Believe: a Catechism for the Churches of Evangelical Christians-Baptists)* 96.

that the question –"Does water baptism save?"– is misplaced. The formulation is wanting in that baptism is singled out and set apart from the other aspects of the salvific process. The Scripture affirms that only Christ saves. He is the Savior; everything else is only the instruments he works with.

Tearing one element out of the living fabric of salvation makes the picture of salvation flawed, destroys its integrity, and traps theology in endless fruitless discussions. The correct questions should be framed differently: Does water baptism play a part in the process of salvation? Is it an integral part of salvation and the church's mission or not? One can find proper biblical and theological answers to these questions by analyzing different discourses and diverging viewpoints.

Water Baptism in A Biblical Context

In its specific ritual and metaphorical sense, the New Testament concept of baptism certainly has a long preceding history, Old Testament connotations, and roots in Greco-Roman religious culture. Numerous theological studies have examined and described the background and context of New Testament baptism.[22] The majority of experts are strongly inclined to believe that such a rite existed before John the Baptist's time, although it is not found in the Old Testament. According to Adela Yarbro Collins,[23] one may discover the roots of both Christian and rabbinic baptism in the washing practices that come from, and are described in the book of Leviticus. The other foundation of baptism, according to some experts,[24] was the Jewish practice of proselyte baptism, that is, the use of water baptism as part of the initiation ritual whereby Gentiles converted to Judaism. However, it is impossible to derive the New Testament practice of water baptism from the Jewish ritual washing or proselyte baptism, even though it has some genetic connection and connotations with these actions. Still, the differences between these types of water immersion are substantial. Foremost among them is that New Testament baptisms always required two agents: the one who administered the "sacrament" and the one who underwent it, whereas all Jewish rites were self-performed.

---

22. See Beasley-Murray, *Baptism in the New Testament*, chapter 1; Pearson, "Baptism and Initiation in the Cult," 42–62; Petersen, "Rituals of Purification, Rituals of Initiation," 3–40.

23. Collins, "The Origin of Christian Baptism," 28–46.

24. Especially enthusiastically this viewpoint is defended in Jeremias, *Infant baptism*. Also, see his response to criticisms in Jeremias, *The Origins of Infant Baptism*.

According to the gospel tradition, John the Baptist uses the language of baptismal theology to describe the actions of the coming Messiah, presenting him as a baptizer who is going to be greater than John himself (John 1:27). John conceives of the Messiah's entire mission to redeem and save humankind and to build the kingdom of God in terms of baptism. First of all, it is the baptism of the Holy Spirit, which in the Baptist tradition is almost universally understood as one's immersion into the body-church of Jesus Christ. Then there is also the baptism of fire, which many[25] interpret as the fire of eternal torment reserved for "straw," that is, for those who have not accepted Christ's sacrifice and received salvation. Others[26] interpret the baptism of fire in the opposite sense – as an immersion into the infinitely flaming love of God in which impurities are dealt with.

John's preaching about the imminent coming of Yahweh (in the person of the Messiah) and the necessity to repent caused an unexpectedly wide response in the Jewish society, which culminated in Jesus's own baptism (Matt 3:13–17; Mark 1:9–11; Luke 3:21–22[27]). Jesus continued John's ministry of calling people to repentance and administering baptism by the hands of his disciples (John 3:26; 4:1). However, this practice apparently did not last long, as Jesus returned soon to Galilee.[28]

For Baptists, the most significant account of water baptism is found in the gospel narratives. This pride of place belongs undoubtedly to Christ's command – the so-called Great Commission – to the apostles to go and make disciples of all nations, "baptizing them in the name of the Father and of the Son and of the Holy Spirit" (Matt 28:19). These words are something more than a statement about global mission and the call to spread the gospel message to the ends of the earth. The Great Commission defines the role of baptism as an authentication of one's discipleship. The only way a person can become a true disciple of Jesus is through water baptism; thus, it becomes a pivotal moment of Christian discipleship.

The book of Acts clearly demonstrates that baptism is the moment of initiation and the beginning of one's Christian life. In this book, the word βάπτισμα (and its cognates) is used more often than in any other book of the

---

25. See Duzdal', *Kreshcheniye po Vere (Baptism by Faith)*, 15; Dudnik, *Nachatki Ucheniya Khrista (The Beginnings of Christ's Teachings)*, 113–114; etc.

26. Sibanda, "Why Is the Doctrine and Experience?," 114.

27. The fourth gospel does not describe the event of Christ's baptism but the text implies it as John the Baptist's words in John 1:29–34 indicate.

28. Beasley-Murray argues for the historicity of this narrative, although some biblical scholars question it.

New Testament, but unlike the apostolic epistles, the author does not explain the meaning of water baptism; he merely describes the practice of it. When reading the narratives of the book of Acts, one is immediately struck by the connection of one's water baptism with their repentance (Acts 2:38; 9:18–20; 19:5), with their faith (Acts 8:37; 16:30–33), and with the work of the Holy Spirit (Acts 2:38; 10:44–45; 19:2–6). All the accounts emphasize the indissoluble connection all these actions have with the forgiveness of sins (Acts 3:19; 5:31; 10:43; 26:18 compare with verse 20).

The apostolic epistles provide the theological grounding for the idea of baptism. Of particular relevance are Paul's letters, where he connects baptism with the concept of being "in Christ."

Thus, Romans 6:1–4 refers to Christ's death and resurrection on the cross, calling believers to leave a life of sin behind and begin a life of holiness. Baptism plays a crucial instrumental role in this case because it inducts one into, or unites them to Christ. In Galatians 3:27, Paul continues this train of thought. The apostle uses the vivid imagery of changing one's vestments, which serves as a symbol of spiritual change. For the Old Testament prophets, the idea of renewal was frequently associated with putting on the "garments of salvation" and "a robe of righteousness" (Isa 61:10; Zech 3:4). Paul uses the same symbolism when he says that those who have been baptized into Christ have put him on. Their old garments, which symbolize their old stained, sinful life, have been taken off and put away. Now, the Christians have clothed themselves in the righteousness of Christ as pure garments of holiness.

In Colossians 2:11–14, the apostle describes the decisive abandonment of the new believer's past sinful life by using the metaphor of circumcision as the putting off of "your whole self ruled by the flesh" (Col 2:11). He points out that the outward circumcision of the Old Testament was only a prototype of the true circumcision when "you were circumcised by Christ." This spiritual circumcision, that is, one's complete separation from sin, is reflected in the material world through one's being "buried with him through baptism into death" (Rom 6:4). Having accomplished the circumcision of the heart, Christians enter the new covenant by faith through baptism. Consequently, those who deliberately fail to exercise faith do not enter the covenant, even if they have performed outward acts.

In 1 Corinthians 12:13, Paul emphasizes that the fellowship people of different social, sexual, ethnic, and other backgrounds have in the Christian community is not created by a shared property or interest. This unity is created by the Holy Spirit's baptism into one body, which, as the context makes clear, refers to Christ's church. According to Beasley-Murray,

The similarity between Gal 3:27 and 1 Cor 12:12–13 is reproduced in Paul's emphasis that baptism to Christ and his Church entails an obliteration of social distinctions. If in Gal 3 this happy result follows on Christian baptism and in 1 Cor 12:13 it follows on baptism in the Spirit, the inference is not unreasonable that the two baptisms are one.[29]

One of the most important texts for the theology of baptism is 1 Peter 3:21, the analysis of which often depends on the scholar's doctrinal presuppositions. Peter points to the salvation of Noah's family as the *antitype* – ἀντίτυπον, a prototype, proto-image – of Christian baptism. The flood that destroyed all living things symbolizes the death of the past sinful life, while Noah's miraculous salvation serves as a sign of the resurrection to a renewed state of holiness. Peter's text explicitly states that water baptism saves New Testament believers, but not in and of itself. Peter immediately specifies that it is not the water of baptism, which can only wash the body, but the power of Christ's resurrection that saves people. From this indisputable position, the proponents of anti-sacramentalism immediately conclude that water baptism has no part in the salvation process whatsoever[30] but that only the resurrection of Jesus Christ saves believers. Grammatically, however, the phrase "by the resurrection of Jesus Christ" modifies the noun "baptism." Thus, the text does not deny baptism's importance but, instead, points to the instrumental role of the resurrection in the process of salvation. Baptism through (δι') resurrection brings one into a new life. It is what the text literally says; consequently, dismissing baptism's contribution to one's salvation is impossible.

The Johannine corpus contains no direct references to Christian baptism but has several allusions. The most important passage that often appears in theological reflections on the nature of baptism is the account of Christ's conversation with Nicodemus (John 3:1–21). Here, water is presented as an element of the saving action by which Jesus, through the Holy Spirit, gives eternal life to men. The Holy Spirit is the primary agent of spiritual regeneration. Nevertheless, Everett Ferguson, one of the most respected scholars of baptism, writes: "Reading John 3:5 as a reference to baptism does not 'tie' or

---

29. Beasley-Murray, *Baptism in the New Testament*, 169.

30. For example, James Dunn writes: "Baptism is 'the washing away of bodily pollution', but that operation of the water has nothing to do with the salvation effected." Dunn, *Baptism in the Holy Spirit*, 217.

limit the work of the Spirit to the water."[31] But then, what does water mean in the context of the birth from above?

Beasley-Murray[32] has no hesitation in stating that water undoubtedly refers to water baptism, which is part and parcel of the process through which one receives eternal life. A number of Eastern Orthodox[33] and some Baptist theologians subscribe to this position. Reformed tradition, with which many Baptists agree, most often identifies the concept of water with the Spirit. Another common interpretation of the notion of being "born of water" has to do with physical birth, referring to either the efflux of male semen or the amniotic fluid at the birth of a child. More commonly, however, Eastern European Baptists identify the water in this text with the word of God, similar to the view William MacDonald expresses in his *Believer's Bible Commentary*:

> Some suggest that water in this verse refers to the Word of God. In Ephesians 5:25 and 26, water is closely associated with the Word of God. Also, in 1 Peter 1:23 and James 1:18, the new birth is said to take place through the Word of God. It is quite possible, therefore, that water in this verse does refer to the Bible.[34]

This view is the most widely accepted.

Thus, the key biblical texts that discuss water baptism – namely, 1 Peter 3:21 and John 3:3–6 – suggest, according to many scholars' views, a link between water baptism and salvation as a means of entering the ark-church and to regeneration as the only means of reaching the kingdom of God.

Baptism in the Pre-Nicene Period

The ecstatic enthusiasm and miraculous manifestations of God's power that highlighted the first decades of church history gradually gave way to institutionalized forms of communal life. During the lifetime of the apostles and eyewitnesses who heard Jesus in person, the conversion of neophytes, which included their coming to faith, repentance, and water baptism, occurred almost instantaneously, and only afterward did their sojourn in the apostles' teaching begin (Acts 2:42). In other words, instruction followed baptism. The role of

---

31. Ferguson, *Baptism in the Early Church*, 144.
32. Beasley-Murray, *Baptism in the New Testament*.
33. See the commentary on the Gospel of John 3:5 in St. Athanasius Orthodox Academy, *The Orthodox Study Bible*, 1427.
34. MacDonald, *Believer's Bible Commentary*, 1432.

water baptism in this period was especially great, for it represented the visible sign through which the formation of congregations took place. Numerous studies analyzing this period[35] show how baptism became a normative component of church life and practice, although it gradually acquired a rather exclusive character.[36]

As communities grew and were being institutionalized, they became more enclosed and "otherworldly" with respect to the society around them. This tendency is clearly seen in the later epistles of apostle John, who draws a sharp distinction between the world of sin and the church's holiness (John 2:15–17). Similar emphases are found in the text of *Didache*. By definition, entry into such cloistered communities required a long and rigorous procedure of preparation and selection. This requirement seems to have been the main reason for the division of discipleship into two phases: pre-baptismal and post-baptismal training. It both shaped the catechetical practice and introduced a new, additional element – the testing of neophytes, that is, probation of their sincerity, evidence of changes in their life and behavior, and some examination of their knowledge of orthodox doctrine. After this practice took shape, giving the congregations some sense of security, there arose a need for theological reflection. As a result, the visible sign of the conversion process, namely water baptism, acquired an exceptional significance.

It is quite possible that another factor in giving special significance to baptism was the influence of apostle Paul, who, in recounting his conversion, stressed the connection between the washing away of sins and water baptism (Acts 22:16). It seems that Paul repeated his testimony more than once, in different contexts and before different witnesses, linking the forgiveness of his sins not to the moment of repentance (inner change), which undoubtedly occurred during his encounter with Christ on the road to Damascus (Acts 9:4–6), but to the fact of water baptism, which he received a few days after his repentance (Acts 9:17–18). For the communities that emerged in the wake of Paul's mission, his word always had an exceptionally important meaning. It is,

---

35. This development is well documented and evident in a collection of primary sources (a reader) Steve McKinion published: McKinion, *Life and Practice in the Early Church*. Note also another collection of primary sources on the history of baptismal rituals: Whitaker, *Documents of the Baptismal Liturgy*.

36. See the article by Aubrey Argyle on this topic, who showed how pagan superstitious beliefs about baptism began to enter Christian communities and how this led to a magical view of baptism and, later, infant baptism. However, it did not cause him to abandon his sacramental view of baptism as a sacrament of repentance and faith that leads to the reception of the Spirit. Rather, his criticism is aimed at the idea of regenerate baptism without faith and repentance. Argyle, "Baptism in the Early Christian Centuries," 187–222.

therefore, no accident that in the texts by Barnabas, Origen, and other early Christian writers, the Pauline phrase "ἀπόλουσαι ἁμαρτίας" (the washing away of sins) often occurs in the discussion of baptism.

Put another way, during the first few centuries of the Christian era, there occurred a shift in the theological understanding of baptism. It evolved from a sign of entry into the covenant through the union with Christ in his death and resurrection, to a sign of the forgiveness of sins. By the end of the pre-Nicene period, the notion of the sacred-instrumental action of baptism per se received wide acceptance, and thus, the idea of *ex opere operato (from the work performed)* began to take shape.

The Theological Meaning of Baptism

Eastern European Evangelical churches are home to different approaches to and interpretations of water baptism. Due to the traditional Baptist principle of hermeneutical freedom, they complement each other and create a beautiful, integrated portrait of this ecclesial sacrament. Following this pattern, my study presents seven theological facets or dimensions of water baptism that together provide a comprehensive picture of the phenomenon.

A Convention or Reality? Baptism as a Symbol

The belief that water baptism is a symbol is clearly the most common feature that distinguishes the Baptist theology of baptism. Many Baptist authors share this view. In presenting his version of the Baptist understanding of baptism at the *Understanding Four Views on Baptism* symposium, Thomas Nettles emphatically maintained that water baptism was nothing more than a symbol and only metaphorically testified to a previously accomplished act of salvation. He wrote of baptism: "No saving efficacy inheres in either the form or the matter itself. The person baptized has no scriptural warrant to believe that in baptism Christ's saving activity is initiated, augmented, or completed."[37] Charles L. Quarles, professor at Southeastern Baptist Theological Seminary, adds: "Baptists insist that baptism is a mere symbol of our union with Christ and our participation by faith in his death, burial, and resurrection. Baptism pictures but does not produce the washing away of our sin."[38]

---

37. Nettles, "Baptism as a Symbol," 25.
38. Quarles, "Ordinance or Sacrament?," 48.

The present-day *Confession of Faith* of the Ukrainian Baptist Union also describes baptism in traditionally symbolic terms but more cautiously: "Baptists insist that baptism is a mere symbol of our union with Christ and our participation by faith in his death, burial, and resurrection."[39] However, the early Baptists, while rejecting the *ex opere operato* principle, did make clear that there was a real connection between baptism and incorporation into Christ, union with his death and resurrection, and the forgiveness of sins. Put differently, they expanded the concept of baptism as a symbol. For example, the *Second London Confession* of 1677–1679 states in chapter XXIX that "Baptism is an Ordinance of the New Testament, ordained by Jesus Christ, to be unto the party Baptized, a sign of his fellowship with him, in his death, and resurrection; of his being engrafted into him; of remission of sins."[40]

The insistence on the metaphorical and symbolic meaning of baptism was not typical of the first generation of Baptists. As Stanley Fowler and other authors have shown, the early Baptist John Smyth and his followers spoke of baptism using the language of Christ's actual presence and real union with him.[41] They even explicitly called it a sacrament: "Therefore, the baptism of water leadeth us to Christ, to his holy office in glory and majesty."[42] This expression clearly articulates baptism's instrumental power, which is not a mere conventionality. It accomplishes something – it leads the person being baptized into Christ's presence. The *Baptist Catechism* of 1689 explains that baptism, along with the word, the Lord's Supper, and prayer, conveys to believers the "benefits of Redemption."[43]

If baptism is only a symbol, can it convey or accomplish anything? Many believe it is only a testimony of faith and obedience, a sign of a previously

---

39. Uchbova Rada (Educational Council of the All-Ukrainian Union of Churches of Evangelical Christian Baptists (AUCECB), *Vyznannia Viry Yevangel's'kykh Khrystyian-Baptystiv ta Praktyka Khrystyians'kogo Zhyttia i Slyzhinnia (The Confession of Faith of Evangelical Christians-Baptists and the Practice of Christian Life and Ministry)*, 25.

40. Lumpkin, *Baptist Confessions of Faith*, 290–91.

41. Fowler, *More Than a Symbol*.

42. Article 30 of "A Short Confession of Faith" of 1610 that John Smyth and forty-three members of his group signed. In Lumpkin, *Baptist Confessions of Faith*, 110.

43. Question 95 and the answer to it in the *Baptist Catechism*, written for the *Second London Confession of Faith* in the late seventeenth century and known as the Keach Catechism (after Benjamin Keach, 1640–1704), states: "The outward and ordinary means whereby Christ communicates to us the benefits of redemption are His ordinances, especially the Word, Baptism, the Lord's Supper and Prayer." Keach, *The Baptist Catechism*, 23.

accomplished death to sin and rising to new life.[44] Ivan Prokhanov writes in his *Evangelical Christians' Doctrines* of 1910: "Baptism with water is an outward sign of the baptism of the Holy Spirit, or death to sin and resurrection to righteousness, which had previously taken place in one's soul."[45] He separates the moment of the Spirit baptism, which, in his opinion, accompanies the regeneration (birth from above), and the act of water baptism, without explaining why it is necessary to separate the sign and signified in time. Prokhanov's view gained ground and lived on among the Prokhanovtsy (evangelical Christians) who, following his lead, tended to undervalue the role of water baptism (and other church rituals). For this group, conscious water baptism was not considered mandatory, and in the first decades of this movement's history, it led to some tension with Ukrainian and Caucasian Baptist churches.

Unlike these evangelical Christians, Baptists were inclined to a more sacramental-realistic view of water baptism, influenced by the *Hamburg Confession* of 1847. The *Confession of Faith of Christians-Baptists* (1906) states that baptism "is the solemn declaration, the confession of the sinner . . . that he surrenders himself – both body and soul – to Christ and puts on Him as his righteousness and strength, putting his old man to death with Christ and desiring to walk with Him in newness of life."[46] This wording proved acceptable to the leaders of the Transcaucasian Baptists, most of whom were former Molokans in conflict with the theology of spiritual Christians who denied water baptism altogether. Baptists constantly disputed these matters with the Molokans and, therefore, had to defend baptism's necessity and deep sacramental meaning.

By emphasizing that the outward act of baptism is of no avail without a proper inward state, many contemporary Eastern European Baptist authors point to the necessary unity of the outward act and the inward state. Thus, Nikolai Khrapov, one of the most authoritative Baptist ministers of the Soviet period, writes about water baptism: "Although the blood of Christ, which cleanses us from sin, is the only means of salvation for sinners, nevertheless our salvation is secured and actualized by baptism into the Lord's death. The resurrected life of Jesus is actualized in us only through baptism into his death."[47]

---

44. See "Veroucheniye Evangel'skikh Khristian-Baptistov, 1985 (The Beliefs of Evangelical Christians-Baptists, 1985)," in Sannikov, ed, *Istoriya Baptizma* 467; also, Uchbova Rada (Educational Council of the All-Ukrainian Union of Churches of Evangelical Christians-Baptists - AUC ECB), *Vyznannia Viry Yevangel's'kykh Khrystyian-Baptystiv (The Confession of Faith of Evangelical Baptist Christians)*, 25; and other similar documents.

45. Sannikov, ed., *Istoriya Baptizma (The History of Baptist Movement)*, 451.

46. Sannikov, ed., 426.

47. Khrapov, "Dom Bozhyy i Sluzheniye v Nyom (The House of God and Ministry Therein)."

The well-known preacher Alexey Kolomiytsev writes: "Baptism is neither a rite nor a religious disposition. It points to a deep, inner process, which Paul compares to death and burial. . . . True baptism is an internal process expressed externally in the act of immersion in water."[48]

What are the strengths and weaknesses of this understanding? The strengths of the symbolic approach to baptism are undoubtedly its emphasis on one's conscious faith and personal decision that translates into one's responsibility and the affirmation of adherence to the classic Reformation principles of *Sola Fides* and *Sola Gratia*.

The symbolism of water baptism also demonstrates a more spiritual and democratic manner of thinking. "Officially recognized" church membership becomes optional, and the clerical control of the congregation is loosened, resulting in less legalism and sectarianism. The absence of a clear-cut link between one's baptism and one's salvation makes it possible to regard a wider range of people whose baptisms have no official confirmation and whose faith is proved only by their moral behavior as "saved" ones and, consequently, as admitted into fellowship.

The symbolic approach is free from the danger of idolatry. One hears in the insistence on baptism as a symbol, the pathos of the Old Testament prophets who opposed idolatry and demanded worship that would not necessarily be accompanied by visible rituals. This understanding continues the tradition of Hezekiah destroying the brass serpent, Nehushtan (2 Kings 18:4), which was created at the command of God himself but, because of the sinful nature of men, became an object of idolatry. In fact, symbolism represents a conscious attempt to distance oneself and move as far away as possible from the perilous path that might lead to idolatry, where the incomprehensible God is replaced with his visible sign, the idol of God. Ultimately, it is a program of demythologizing all churchliness/ecclesiality and Christian traditionalism on the way to attaining "the pure Spirit."[49]

As many critics of this approach have pointed out, the main weakness of the symbolic model of baptism is the lack of biblical grounding. Proponents of the symbolic approach are at pains trying to offer a viable exegesis and reinterpreting at least a dozen plain biblical texts that directly link baptism

---

48. Kolomiytsev, "Tsel' i Zhacheniye Vodnogo Kreshcheniya" ("The Purpose and Significance of Water Baptism").

49. A perfect recent example of this approach, which denies all institutional and corporate dimensions of the church and reduces faith to individual responsibility and personal conviction alone, is the following book: Nesterenko, *Institutsyonal'noye Pleneniye Tserkvi* (*The Institutional Captivity of the Church*).

and salvation. Symbolists have always faced the problem of so-called "difficult" texts[50] that do not fit into their rigid dogmatic system, while the explicit teachings of Christ, the practices of the book of Acts, and the witness of pre-Nicene Christianity speak against their view.

Another weakness of the symbolic view of baptism is excessive spiritualization that renders all processes relating to the work of God in the New Testament entirely spiritual. Such a view severs the unity of the material and spiritual worlds and makes God the Lord of the spiritual realms alone. In this regard, the symbolic understanding of baptism is somewhat dualistic and partly gnostic. It does not take into account the integrity of human nature, which experiences physical reality and is in need of communicating through material signs and rituals in addition to purely spiritual means.

Equally, the symbolic model of baptism leads to some practical weaknesses. Among them are the desacralization of worship, the reductionist view of church life as a cultural phenomenon, and its relegation to a mere secular performance. Rationalization and deritualization inevitably lead to a diminished value of baptism, its authority, and its importance. In practice, this is manifested in the increasing number of people who are not willing to receive water baptism but still consider themselves practicing Christians.

The Door to the Church: Baptism as Initiation

Baptism may be "read" as the new believer's acceptance into the congregation. This concept of initiation allows us to consider entering the church as both a process and an event. It also gives us the opportunity to analyze the objects and subjects of entry into the church and evaluate each participant's role.

Christian baptism is the climax of one's conversion and the ultimate initiation rite. It is an event that completes a long and complex process the would-be baptized has gone through. By now, one has mastered some basic theology and demonstrated the behavior and traits of the church culture that this particular community of believers approves of. In other words, the initiate must have mastered the "mother tongue of the church" and is now ready to bear witness to this through a particular ritual act. The result is the initiate's new identity, on the one hand, and the confirmation by the community of its willingness to accept the new member, on the other. Baptism then represents a moment of radical transformation in the existential status of the neophyte, which not only

---

50. 1 Pet. 3:21; Mark.16:16; and so on.

ushers him into a new community of the elect and initiated but also separates her from the outside world of the uninitiated.

Gerard Kelly, drawing on the work of Chauvet, divides initiation into three main stages.[51] The first involves listening to and internalizing the stories that the new community lives by. These stories explicate the community's cultural traits, traditions, accepted behaviors, customary appearances, and other subcultural elements. They also help to understand how this community perceives, views, and evaluates the people and society beyond its boundaries. Usually, this stage involves purposeful training that takes the form of verbal instruction as well as non-verbal pedagogical techniques, which are often much more effective than verbal ones. Neophytes at this stage often subconsciously adopt behavioral stamps, approved normative vocabulary, specific language, and characteristic narratives that are incomprehensible and, in a sense, mysterious to the uninitiated.

The second stage of almost all initiatory procedures is a test, an examination in which the initiate's preparedness to enter a new community is tested. In traditional or primitive cultures, this often involves inflicting bodily mutilation and demonstrating the neophyte's ability to bear it and live in accordance with the new community's norms. In the Eastern European Baptist tradition, the neophyte's examination typically involves an interview when the person preparing for baptism answers the questions the entire congregation or the extended church council asks. Such interviews aim to get to know the neophyte and test their readiness to become a community member.

The third element of initiation is the ritual itself. It is an event that usually takes place in the presence of the whole community and its most authoritative members, which is as solemn as it could be. Additionally, the event may incorporate some material tokens or certificates that the initiates receive.

Not all scholars agree with this interpretation of initiation. For example, Dunn says: "I describe the event of becoming a Christian by the inelegant title 'conversion-initiation.'"[52] He considers only the rite of baptism itself to count as initiation. In this way, he attempts to separate the spiritual processes he calls "conversion to Christianity" from the ritual of baptism itself, which he does not recognize as having any spiritual component. However, one can hardly agree with Dunn on this since initiation is not limited to the event of water

---

51. Kelly, "Baptism in the Roman Catholic Church," 35. We present the three stages of initiation Kelly outlined in a different sequence that seems more logical and natural.

52. Dunn, *Baptism in the Holy Spirit*, 5.

baptism alone. Rather, it corresponds well to the traditional Baptist notion of "entering the church."

In the Baptist tradition, water baptism as the door or gateway to the church is one of the most beloved and common images explaining this sacramental act. Already, the early Baptist confessions of faith emphasized this aspect of baptism. For example, the 1651 "The Faith and Practice of the Thirty Congregations" reads in paragraph 50: "That those which received the word of God preached by the Ministrie of the Gospel, and were Baptized according to the Counsel of God, at the same time or day they were of the visible Church of God."[53] One finds the same statement in many other early Baptist documents, for example, in Article XI of the so-called "Standard Confession" of 1660.

Likewise, from the very beginning of their history, Eastern European Baptists have emphasized the importance of water baptism as an instrument of admission to the church. "The Newly Converted Russian Brotherhood's Rules of Faith" by Mikhail Ratushnyy and about one hundred other Ukrainian Stundists, signed and handed to the Russian tsar in 1871, states in paragraph 5: "By means of baptism we are received into the visible church of Christ on earth."[54] Similarly, the *Confession of Faith of the Odesa Theological Seminary* states: "Admission to the local church is made through water baptism, which is the first fruit of faith, love, and obedience to Christ, [and] a visible indication of one's joining His universal church."[55] This is also what the 1985 *Beliefs of Evangelical Christians-Baptists*[56] and other confessional documents teach. In an abstract he read at the 41st Congress of the All-Union Council of Evangelical Christians-Baptists, Mikhail Zhidkov pointed out: "Baptism is the doorway to entering the local church, where all those who love the Lord Jesus Christ are united into 'one body' of holy fellowship."[57]

The idea of baptism as initiation inevitably leads to several important practical implications. First of all, the idea of joining a local congregation presupposes the *church's presence*. This is why, most often, baptism is performed in the presence of the whole community or its larger part. Typically, a celebration is held on the occasion, and those who have been baptized are presented with commemorative signs and certificates. Theologically speak-

---

53. Lumpkin, *Baptist Confessions of Faith*, 182.

54. Zhabotinskiy, "Prosheniye Ivana Ryaboshapki (Ivan Ryaboshapka's Plea)," 143.

55. Sannikov, ed., *Istoriya Baptizma (The History of Baptist Movement)*, 479.

56. Sannikov, 405.

57. Zhidkov, "Vodnoye Kreshcheniye i Vecherya Gospodnya (Water Baptism and the Lord's Supper)," 57.

ing, one should explain this attitude by the fact that at baptism, the congregation publicly welcomes new members and that the laying on of hands on the baptized is a special demonstration of that acceptance. Therefore, Baptist ministers have been reluctant to allow private, secret baptisms and only under compelling circumstances.

Another important practical implication of such an understanding of baptism as initiation is the practice of preparation for baptism and "examination" of those to be baptized before the act of baptism itself is administered. This practice is a surprising exception to the traditional Baptist approach, whereby all church ordinances or practices are necessarily justified by reference to explicit biblical texts. It is difficult to find unequivocal biblical instructions or New Testament examples supporting this kind of lengthy catechesis prior to baptism. Even the so-called "Great Commission" (Matt 28:19), often cited to justify the training of new believers before baptism, cannot support such a practice. Any rigorous exegesis will make it clear.

It is time to look at the strengths and weaknesses of the initiatory understanding of baptism. One of the greatest strengths of this interpretation of baptism is its wide acceptance not only among various Baptist groups but also across virtually all Christian denominations. The crucial element of this theory is its emphasis on the collective rather than individualistic understanding of water baptism. Initiation implies the ecclesial community's involvement and the baptized person's incorporation into that community.

If baptism refers to one's entry into the ecclesial community, speaking of the training the neophytes need to prepare for this special moment makes perfect sense. This training, then, helps to form the church as a community of like-minded people, not only in orthodoxy but also in orthopraxy. There is not only the possibility but also the demand for serious catechetical training, which includes various testing elements – for example, hearing the testimonies of the candidate and those from their circle, conducting oral interviews, and so on.

This understanding allows one to easily distinguish between church and non-church, to draw a visible and clearly distinguishable line between different communities, to build a stable institutionalized form of ecclesial existence, and to give the church organism a shell of organization, without which a spiritual organism cannot survive long in the material world. Through this, a stable local church is formed as a community of the faithful with a fixed membership.

Initiation entails a moral commitment to holy living in Christ and the community of saints, that is, in the church. It is why Beasley-Murray specifies that "baptism in the Apostolic Church is a moral-religious act."[58] In other words, baptism imposes certain moral and ethical obligations on the baptized.

Nonetheless, this understanding of baptism certainly has its weaknesses. Considering water baptism to be a systemically significant attribute of churchliness/ecclesiality, one can easily fall into error by creating the appearance of the church while losing its most essential ontological qualities, such as spiritual "otherness." The focus on water baptism as a sign of the church opens up the possibility (and fosters the reality) of instances of hypocrisy and self-deception, wherein a person who has been baptized has never actually experienced regeneration. Preparatory talks and final tests are a fairly unreliable filter that often lets in some underprepared candidates.

Also, the understanding of baptism as initiation is exclusive rather than inclusive. According to Fiddes, it does not include in the church those who are still on the journey of faith or those who have long led a virtuous Christian life but have not been baptized or have been baptized in another denomination. Consequently, it excludes a large group of Christians from the church even though they themselves believe they have the faith and its fruits. While many consider this exclusivity a strength, Paul Fiddes, following Jürgen Moltmann, looks at it from a different angle. He views the church as a group capable of accepting the unpleasant and the unlovable, stepping out of the comfort zone, and lifting the restrictions.[59] From this perspective, as these researchers show, exclusivity is a weakness.

The Seal of the Covenant: Baptism as a Promise

Traditionally, most Eastern European Baptists have viewed baptism as a promise one makes to God to keep a good conscience by entering into a covenant with him. The *Bratskiy Vestnik (Brotherly Herald)* journal[60] regularly published information about the past acts of water baptism in local congregations in the section "About local churches' life." The reports often took the following form: "The city of Poti. Newly converted souls made a covenant with the Lord and entered the church through water baptism by faith. The act of baptism was performed by the elder of the church, Brother I. D. Varavin,"[61] or "Recently,

---

58. Beasley-Murray, *Baptism in the New Testament*, 284.
59. Fiddes, *Tracks and Traces*, 14.
60. It is the official and only periodical of Evangelical Christian Baptists in the Soviet Union.
61. "Iz Zhyzni Pomestnykh Tserkvey (About Local Churches' Life)," *Bratskiy Vestnik* (1978), 60.

a solemn service was held in the Yuzhno-Sakhalinsk church, where newly converted souls made a covenant with the Lord through the holy water baptism. It was administered by brother Yu. A. Maksimchuk."[62] One can find such descriptions in most reports about local baptisms.

Nikolai Kolesnikov, a well-known minister of the Baptist Brotherhood, writes: "By receiving water baptism, we have made a covenant with God. Thus, we have received the right to participate in the gracious sacrament of the remembrance of Christ's death – the Lord's Supper – and to be called 'children of God.'"[63] Brewer of Baylor University, in his historical and theological study titled "'Signs of the Covenant': The Development of Sacramental Thought in Baptist Circles," notes that based on seventeenth- and eighteenth-century documents, "many Baptist groups and leaders held that the rites of baptism and the Supper were effective covenantal signs which encompassed both human and divine action during their enactment."[64]

It would seem that the proclamation of baptism as a sign of man's covenant with God is a well-established truth in Baptist theology of baptism, yet the attempt to find explicit references to baptism as a covenant in Baptist confessions of faith proves unsuccessful. All early English confessions of faith, as well as the creedal texts of Eastern European Baptists, link the concepts of baptism and covenant rather loosely. A rare exception is *The Orthodox Creed* of 1678, which the General Baptists of England prepared in response to the *First London Confession* that Particular Baptists had published in 1677. It declares that Jesus Christ instituted baptism as "a sign of our entrance into the covenant of grace, and ingrafting into Christ, and in the body of Christ, which is his Church."[65]

Oncken's *Confession* (both the original text and Pavlov's Russian translation) contains only a hint of the covenantal relationship when it describes the responsibility of the one being baptized and God's response. Thus, this confession still uses covenantal language while avoiding direct reference to baptism as a covenant. The later St. Petersburg confessions of faith of evangelical Christians (Prokhanov's and Kargel's *Confessions*) do not even allude to baptism as a covenant. Consequently, we observe a paradoxical situation. At the level of church consciousness, in liturgical texts and other universally accepted Baptist documents, the act of baptism is clearly presented as a moment of covenant.

---

62. "Iz Zhyzni Pomestnykh Tserkvey (About Local Churches' Life)," *Bratskiy Vestnik* (1988), 86.

63. Kolesnikov, "Pospeshym k Sovershenstvu (Let Us Hasten to Perfection)," 35.

64. Brewer, "'Signs of the Covenant,'" 419.

65. Lumpkin, *Baptist Confessions of Faith*, 317.

In contrast, the official dogmatic texts of both English and Eastern European Baptists carefully avoid this interpretation.

Perhaps one reason for this state of affairs is that the authors of the early Baptist creeds drafted them in opposition to the theology of paedobaptism. The proponents of that view usually emphasized that baptism was a sign of the covenant based on Colossians 2:11–12, which was their central theological argument. Suppose baptism as a sign of the Christian's covenant with God replaces Old Testament circumcision, which was the sign of God's covenant with Abraham and his descendants. In that case, baptism would be not an individual but a corporate act and could, by analogy with the Old Testament, be administered to children on the basis of the covenant rather than on the basis of their faith. It is probably why Baptist ministers have carefully avoided direct analogies between baptism and covenant, even though there was a biblical basis for such a connection.

The image of Christian baptism as a sign of the covenant identifies water baptism as the "territory" where the official meeting (encounter) between God and man occurs. It is like a ceremony of a man signing an eternal and irrevocable covenant in the presence of many witnesses, both on the part of man in the form of the community and on the part of God in the presence of many spiritual authorities. The terms of the covenant were proclaimed by Christ during his earthly sojourn and preaching in Israel. The covenant itself was sealed on Calvary through the shedding of blood. However, the new believer's personal acceptance of the covenant is carried out in the act of baptism. Therefore, there is a divine side to it – God dictates the terms and promises the washing away of sin, eternal life, blessings, and an imperishable inheritance. There is also a human side, which consists of accepting these conditions by faith and confirming one's consent in water baptism.

Just as the Old Testament circumcision was an indication of the faith Abraham had prior to circumcision, so the New Testament baptism implies the believer's faith and is meaningless without one's preceding faith. Circumcision demonstrated that one belonged to Abraham's children according to the flesh. Baptism, in turn, indicates that one belongs to God's children according to the Spirit. But just as not all the Israelites who had the sign of circumcision were the true people of God (Rom 9:6), not all those who have received the sign of water baptism are true members of the New Testament church. Yet, many analogies notwithstanding, the most profound difference between these signs lies in their opposite spiritual meaning. The former was earthly and fleshly; the latter is heavenly and spiritual. Commenting on relevant Pauline texts, Schreiner summarizes it as follows: "Paul does not establish a connection between physical circumcision and baptism, but *spiritual circumcision and baptism*."[66]

Now, let us consider the strengths and weaknesses of the covenantal view of baptism. The major strength to note is this view's emphasis on the responsibility of the person being baptized to enter into the covenant. For the covenant to be valid, one must not only perform the ritual but also make a pledge to obey the terms of the covenant and, in particular, promise God a good conscience. For Eastern European Baptists, this component of baptism is very important. A sense of duty constitutes a crucial element of social conscience in this part of the world. From a pastoral point of view, a reminder of the commitments made, the high responsibility, and the price of the covenant can discipline a church member and help them through difficult moments of spiritual weakness. This interpretation of baptism opens the door to its contemporary presentation in terms of an encounter, a place where God and man work together. Also, the covenantal view of baptism provides an opportunity for a productive dialogue among different perspectives and traditions.

A weakness of this understanding of baptism is that it gives room for possible false correlations based on the analogy of covenantal signs. True, Colossians 2:11 clearly refers to spiritual circumcision (the putting away of sin) as a prototype of water baptism. But many theologians read this text as indicating a correlation between literal circumcision and literal baptism and infer from it a possibility for and legitimacy of paedobaptism. This interpretation is alien to the Baptist theology of baptism.

Another weakness lies in the ambiguity found in one of the key biblical texts this approach favors, 1 Peter 3:21. The particular challenge is how to interpret its keyword *eperotema*. It can mean both one's promise and plea (pledge, appeal).

The promise to have a good conscience one makes during baptism is often interpreted as a promise to live a sinless, holy life, which is unrealistic for an honest Christian. The *Preparation Manual for Water Baptism*, edited by Mikhail Ivanov, hints at such an interpretation:

> Baptism is a promise of a good conscience to God, i.e. a conscience that is pure and clean. And our conscience is clear when there is no burden of sin, which torments and tortures a person.

---

66. Schreiner, "Baptism in the Epistles," 78.

Baptism is a promise made to God to avoid sin and to live a holy and righteous life (1 Pet. 3:21).[67]

Such wording, although quite cautious, still bewilders perfectionists who realize the impossibility of avoiding sin in an absolute sense and, therefore, do not want to take the responsibility of making such a baptismal covenant.

This difficulty may explain the eager desire of the younger generation of Baptist theologians to interpret the word *eperotema* in the sense of a request or prayer rather than the covenantal sense of agreeing to the covenant terms. Their vigorous struggle is understandable but is directed more toward an incorrect understanding of the phrase "the promise of a good conscience," which is taken to mean a promise of sinlessness. In fact, the promise to *have* a good conscience is a promise to be sensitive to sin, to understand it, to recognize its manifestations, and to react appropriately to it. In modern terms, it is a promise to have a tool that can detect any departure from true Christianity, not a commitment to never depart from it. In addition, there are many cases when some people distort the baptismal formula in the Eastern European context so as to require the candidate to promise to "serve God in good conscience"[68] rather than to have a good conscience, as the Scripture says. No doubt, the terms "to serve" and "to have" when modifying the phrase "a good conscience" have entirely different meanings. No Christian can promise to *serve* because one's service or ministry begins with God's calling and his gift, not the Christian's arbitrary choice. Thus, a distortion of the baptismal formula does not encourage the Christian to enter the covenant with God but, on the contrary, often produces the opposite reaction when a person completely rejects the idea of a covenant and sometimes even the baptism itself.

Death and Resurrection: Baptism as Union with Christ

Although most Baptists reject any element of sacramentalism in water baptism on a theological level, almost all of them share a common understanding of baptism as union with Christ in his death and resurrection. It is to say that they define the essence of baptism in terms of union with Christ. Already the earliest Baptist confession of faith, the first Baptist John Smyth, penned in 1609,

---

67. Ivanov, ed., *Posobiye Dlya Podgotovki k Vodnomu Kreshcheniyu (Preparation Manual for Water Baptism)*, 35–36.

68. See the 1985 edition of the *Beliefs of Evangelical Christians-Baptists* that suggests the following question to be asked at baptism: "Do you promise to serve God in good conscience?" Sannikov, ed., *Istoriya Baptizma (The History of Baptist Movement)*, 468.

reveals it. Article 14 of the *Short Confession of Faith* affirms, "That baptism is the external sign of the remission of sins of dying and of being made alive, and therefore does not belong to infants."[69] A similar statement is found in the 14th paragraph of Smyth's *Declaration of Faith* of 1611. That baptism is a sign of union with Christ's death and resurrection is literally repeated in chapter XXVIII of the 1678 General Baptists' *Orthodox Creed* and other widely recognized early Baptist confessions of faith.[70] The Particular Baptists' *Second London Confession* of 1688–89, in Chapter XXIX, declares that baptism is "a sign of his fellowship with him (Christ), in his death and resurrection."[71]

The earliest Eastern European Baptist confessions of faith display the same conviction. For example, the 1871 petition Ivan Ryaboshapka and Michaïl Ratushnyy submitted to the Russian Emperor speaks of baptism in the following terms: "Baptism is a symbol of the entombment and resurrection of Jesus Christ, which the apostle Paul clearly proves in Rom. ch. 6, vv. 4.5.8."[72] Ivan V. Kargel's statement of doctrine he composed in 1913 for the Second St. Petersburg Community of Evangelical Christians says that baptism is "a sign of burial and resurrection with Christ (Rom. 6, 2–4)."[73] The same idea is repeated almost verbatim in the 1906 *Baptist Confession* (ch. 8), the 1910 *Confession of Evangelical Christians* by Prokhanov (ch. 14), and the 1985 *Beliefs of the Evangelical Christians-Baptists* (ch. 8). They all refer to Paul's epistle, in Romans 6:2–4, considering it to be one of the most significant biblical texts that explicate the meaning of water baptism.

The idea of baptism as a union with Christ raises several important theological issues. In what sense is the often-used phrase "in Christ" to be understood? Is it a physical reality? A metaphor? A synecdoche? A metonymy? Or another trope of speech semantics? Furthermore, in what ways can one accomplish entering and abiding in Christ?

The expressions "in Christ," "with Christ," and its derivatives occur very frequently in the pages of the New Testament (about eighty times in total). They are particularly prominent in Paul's theology and, above all, in his soteriology. Jack Cottrell, an active writer of the Churches of Christ in the US, emphasizes that this idea unequivocally affirms that it is only "in Christ" that people receive

---

69. Lumpkin, *Baptist Confessions of Faith*, 101.
70. Lumpkin, 317.
71. Lumpkin, 291.
72. Quoted according to the edition: Zhabotinskiy, "Prosheniye Ivana Ryaboshapki (Ivan Ryaboshapka's Plea)."
73. Kargel, *Kratkoye Izlozheniye Veroucheniya Evangel'skikh Khristian (A Brief Exposition of the Evangelical Christians' Beliefs)*, 8.

redemption and forgiveness of sins (Eph 1:7; Col 1:14), gain eternal life (Rom 6:23; 1 John 5:11), are "enriched in every way with all kinds of speech and with all knowledge" (1 Cor 1:5), are made heirs of eternal benefits (Eph 1:11), etc.[74] It is impossible to interpret these phrases literally in terms of the physical immersion of one person into another. Instead, they should be some kind of stylistic trope reflecting a reality.

Dunn believes that phrases such as "immersion in Christ, in his death and resurrection" are but metaphors.[75] Still, most exegetes criticize Dunn's metaphorical understanding of the phrase "in Christ."[76] For example, Anthony Cross has thoroughly and carefully analyzed his arguments and shown their fallibility in his *Recovering the Evangelical Sacrament: Baptisma Semper Reformandum*.[77] He demonstrates that the descriptions and arguments Dunn deploys to prove that the saying "baptized into the death and resurrection of Christ" is a metaphor show instead that the expression is not metaphorical but rather is a synecdoche. This is a trope in which the speaker, often unconsciously (but sometimes consciously), implies a whole when speaking of a part, and the hearer, in turn, perceives the part as a whole. For example, Christ invites us to pray for our "daily bread," referring not only to the bread as such but to food in general.[78]

Synecdoche is a special case of metonymy. That is to say that in contrast to metaphor, it is based on the principle of contiguity, according to which two objects belong together to the same conceptual domain (for example, one may refer to a cup instead of its contents, wine), while metaphor is based on a formal similarity between two things from different semantic domains (for example, when a lover calls his beloved's eyes "diamonds"). Thus, synecdoche differs

---

74. Cottrell, *Baptism: A Biblical Study*, 80.

75. Usually, a metaphor is a word or phrase that transfers meaning from one concept to another, based on their perceived similarity. Biblical language is filled with metaphors that seek to explain spiritual phenomena in terms of their similarity to some physical phenomena. For example, Christ said, "You are the salt of the earth," referring to the many properties salt has that his disciples should possess. One of them is that salt protects against decay, and Christ's disciples should restrain evil in the society around them.

76. Hartman even says that Dunn "is virtually alone in regarding 'baptise' as a metaphor here." Hartman, *Into the Name of the Lord Jesus*, 55 n.7; K. McDonnell and G.T. Montague use similar expressions in McDonnell and Montague, *Christian Initiation and Baptism*, 42.

77. Cross, *Recovering the Evangelical Sacrament*, 136–153.

78. Another example of synecdoche, when the whole is substituted for its part is Matt. 3:5: "People went out to him from Jerusalem and all Judea and the whole region of the Jordan." It is clear that not all the inhabitants of Judea went out to listen to John the Baptist but the synecdoche demonstrates the idea of multitude in a more emotional and expressive way that is appropriate here.

from metaphor in that it implies a greater reality of the object or thing being substituted with its aspect or part; it involves the transfer of a property from one object to another on the basis of a real logical connection that obtains between the two. Cross contends that New Testament descriptions of baptism with their references to the believer's immersion into Christ have all the characteristics of synecdoche rather than metaphor. He points out that in this case, the part – baptism – substitutes for the whole – becoming a Christian and being united to Christ.[79] If this is so, there is a much closer connection between being baptized and being immersed in Christ than a merely metaphorical connection. It is an example of contiguity rooted in the objective link between the two phenomena, not in their outward resemblance. In other words, water baptism is baptism into Christ not so much because of their external similarity but because the latter is truly related to the former.

The notion of union with Christ, of living in him, usually implies two aspects: first, a purely personal aspect, namely the mystical unity of two persons, and second, a corporate aspect, wherein one joins the body of Christ, the church. The Christian mystical tradition speaks of the personal aspect of being in Christ in various ways. But the focus is always on special techniques that allow one to identify with and find oneself in the supreme being. For this purpose, a Christian is usually invited to follow the fourfold path and choose at least one of its ways: (1) *asceticism* – here one is advised to use different methods of prayer, spiritual meditation, contemplation, and so on; (2) *imitation* – it is demanded that a Christian should have the same thoughts, feelings, desires, and motivations that Jesus had; (3) *morality* – one is expected to live a life according to the principles Jesus gave us (for example, be a peacemaker, forgive others, practice non-resistance, etc.); (4) *behavior* – to act as he did, in accordance with the golden rule and the highest commandments of love for God and one's neighbor.

The second aspect of union with Christ is corporate: it implies union with his body-church. To enter into Christ means achieving unity with him not only personally (here am I and the Lord) but also corporately (here am I with others and the Lord). To unite with Christ is to enter his body, be nourished by his Spirit, become a member of his organism, and interact with other members of that community. In his letter to the Corinthians (1 Cor 15:18-22), apostle Paul contrasts life in Adam with life in Christ. This is a typical double or contrastive synecdoche: by saying "in Adam" (who was a particular person, part

---

79. Cross, *Recovering the Evangelical Sacrament*, 76. This view is shared by Schreiner: Schreiner, "Baptism in the Epistles."

of the whole of humanity), the apostle refers to the mode of one's existence in ordinary human society (the whole). A person becomes a member of this community by birth. At the same time, each member of this society has more than just a metaphorical connection to the first man, Adam, by virtue of their physical resemblance. There is also a genetic connection, the one of descent, since the entire human race was once in "the loins of Adam," as the Scripture says. The unity "in Christ" is formed along the same lines, in the apostle's opinion: the particular person of Jesus, the teacher from Nazareth, embodies the integral phenomenon of the God-manhood that has both the head and the body. This body consists of many members, that is, individual Christians who are "joined and held together by every supporting ligament" (Eph 4:16), thus united with each other and with their head Christ. In this case, the bond is established not by outward resemblance but more organically, by the blood the Son of God shed.

Yakov Vins, a well-known teacher and missionary in the Eastern European evangelical context, explained some of the key Baptist principles to the youth as follows:

> Baptism is also the external expression of the believer's inner spiritual experience. The believer's immersion into the water indicates that he has spiritually died and is now buried for the world and sin, just as Jesus Christ died and was buried. But the believer's coming out of the water denotes his renewed life, in which he now lives by the power of the Lord Jesus Christ's resurrection (Col. 2:12–13).[80]

Thus, Vins views the material and spiritual processes holistically.

The Eastern European Baptist tradition most often interprets immersion into Christ as joining his body-church in terms of the baptism of the Holy Spirit, citing 1 Corinthians 12:13. According to this understanding, water baptism and spiritual baptism are seen as interrelated, being the outward and inward manifestations, respectively, of a single process of one's incorporation into Christ. One can find the same view in the writings of the early English Baptists, who clearly and unequivocally linked the two baptisms. The *Short Confession* of 1610, written on behalf of the First Baptist congregation of Amsterdam, states in Article 30:

> The whole dealing in the outward visible baptism of water, setteth before the eyes, witneseth and signifieth, the Lord Jesus doth inwardly baptize the repentant, faithful man. In the laver of regen-

---

80. Vins, *Nashy Baptistskiye Princypy (Our Baptist Principles)*, 27–28.

eration and renewing of the Holy Ghost, washing the soul from all pollution and sin, by the virtue and merit of his bloodshed; and by the power and working of the Holy Ghost, the true, heavenly, spiritual, living Water, cleanseth the inward evil of the soul, and maketh it heavenly, spiritual, and living, in true righteousness or goodness.[81]

Cross, analyzing different views on the connection between water baptism and spiritual baptism, places the leading theologians into two camps: those who tend to link the two baptisms together and those who deny the real connection between them. On the one hand, Cross presents the arguments made by Beasley-Murray, the most authoritative defender of the close link between the two baptisms, and on the other hand, he cites Dunn and Gordon Fee, who deny this connection. In the end, he concludes:

> It is difficult to accept that 1 Cor. 12.13, which refers to Christian initiation in which water-baptism is an essential component (cf. Acts 2.38), excludes any reference to water-baptism. While it is not necessary to reject the metaphorical (in the broadest sense) application of the reference to baptism, recognition that "baptism" is here an example of synecdoche (which is the more precise term than metonymy) is strongly suggestive that the referent is to both Spirit- and water-baptism and the rest of the conversion-initiation process.[82]

An important element of this discussion is the attempt to properly understand Luke's narratives describing water baptism in the book of Acts. These accounts irrefutably demonstrate that there were instances when water baptism occurred before spiritual baptism (the Samaritans' case, Acts 8:5–17), cases when it happened later than spiritual baptism (the house of Cornelius's case, Acts 10), and the most copious evidence showing that water baptism coincided with spiritual baptism (the conversion of three thousand at Pentecost, Acts 2:37–41; the baptism of the Ethiopian eunuch, Acts 8:28–39; the story of the believers in Ephesus, Acts 19:1–5).

Thus, even though according to the Lukan accounts of water baptisms in the apostolic church, it is statistically more plausible to assume that water baptism and spiritual baptism should coincide, there is no unambiguous dependency between these phenomena. God is not bound by theological constructs

---

81. Lumpkin, *Baptist Confessions of Faith*, 110.
82. Cross, "Spirit- and Water-Baptism," 147–48.

and acts entirely freely in accordance with historical and cultural circumstances, the state of faith of those wanting to be baptized, and many other factors.[83] Paul Fiddes warns us to be careful when we try to unequivocally link one's spiritual baptism and the "completion of one's initiation" in water baptism. He cites Karl Barth, who emphasizes, when speaking of baptism, that the Spirit has many different ways to begin and complete his work in a person. Fiddes then continues, "We may say that there are different comings of the Spirit appropriate to various stages of the process of initiation, as well as to the whole life-long journey of Christian growth."[84] Consequently, if all spiritual processes go as they should, water baptism should represent and bring into focus spiritual baptism, although many variations are possible in real life.

Let us now conclude this section by considering the strengths and weaknesses of the view that sees baptism as a union with Christ. The major strength of this understanding is its deep roots in the New Testament imagery and especially in Pauline theology. A literal and straightforward reading of the biblical verses that speak of the ones "baptized into Christ" and "clothed in Christ," as well as a large number of phrases that refer to believers being "in Christ," suggests the unity of spiritual and physical baptism. It is a much more natural reading of the biblical text than the theory of a fundamental separation of these two processes. The Acts narratives, in the vast majority of cases, demonstrate that spiritual baptism, regardless of the signs that accompany it (joy, tongues of fire, new tongues, etc.), takes place simultaneously with water baptism. Of course, Christ, who baptizes with the Spirit, performs this action in response to the recipient's faith and not simply observing some external ritual, and, therefore, the Spirit baptism can take place earlier or later than water baptism. It cannot even happen at all if there is only a person's desire to become a Christian but no genuine faith.

It is also important to note that by linking water baptism with joining the body of Christ, the Scripture suggests a broad ecclesiological perspective. The time of one's water baptism is a moment when a person not only enters a particular local congregation and the invisible body of Christ but also joins the entire Christian community. That is to say that, by becoming a member of a particular congregation, a Christian becomes a member of the whole body

---

83. For a more detailed discussion of the differences between spiritual and water baptism, see Sannikov, *Kreshcheniye Dukhom i Dary Dukhovnyye* (*Spirit Baptism and Spiritual Gifts*), 13–14.

84. Fiddes, *Tracks and Traces*, 149.

of Christ within the boundaries they perceives. It helps one to gain confidence and find support on a broad scale.

By viewing water baptism as the culminating point of a person's journey of conversion to God, which concludes with the immersion into Christ and rising to new life, Christians acquire an outward sign that validates the invisible spiritual process. Thus, this interpretation of baptism reduces the risk of focusing on visible signs, wonders, and sensual experiences and helps to focus on Christ and the believer's growth in holiness.

At the same time, however, the close association of spiritual and water baptism has many weaknesses. The main risks are the Christian's complacency and the overemphasis on the event of water baptism. In other words, when stating that spiritual baptism is confirmed by water baptism, one must always remember that the opposite is not true. Water baptism does not necessarily bring about one's spiritual baptism. As already stated, the connection between the two baptisms hinges on the recipient's faith. Therefore, one cannot infer that a person was baptized by the Spirit from their water baptism. Unfortunately, in practice, many people tend to reassure themselves that they have received water baptism and, therefore, have been immersed in Christ. It often leads to formalism in church life and a satisfaction with ritual.

Coupling the spiritual and emotional experience of union with Christ with the moment of water baptism yields joy and emotional intensity, but it is a one-time burst, often followed by an excessively long period of complacency. This attitude may result in spiritual failure and is undoubtedly a weakness of this understanding of baptism.

A Sign of Grace: Baptism as a Means of Grace

Classical Baptist doctrine enlists water baptism as the means of grace. The 1906 *Confession of Faith of Christians-Baptists*, penned by Vasiliy Pavlov, devotes an entire section (VI) to the means of grace and their order, declaring that they are not ordinary human devices but God's institutions whose order is unchangeable. The first of the gracious means of salvation is the word of God, and the second is baptism.[85] The *Concise Exposition of Beliefs of Evangelical Christians*, compiled by M. P. Friesen and appearing in the E. Grositskaya case in Kyiv in 1903, states basically the same. This exposition of Baptist doctrines is strongly influenced by Oncken's earlier *Confession of Faith*. In 1908, Prokhanov submitted it to the Odesa Congress of Evangelical Christians, and the

---

85. Sannikov, ed., *Istoriya Baptizma (The History of Baptist Movement)*, 425.

following year, it was published by the Sevastopol congregation. This document's reception shows that it obviously satisfied both Baptists and evangelical Christians, despite the fact that neither Prokhanov's *Confession of Faith* nor Kargel's confession makes any mention of the gracious effect of baptism.

The *Concise Exposition of Beliefs* declares:

> The means of grace the Holy Scripture has established and through which the Holy Spirit works [act] in virtue of Christ's atoning sacrifice [and play their part] in the work of one's conversion and sanctification. They are: the Word of God (preached) at conversion; [and] the Word of God, Holy Baptism, and the Holy Lord's Supper [intended] for believers in the fellowship of the Church of Christ. Prayer is inseparable from all these means of grace and from all manifestations of the spiritual life of the Christian and the Church.[86]

This text clearly divides the means of grace into two classes: (1) the means of saving grace, which is identified with the word of God, that is, the preaching that impacts the heart of the unbelieving sinner, and (2) the means of sustaining grace which is intended for the church members, with baptism taking pride of place in this category.

Conceiving of baptism as a means of grace should look rather odd to a typical Baptist anti-sacramentalist because Baptists have emphatically rejected the paedobaptist belief that during the act (or rite) of baptism, grace is imparted to or acts upon the believer. Sometimes, these anti-sacramentalists have even denied that anything really happened at baptism. However, upon closer examination, it becomes clear that they are rejecting an "automatic" or non-participatory operation of grace, that is, the grace that works by itself without the believer's participation. But they do not discard the notion of grace working through the faith of the person receiving baptism.

Why is baptism called a means of grace? Usually, the concept of grace and gracefulness is associated with the concept of a gift. It is a good, wonderful, undeserved, and surpassing all understanding gift that comes down from above (2 Cor 9:15). The Greek word χάρις, meaning grace, has many nuances and connotations and is one of the most frequently occurring concepts in the New Testament. Most often, grace is described as the means through which God

---

86. *Kratkoye Veroucheniye Khristian Yevangel'skogo) (The Concise Exposition of Beliefs)*, 4.

works in the world. General grace is said to extend to all people, bestowing upon them God's favors, while special grace is operational in people's salvation.[87]

Such a narrowly instrumental view of grace can mislead rather than clarify its nature. It would be incorrect to conceive of grace as a mere tool or a given, that is, as something produced by God but existing apart from him, though under his control. In this view, grace-givenness is simply a static reality that becomes a fact following God's command at some point. Real grace has a different nature. It is a gift, not a given. It is not a thing but an outflow of God's life, a link with his transcendent reality. God does not merely act in the world through his grace but is in it. God's grace and God himself are ultimately inseparable from each other. God reveals himself in his gift. In fact, he is simultaneously both the gift and the giver.

If one turns grace into a separate thing from God, dissociating it from God, then a phenomenon of a different, lower order emerges, which is not God but risks turning into His similitude, that is, into an idol of God. But in fact, grace is *causa sui*, the cause of itself. Nobody and nothing can force God to reveal his gift of grace. Rather, he willingly gives himself because it is his intrinsic nature. Just as he gives himself to himself within the Trinity through *perichoresis*, one's life in the other, in a similar analogous manner, he gives himself to men and his Creation, being present by his absence, as Jean-Luc Marion explains. "Now, such a presence without limit (without horizon), which alone suits givenness without reserve, cannot present itself as a necessarily limited object. Consequently, it occupies no space, fixes no attention, attracts no gaze. In this very bedazzlement, 'God' shines by absence."[88] God is present everywhere in and through grace, but not as a finite object or phenomenon, and, therefore, grace is invisible by virtue of its obviousness. Grace is overlooked and neglected. Yet without it, life, space, time, and all things would simply disappear.

Baptism is the trace or sign that grace, itself elusive, has left behind. But without a materialized imprint, grace does not manifest wholeness. Since God uses the material world as his imprint, as a trace of his creative gracious power, he wishes to see the human being sanctified in its entirety, "through and through," with their spirit, soul, and body imprinted with the workings of grace until the day of "the coming of our Lord Jesus Christ" (1 Thess 5:23).

If we view baptism as a moment of divine giving in which the person being baptized receives the giver and gives him- or herself to him at the same

---

87. See Hughes, "Grace."

88. Marion, "Métaphysique et Phénoménologie," 95 [English translation: Marion, *The Visible and the Revealed*, 63.]

time, then we can justifiably call this event an encounter of God and man. In other words, it is a bilateral process of giving and receiving. It is not merely a meeting of two partners or contracting parties but a meeting of two lovers. It is no accident that Beasley-Murray calls baptism by the old-fashioned word "trysting-place."[89] But such a tryst happens only when trust and love exist on both sides. God has loved every human since the world's foundation and gave his only begotten son to prove his love, but humans have not always loved God in return. Divine self-giving and openness to people call for similarly conscious self-giving on the part of man.

In his article "The Evangelical Doctrine of Baptism," John Stott examines water baptism from three perspectives. The first is *ex opere operato*, an approach in which grace is inevitably and unconditionally imparted to the believer by the power and efficacy of the sacrament itself or by virtue of God's promise shaping the sacrament. Stott shows this is an entirely unacceptable view, for the nature of the church and the essence of grace discussed above do not admit of such an interpretation.

The second perspective is the so-called Bare Token approach. It is the view that holds that grace has nothing to do with baptism, and baptism, in turn, is an empty symbol. Stott rejects it by stating that if baptism conveys nothing to the recipients, the apostles would never have attributed any effect to baptism. Nonetheless, they did say, for example: "Repent and be baptized . . . for the forgiveness of your sins. And you will receive the gift of the Holy Spirit" (Acts 2:39, etc.). Put differently, they were pointing to a certain effect of baptism. Thus, this second view, just like the first one, fails to reflect biblical reality adequately.

There is also the third approach that regards baptism as a sign of grace. It is the understanding that Stott calls evangelical, explaining its operation this way:

> The third and evangelical view is that the sign not only signifies the gift, but seals or pledges it, and pledges it in such a way as to convey not indeed the gift itself, but a title to the gift – the baptized person receiving the gift (thus pledged to him) by faith, which may be before, during or after the administration of the sacrament.[90]

In other words, in Stott's opinion, baptism confers grace. However, it does not do this mechanically, but conveys a kind of "title to the gift" and then, when the baptized person truly obtains faith, they actually inherit the blessings the act of baptism conveys.

---

89. Beasley-Murray, *Baptism in the New Testament*, 305.
90. Stott, "The Evangelical Doctrine of Baptism," 51.

Stott explains that in baptism, people receive the right to the gift first and foremost, while the ritual itself is only a sign, imprint, or, in a sense, a document (certificate) confirming this right. Therefore, one's acquiring the "title to the gift" and one's actual receiving it may not be linked in time. If the candidate for baptism has wholehearted faith at the time of baptism and is legally qualified (able to bear responsibility for his actions), then in the act of water baptism, they receive both the right to and the gift of grace – Jesus Christ himself. If the person does not have the fullness of faith at the time of baptism but comes to believe truly after the ritual has been performed and, thus, opens their heart to the overwhelming grace later, they should not be re-baptized. Instead they are to be considered as taking ownership of their right. That is to say, the right to possess a gift one received earlier translates to a valid possession of that gift only at the moment of one's faith and self-giving to the giver. One could argue similarly in the case of faith preceding baptism. If a person's actual encounter with the giver took place prior to water baptism, and they had already given themselves to the grace of God, then they had become the actual possessor of the gift before they received the legal title to the ownership of this treasure. A person, as it were, gets the title to the gift later and thereby completes the whole process.

This idea of baptism as a material sign or trace of grace, which captures its legal meaning and juridically secures the relationship between the giver and the receiver, explains the idea of a single and unrepeatable baptism. Even when a Christian offends grace by his careless, sinful behavior and turns away from the giver of grace by his words and transgressions, his entitlement to grace remains intact, and the Lord continues to work upon and in him. Unity with Christ that water baptism confirms is indissoluble as long as the person has not fallen away from grace by sinning against the Holy Spirit. Therefore, the early Christian communities welcomed back even the apostates who had committed idolatry and then repented without requiring their rebaptism, although this led to schisms and long-lasting debates within the church.

The image of baptism as a legal act signaling a spiritual process was widespread among Eastern European Baptists in the Soviet period. Thus, Khrapov wrote:

> The validity of the New Testament applies only when we attach to this document our seal – baptism. The bride and groom have fallen in love; friends and relatives have prepared everything for their life, including accommodations and household items; they have legally formalized their marriage in the appropriate venue;

however, they enter into married life only after the wedding, when their promises are enshrined before God and the Church. Baptism is a kind of uniting of a Christian with the Body of Christ – the Church.[91]

Alexander Dudnik continues this thought:

> What gives you the right to call the Lord your 'bridegroom'? It is common knowledge that a young man can love a girl with all his heart and enjoy reciprocity on her part, and yet he cannot call her his bride until he officially proposes to her and she consents to be his wife. We call this act betrothal. . . . In baptism, the Church, as well as each of its members individually, is betrothed to Christ as their heavenly Bridegroom."[92]

What are the strengths and weaknesses of the view that conceives of baptism as a means of grace? First of all, it allows us to focus on two key concepts: grace and trace.

Since the primary baptismal texts speak of union with the church, the body of Christ, and with Christ himself, identifying grace as a gift allows us to see Christ reflected in his gift. All graces and blessings the Christians experience in their earthly and eternal life are the effects of union with Christ. For both life and all blessings are found in him alone, and outside of him, there is no true life. Thus, the giver of the gift reveals himself in the gift, that is, in Christ. It is definitely this approach's strength. It helps one to see both the gift and the giver in the union that unites the son of God with the believer and the believer with him, redoubling and intensifying this unity.

The concept of the trace of God's grace allows us to understand and explain the time gap between one's coming to faith and being baptized. If baptism is seen in legal terms as the acquisition of one's title to a gift, it opens up the possibility to theologically justify the belief that baptism is performed once and for all and cannot be repeated, the idea to which the apostle Paul refers in Ephesians 4:5. Baptism gives the right to receive and possess the gift. Still, it is possible to take full possession of it only if the complex of conditions is met and, above all, if one has faith and wholeheartedly assents to the terms of the covenant. Therefore, true union with Christ occurs only when the integral completeness of all necessary conditions has been achieved.

---

91. Khrapov, "Dom Bozhyy i Sluzheniye v Nyom. (The House of God and Ministry Therein.)"

92. Dudnik, *Nachatki Ucheniya Khrista (The Beginnings of Christ's Teachings)*, 32–33.

However, explaining water baptism as a sign or trace of grace has some weaknesses. The main one is that a person may mistakenly infer that they possess grace based on an external sign only. One can embrace a false idea that their union with Christ is complete simply because their water baptism has been completed. This thinking lays the foundation for the principle of *ex opere operato*.

Another weakness of the theory in question is the purely instrumental view of grace as a power or instrument in God's hands. The pivotal aspect of baptism, the encounter with Christ, seems overshadowed and obscured. It looks as if, in baptism, people merely receive something from God rather than enter into a mysterious encounter with him.

Proclaiming the Word: Baptism as a Confession of Faith

In London on 5 June 1864, Charles Spurgeon delivered his famous sermon "Baptismal Regeneration." There, he sharply criticized the sacramentalization of baptism and its separation from faith and stated: "Baptism is the avowal of faith; the man was Christ's soldier, but now in baptism he puts on his regimentals. . . . It is the avowal of his faith."[93] The *First London Confession of Faith* of 1644 states in Article XXXIX: "That Baptism is an Ordinance of the new Testament, given by Christ, to be dispensed onely upon persons professing faith, or that are Disciples, or taught, who upon a profession of faith, ought to be baptized."[94]

It is a confession or public declaration of one's faith. This description of baptism is practically standard in Baptist theology. In 1924, the authoritative Baptist missionary Vins published a booklet, *Our Baptist Principles*, which is still popular among Eastern European Baptists. In it, he wrote:

> In a word, baptism is a public profession of faith in the Lord Jesus Christ as the personal Savior and a solemn act of voluntary self-surrender to the service of God. No religious practice or rite could express the believer's spiritual experiences and feelings; only the careful performance of holy baptism according to the teaching and example of the New Testament [can do that].[95]

---

93. Spurgeon, *Baptismal Regeneration*, 40.
94. Lumpkin, *Baptist Confessions of Faith*, 167.
95. Vins, *Nashy Baptistskiye Princypy (Our Baptist Principles)*, 28.

These and similar statements echo the Anabaptist tradition, which emphasized that baptism was primarily about public confession. One of the most influential Anabaptist theorists, Balthasar Hubmaier, wrote: "Water baptism . . . is an external and public testimony of the inward baptism of the Spirit, set forth by receiving water. By this not only are sins confessed, but also faith in their pardon, by the death and resurrection of our Lord Jesus Christ, is declared before all men."[96] That baptism amounts to a public confession of both the person's sins and their faith is very important for Baptists. They ground this idea in their reading of the New Testament and, especially, apostle Paul's words: "If you declare with your mouth, 'Jesus is Lord,' and believe in your heart that God raised him from the dead, you will be saved" (Rom 10:9).

The confession of faith, first, should be personal, and second, must necessarily manifest itself in outward actions: in words and deeds. From the perspective of Baptist theology, faith cannot be communal, nor can it be merely a conviction, a mental process, or a system of beliefs. Eastern European Baptists categorically reject the Lutheran view that external rites can generate faith.[97] Nevertheless, they admit that outward confession, works of faith, and church ordinances strengthen pre-existing faith, enrich it, and make it more solid and confident. Thus, notwithstanding the Zwinglian influence with its tendency to separate the external and the internal, the two realities are tightly bound together when it comes to baptism. Faith and its profession should go hand in hand and, by definition, be personal.

Furthermore, one's confession of faith should be public. Baptism is believed to be a testimony one bears before people and the spiritual world. Note how the well-known Baptist preacher Dudnik recalls his baptism:

> On the day of my baptism, the banks of the river were dotted with a crowd of many thousands. The choir was singing: 'All of you who have been baptized into Christ, you have put on Christ!' The sun was shining brightly as if it rejoiced at my betrothal to the Savior. And it seemed as if He Himself stood in the cloudless sky, accompanied by countless holy angels, accepting my solemn vow and looking at me affectionately.[98]

---

96. Vedder, *Balthasar Hubmaier*, 202.

97. There is an ongoing debate among Baptists about the way faith is born. Typically, Particular Baptists emphasize that faith is a gift from God, while General Baptists largely point out that "faith comes from hearing the message, and the message is heard through the word about Christ" (Rom. 10:17).

98. Dudnik, *Nachatki Ucheniya Khrista (The Beginnings of Christ's Teachings)*, 34.

The idea that baptism is a confession one makes not only before people but also before the spiritual world is often present in the water baptism accounts various Eastern European authors give.

What does the person receiving baptism testify to? The so-called *Standard Confession of Faith* explains in Article XI who qualifies as a candidate for baptism. The answer is: "such only of them, as profess *repentance towards God, and faith towards our Lord Jesus Christ*"[99] (emphasis in original). That is, baptism as a testimony has to do with one's repentance and reference to Jesus Christ. Anthony Cross observes that since the beginning of the twentieth century, there has been a "significant move within the denomination to see baptism not only as 'acted parable,' but as an 'acted creed.'"[100] He quotes Gilbert Laws: "When a man goes down into the solemn water to be buried with Christ by baptism, and thence is raised in the power of new life, what a tremendous creed he has professed!"[101] That is to say that what counts as the confession of faith is not only the words the one receiving baptism and the one performing it speak but also the act of baptism itself. Still, the oral confession of faith is considered the principal and mandatory confession. Therefore, from the Baptist point of view, it is more appropriate to speak not of baptism "by faith" but of baptism by *profession of faith*.

The phrase "baptism by faith" is quite inclusive and, theoretically, includes nearly all Christians, including those who practice infant baptism. The Reformed, Lutherans, Catholics, and the Eastern Orthodox would not deny "baptism by faith" on a theological level. Their difference with the Baptist tradition would be in the way they define the phenomenon of faith, not in the concept of baptism by faith. The particularity of the Baptist understanding, however, lies precisely in the term "credo-baptism," that is, baptism by profession of faith at the time of baptism. It is something that no one who professes paedobaptism can embrace.

An essential feature in this credo-baptism is the performative character of the speech acts that occur during the rite. The words spoken in the context of the solemn baptismal ceremony are effective in themselves, without involving other instruments. One's baptism is accomplished through the unity of external immersion in water and the baptizer's performative speech act if, of course, both the context of the ceremony and the intentions of the one to be baptized

---

99. Lumpkin, *Baptist Confessions of Faith*, 228.

100. Cross, *Baptism and the Baptists*, 31. Cross cites Robinson, *The Confessional Value of Baptism*, 121; and other sources.

101. Cross, 32.

are correct. In this case, the words produce an effect. They do it not indirectly, through some additional instruments, but directly, when they are uttered. This is why the concept of "visible word," or "visible speech" often features in older confessions of faith. For example, Article 74 of the *Proposition and Conclusions Concerning True Christian Religion*, published in 1612–14, states that "sacraments have the same use that the word hath; that they are visible words, and that they teach to the eye of them that understand as the word teacheth the ears of them that have ears to hear."[102]

Baptists believe that the words pronounced in the rite of baptism have an effect similar to the words spoken when taking vows, in solemn betrothal ceremonies, weddings, or legal declarations. This is the similarity that Tertullian probably had in mind when introducing the word *sacramentum* (sacrament), which meant a military oath or vow, into Christian theology.[103]

When the baptized person accepts by faith the words the baptizer has said and confirms it with a loud "Amen," they enter into a new spiritual reality. Now, the person is lawfully united with Christ, or in Spurgeon's words, officially becomes the warrior of Christ. It is important to note that the words spoken must be heard. Therefore, the argument against paedobaptism in the old confession of faith of 1612–14 states that "the word teacheth the ears of them that have ears to hear."[104] If infants cannot hear the word, it will have no effect on them either.

What are the strengths and weaknesses of baptism as a confession of faith? One of the strengths of this understanding is that it presupposes repentance as one's declaration that one's lifestyle has been sinful and that one is now renouncing it. The candidate seeking baptism, in this case, realizes that they must abandon their old way of life with its engraved habits, norms of conduct, and words. Baptism becomes a visible turning point, a moment of radical change (μετανοία in Greek), and a transition from sin to holiness.

Metanoia (the turnaround) commences with one's repentance and culminates in one's baptism. Hence baptism's radicality and irreversibility. Before baptism, even after the prayer of repentance and confession of sin, a person may not yet be able to break with all his sinful habits and elements of the old way of life. But the closer one gets to baptism, the better one understands that their decision is going to be irrevocable. A would-be baptized person should be fully aware that there is no turning back! Perhaps this was the understanding

---

102. Lumpkin, *Baptist Confessions of Faith*, 138.
103. Van Roo, *The Christian Sacrament*, 37.
104. Lumpkin, 138.

pre-Nicene Christians had, and this attitude forced candidates for baptism to postpone this most important step almost indefinitely, sometimes until death, as the classic example of Emperor Constantine demonstrates.

The congregations did not rush to baptize neophytes either, testing the firmness of their commitment sometimes for years. Thus, the performance of baptism was a borderline, a boundary separating the old from the new. This approach tested the neophyte's determination. It is common knowledge that society assesses one's conversion to Christianity solely on the basis of their baptism. It is especially evident in conversions to Christianity in an Islamic context. The full-fledged persecution begins and becomes unrelenting precisely after a person has been baptized, not after their repentance (initial conversion). If a candidate for baptism understands the consequences of his deed, he must make a final and courageous decision to go through the baptism.

A clear, courageous, and public declaration of the baptized person's decision to be united to the church and Christ has, without a doubt, a crucial missional dimension. It signals to the neophyte's immediate circle their radical break with the past and the beginning of a new life and serves as a model for those seeking to learn more about Christianity.

Another very powerful aspect of this confessional understanding of water baptism is the baptismal creed's focus on Christ and on the fundamental truths of Christianity. It gives one's faith a clear focus and defines its proper object. It also teaches one to articulate their faith and be prepared to explain it to others, "to give the reason for the hope that you have" (1 Pet 3:15).

A weakness of this view of baptism is the risk of substituting the confession of faith for the faith itself. Indeed, a profession of faith is an outward act that may be performed (intentionally or unintentionally) without sufficient spiritual grounds. Thus, both society and the church community can be misled. It happens in practice from time to time. Nevertheless, such concerns and potential errors should not diminish the profession of faith's importance in administering baptism.

Sometimes, because of their weak faith, some neophytes are not yet ready to make an open confession and need careful spiritual guidance. In this case, a hasty or premature confession of faith in baptism may lead to challenges and temptations that the newly baptized person cannot bear. Therefore, baptism as a confession should be conducted under diligent pastoral supervision.

Humble Receiving: Baptism as an Act of Obedience

Most Baptist descriptions of water baptism begin with the statement, "Baptism is an ordinance of the New Testament, given by Christ."[105] A 1651 confession called *The Faith and Practice of Thirty Congregations* in Article 49 calls baptism an "Action of obedience" and declares: "Then man to refuse it, they are said to reject the counsel of God against themselves."[106] In Eastern European churches, one often hears: "We receive baptism because Jesus commanded it." This is the simplest possible explanation of baptism as it is commonly understood in Baptist churches and is an entirely satisfactory answer to the question about the meaning of and need for baptism. Reflecting on the Baptist sacraments, Viktor Schlonkin writes: "Baptism (Greek: *baptizo*, 'immersion, dipping') is a commandment, an ordinance that Jesus Christ Himself, the head of the Church, instituted."[107] The *Confession of Faith* of the Ukrainian Baptist Union, adopted in 2006, begins the section "Baptism by Faith" with the following words: "We believe that baptism is a commandment of our Lord Jesus Christ."[108] Practically, the same words mark the beginning of the corresponding section in the 1985 *Beliefs of the Evangelical Christians-Baptists*.[109]

The description of baptism as fulfilling the Lord's commandment explains Baptists' use of the neutral term "ordinance" instead of "sacrament." The latter term has obvious overtones with the understanding of baptism that prevails in Roman Catholicism, Eastern Orthodoxy, and the churches of the Magisterial Reformation. The thought that baptism is an act of obedience, first, corresponds to the common Baptist belief that the letter of the New Testament must be strictly followed, and second, reflects the tendency to imitate Christ's actions. Jesus obediently received baptism from John, even though he had no need to repent, and that was why John the Baptist was reluctant to allow him to be baptized. Here, Jesus's words, "[I]t is proper for us to do this to fulfill all righteousness" (Matt 3:15), are the key to and the basis for the imitation of this action at all times afterward. That is to say, Jesus's example of performing a ritual without explaining its purpose forms an important aspect of Baptist

---

105. See the *First London Confession* (1644), article XXXIX; the *Second London Confession* (1677), article XXIX; the *Orthodox Creed* (1679), article XXVIII; etc.

106. Lumpkin, *Baptist Confessions of Faith*, 182.

107. Schlonkin, "Tainstva Yevangel'skikh Khristian-Baptistov (The Sacraments of Evangelical Christians-Baptists)."

108. Uchbova Rada (Educational Council of the All-Ukrainian Union of Churches of Evangelical Christians-Baptists AUCECB), *Vyznannia Viry Yevangel's'kykh Khrystyian-Baptystiv (The Confession of Faith of Evangelical Christians-Baptists)*, 16.

109. Sannikov, ed., *Istoriya Baptizma (The History of Baptist Movement)*, 467.

practice. Although many Baptist ministers believe baptism is not the most important commandment that Jesus gave us, we must still fulfill it literally. After all, Jesus explicitly commanded his disciples to do so (Matthew 28:19), and there are many references to water baptism in the letters of Peter and Paul.

As is well known, the early history of the Baptist movement in Eastern Europe saw a sharp and heated debate about water baptism among the Transcaucasian Baptists, who came mainly from the Molokan congregations. The question was whether it was necessary to fulfill Jesus's commandment literally. N. Lopukhin wrote with an emotional tone about the Molokans:

> It is surprisingly odd that those who call themselves believers are engaged in an open, fierce struggle against baptism; they do not cite anything to prove their case [but insist on the following]: the uselessness of baptism, its abolition like that of circumcision, the fact that it has not yet been revealed to them, and similar absurdities. . . . The Holy Spirit prompts and encourages believers to do and keep the whole will of God, [and] all the commandments of Christ, of which baptism is the first."[110]

The main argument made in this discussion was that people needed to be baptized because it had been the Lord's commandment.

The idea of a humble compliance with Christ's commandment looks very appealing. When Christians make their first steps in life with Christ, simply obeying his will may be quite satisfying. But this answer is not always sufficient for the people of the twenty-first century. In the Baptist-Molokan controversy, it seemed that the main point was to prove that baptism was a Christ-instituted commandment that was on a par with all the other New Testament commandments and that Jesus's disciples could but fulfill it. For the new cultural and historical setting, this is clearly not enough. What is required is an explanation of the nature of this commandment. In fact, the statement that baptism is a divine command does not explain anything, although it answers the question, "Why should one receive baptism?" A younger generation that learned to ask questions instead of accepting ready-made answers is not satisfied with such responses. Therefore, as a rule, all Baptist confessions of faith place an explanation of the nature of baptism right after the declaration that baptism is Christ's institution.

Cross points out that "because baptism is an act of obedience, it is also an act of consecration, and has also been described as a badge or mark of Chris-

---

110. Lopukhin, "Shto Prepyatstvuyet mne Krestit'sya? (What Can Stand in the Way?)," 8.

tian discipleship."[111] Citing the opinion of many authoritative theologians, he reminds us that one of the most significant contributions the Baptist movement has made to the treasury of global Christianity is its persistent practice of discipleship. The disciple is usually the person who obeys his teacher's commands, even when no explanation is given as to why one should do so. From this point of view, baptism as an unconditional act of obedience is indicative of obedient discipleship.

Discipleship per se in the Judean and early Christian context primarily meant fulfilling everything the teacher commanded, not studying his texts. It should be remembered that, unlike the modern Guttenberg civilization, the ancient world not only relied heavily on oral tradition and the personal relationship between the teacher and their disciple, but also disdained the written tradition.[112] To follow a teacher's instructions was a disciple's sacred responsibility. According to Matthew's text, baptism is a part of the process of following Christ and getting the status of a disciple.

The text of Matthew 28:19, linking baptism with discipleship, is quite difficult for exegetical reconstruction. It allows for different interpretations, which, in turn, leads to varying views on the sequence of discipleship and baptism. Daniel Wallace, analyzing the participle of the concomitant circumstance in his advanced course of Greek grammar, cites the text of the Great Commission as a disputed case of such a participle. He points out that the first part of the phrase, "go and make disciples," is common in Matthew (see 2:8; 9:13; 11:4; 17:27; etc.) and then writes: "notice that the first participle, *poreuomai*, fits the structural pattern for the attendant circumstance participle: aorist participle preceding an aorist main verb (in this case, imperative)."[113] According to Wallace, it prevents this participle from being assigned only a temporal meaning but indicates a concomitant action of going and thereby making all men disciples.

The second exegetical conundrum has to do with the syntax of two other participles, "baptizing" and "teaching," immediately following the principal or governing verb in imperative "make disciples" (μαθητεύσατε). Are these participles circumstantial, describing the method or manner of making disciples, or do they function as secondary imperatives, "baptize and teach," that prescribe actions subsequent in time to the explicit imperative "make disciples"? Wal-

---

111. Cross, *Baptism and the Baptists*, 39

112. It is sufficient to remember the second part of Plato's *Phaedrus* in which Socrates demonstrates the limitations of any written text in comparison to the oral word.

113. Wallace, *Greek Grammar*, 645.

lace argues that the two participles βαπτίζοντες (baptizing) and διδάσκοντες (teaching) have the following function and meaning:

> Finally, the other two participles (βαπτίζοντες and διδάσκοντες) should not be taken as attendant circumstance. First, they do not fit the normal pattern for attendant circumstance participles (they are present tense and follow the main verb). And second, they obviously make good sense as participles of means; i.e., the means by which the disciples were to make disciples was to baptize and then to teach.[114]

All this is to say that in terms of the syntax, as Wallace understands it, this phrase speaks of the means by which a person is made Jesus's disciple: they are first to be baptized and then to be taught the rest of Jesus's commandments.

Beasley-Murray endorses the same view and backs it up theologically. He asks how the process of making disciples occurs and answers:

> It might be considered as self-evident that disciples are made by the preaching of the gospel; that such as have become disciples are then baptized, and the baptized proceed to instruction; the two participles baptizing . . . teaching . . . successively follow the action of the main verb. Objection has been taken to this interpretation, however, for since the New Testament Epistles do not appear to reckon with the phenomenon of an unbaptized disciple, how can one become a disciple and then be baptized? Accordingly it is proposed that the participles describe the manner in which a disciple is made: the Church is commissioned to make disciples by baptizing men and putting them under instruction.[115]

Standard Baptist practice currently differs from the just-described model. It interprets Christ's instructions in the following way. First, (1) "go," that is, go on a mission, do not remain idle. Then (2) "make disciples" by preaching about Jesus Christ and his sacrifice that one is called to accept by faith. Next, (3) "teach" through special courses and catechetical training, (4) "baptize" by water baptism, and (5) "teach to obey" all the precepts, commandments, and rules found in the New Testament. Everett Ferguson believes that this interpretation of the Great Commission is neither dictated by the wording of Matthew's text nor consistent with its Greek grammar. He comments: "While

---

114. Wallace, 645.
115. Beasley-Murray, *Baptism in the New Testament*, 88–89.

all the participles derive an imperatival force from the main verb, the participle is coordinate with the main verb (go and make disciples) and two participles subsequent to the verb are circumstantial, describing the means of making disciples, with the 'teaching' accompanying the 'baptizing.'"[116] In other words, Ferguson incorporates teaching and baptizing into the process of making disciples. While there is no consensus on exegetical and theological reading of the Great Commission, one thing is certain: baptism is an indispensable component of making disciples, and no interpretation contends that.

What are the strengths and weaknesses of this approach that sees water baptism as the fulfillment of Christ's commandment? By far, its greatest strength is the obedient, wholehearted, and literal acceptance and application of Christ's words, which demonstrate the humility of both heart and mind on the part of the candidate for baptism. Gentleness and humility have always belonged among the highest Christian virtues. They are the qualities that help to accept by faith those regulations or norms whose meaning is wholly or partially hidden. The humble fulfillment of the commandment to baptize and be baptized is, therefore, an undeniable strength of this interpretation.

Another advantage is its linking of baptism with discipleship. This connection is made crystal clear in Christ's words (Matt 28:19), whatever the sequence of discipleship and baptism. Christians remain disciples throughout their lives, for a Christian is a person who learns constantly and unceasingly. Thus, viewing baptism as a stage and phase of discipleship leads to a proper understanding of the commandments that follow and helps to cultivate the habit of obeying them in humility.

This approach also has a weakness: thoughtless fulfillment of commandments deprives one of initiative and basically halts spiritual growth. Discipleship can quickly degenerate into mindless repetition of authoritative quotations, clichés, and formulae as if they were incantations. Bible study can turn into mechanical memorization of texts in a way one's mentor suggests, and, as a result, a person can memorize all the necessary biblical texts without being able to apply them correctly to real-life situations. For this kind of people, the Bible remains only a book of history, not of real life, and Christ is only a historical person, not a living teacher acting in their lives. Contemporary people, being emancipated and open-minded, want to feel the life of Christ and understand him. They want to hear not only what to do but also why they should do what they are told to do. A person may ask such questions because Christ does not need speechless robots. Instead, he seeks thinking and feeling

---

116. Ferguson, *Baptism in the Early Church*, 137.

individuals equipped to live a healthy spiritual life and prepared to act freely and consciously, not by orders from above, but according to their own inner drive, willingly and lovingly.

Another weakness of this understanding is that it does not really celebrate water baptism, downplaying its festive nature and the emotionality of the once-in-a-lifetime moment. If baptism is nothing more than the obligatory fulfillment of a commandment the Lord once gave, and the New Testament has prescribed, then this ordinance loses all the excitement of the transition from death to life, all the feelings that come with spiritual and mental transformation, and all the joy of entering union with Christ. Instead, it becomes a rather sober experience, being one of many steps in the discipleship process. The drama is gone, the connection with one's eternal salvation fades away, and, in the end, baptism is reduced to an act of pure obedience. The real drama is now exclusively associated with conversion or "repentance" in Baptist terminology.

Such a view demeans baptism and relegates it to the periphery of the conversion process, making us forget the price the first baptized people paid for this seemingly simple act of immersion into water. Perhaps we should remind ourselves of the blood and ashes of the fires, the thousands of deaths and executions of brothers and sisters who gave their lives for consciously accepting water baptism. The executioners of the sixteenth century killed them not for their repentance or inner spiritual experiences of conversion to Christ, but for their visible and conscious water baptism. The drama of baptism is evoked in the emotional cry of Balthasar Hubmaier arguing for conscious water baptism in a letter to Oecolampadius in January 1525. He writes that the inner work of purification of the heart "must, must, must be accompanied by the washing of the body in pure water."[117] Note how emphatically Hubmaier repeats the imperative three times. This is where the crux of the matter lies.

Baptism as Encounter

Through each image of baptism examined so far, its central meaning emerges – the encounter of God and man in the church's presence as a community of the faithful. This event is, so to speak, the juncture where God meets human beings, lifting the person beyond space and time and transforming baptism into a life-changing event. As stated in the final document of the Baptist-Catholic Dialogue (§85), "The sacraments/ordinances are experiences of encounter with Christ that transform the lives of those who enter into these moments of

---

117. Quoted in Rainbow, "Confessor Baptism," 205–6.

worship by the presence and power of the Holy Spirit."[118] This statement means that the sacrament of baptism's primary purpose is to transform the recipient's life during their encounter with God in a community of faith. Baptism, as a confirmation of one's faith, certifies the baptized person in the washing away of sins and union with Christ, marking the beginning of a new joyful life in a different hypostatic state as a person born from above.

According to this view, the proclamation of the good news, its acceptance by faith, repentance, water baptism, and discipleship constitute an inseparable whole. Of course, they can be temporally distinct from each other. Regeneration belongs to the same range of concepts as repentance, faith, and baptism, so any attempt to establish a causal or temporal connection between these processes is meaningless. Formulas like "regeneration through faith," "baptismal regeneration," or "regeneration without baptism," etc. are simply inapplicable to spiritual rebirth. It happens as a result of the holistic process of becoming a Christian.

This understanding existed already in the Apostolic era. It was reflected in a flexible and free-form liturgy, the absence of a fixed baptismal rite, and the use of a simplified confession of faith, which boiled down to the proclamation of Jesus Christ as Lord of life and the universe. Professor of New Testament at Southern Baptist Theological Seminary Robert Stein, in his article "Baptism and Becoming a Christian in the New Testament," describes the earliest church practices very vividly and convincingly. He writes:

> In the New Testament, conversion involves five integrally related components or aspects, all of which took place at the same time, usually on the same day. These five components are repentance, faith, and confession by the individual, regeneration, or the giving of the Holy Spirit by God, and baptism by representatives of the Christian community.[119]

He shows how the New Testament text portrays these five different components as producing the same result of salvation and justification so that in the minds of first-century people, they most often constituted different verbal descriptions of the same process of becoming a Christian.

One finds the same holistic understanding of salvation in the writings of Vasily Ivanov-Klyshnikov, one of the first Caucasian Baptists and a leading

---

118. Commission on Doctrine and Christian Unity BWA, "The Word of God in the Life of the Church."

119. Stein, "Baptism and Becoming a Christian," 6.

figure in the Baptist Union at the end of the nineteenth and beginning of the twentieth centuries. In the *Baptist* journal of 1911, he writes:

> Let us now see, what are the conditions for receiving salvation and all the blessings of God [given] through Christ the Savior?
>
> (1) "Whoever believes and is baptized will be saved, but whoever does not believe will be condemned" (Mark 16:16).
>
> (2) "Repent and be baptized, every one of you, in the name of Jesus Christ for the forgiveness of your sins. And you will receive the gift of the Holy Spirit" (Acts 2:38).
>
> Who does not see here the three indispensable conditions set forth by the Lord – namely, faith, repentance, and baptism – without the fulfillment of which salvation, the forgiveness of sins, and the reception of the Holy Spirit are inconceivable?[120]

V. V. Ivanov-Klyshnikov singles out the threefold condition of one's salvation: faith, repentance, and baptism. Stein, in turn, identifies five components, one of which is water baptism, and the others include repentance, faith, confession of sins, and receiving the Holy Spirit. Strictly speaking, the number of components of the holistic phenomenon of salvation may vary. It depends on the researcher's approach. It is the scholar himself who introduces the method of isolating some of the features of his research object. As a consequence, the final version of its constitutive elements or "components" depends on the author's preconceptions, ideological perspectives, and confessional preferences. The dependence of the theological phenomenon under study on the researcher is so strong that it cannot be eliminated entirely, although it is possible to reduce it as much as possible.

Anthony Cross, a leading expert in Baptist sacramentology, notes that since the middle of the twentieth century, "some scholars had begun to move away simply from the discussion of baptism, which was very often conducted in a way that detached it from the other aspects of conversion, namely faith, forgiveness, justification and the gift of the Spirit, to discussion of the more inclusive subject of Christian initiation."[121] He underscores the recent trend (at least in the British Baptist Union) of changing the language used to describe the Christian life. Instead of discrete rational-subjectivist characterizations

---

120. Ivanov-Klyshnikov, "O Pokayanii (On repentance)," 7.

121. Cross, "'One Baptism,'" 174–5. Notice that here Cross identifies only three elements of a unified conversion experience.

that reflect doctrinal descriptions (justification, faith, adoption, etc.) but fail to capture Christian life itself, theologians now seek to present a more integral, holistic perception of God's actions. Beasley-Murray provides his version of this new language, saying, "faith turning to the Lord receives the grace sought, just as the confession made in baptism receives the salvation of God."[122]

This holistic view is probably the most accurate reflection of New Testament accounts of people's coming to faith. However, in real life, the conversion process always breaks down into separate temporal phases or states. The main point that contemporary Baptist sacramentology makes is that one should not attempt to dismantle the process of personal salvation into its constituent parts but rather perceive it as a whole.

Of course, practically speaking, there is always a sequence of events, but their order is not rigidly fixed. For some, like the Samaritans, baptism may precede the descent of the Spirit; for others, like Cornelius, the descent of the Spirit may come before baptism, and in some cases, faith may save without baptism at all, like what happened to the repentant thief who was crucified with Christ. From a human perspective, salvation is the experience of all the major components of this act (drama), and its integrity is not compromised if one of the parts is omitted due to objective circumstances. What is truly essential is the fact of the divine-human encounter.

---

122. Beasley-Murray, *Baptism in the New Testament*, 103.

3

The Eucharistic Theology

History of Baptist Theology of the Eucharist

Many scholars[1] have noted that the theology of the Eucharist is rather poorly developed in the Baptist tradition. For example, Broadway writes at the beginning of his analysis of Baptist eucharistic theology: "Yet, Baptists have spent few words and little ink discussing the Lord's Supper. They have, in fact, usually had very little to say about the Lord's Supper except to debate about who may participate. The nature and significance of the Supper appear to be minor concerns in the history of Baptist theology."[2]

The lack of a coherent theological picture of the Lord's Supper results in a wide range of views that different Baptist groups hold. Perhaps the only thing that virtually all Baptists unanimously embrace is the rejection of the Catholic and Orthodox views of transubstantiation and the denial of the *ex opere operato* principle, according to which grace is imparted to the recipients during the celebration of the Lord's Supper regardless of their conscious faith or absence thereof.

Baptist theology of the Eucharist has its historical origins in two sources: the Anabaptist and Separatist (Calvinist) legacy. Puritan separatist attitudes toward the Lord's Supper steered early Baptist theology toward a sacramental understanding, while Mennonite influence emphasized the aspects of commemoration and proclamation.

The earliest Baptist confession, the 1609 *Short Confession of Faith*, penned by John Smyth, the leader and ideological inspiration of the Second English Church of Amsterdam and one of the first Baptists, teaches, "*Caenam Domini esse symbolum externum communionis Christi et fidelium ad invicem per fidem*

---

1. See Smith, ed., *The Lord's Supper*, 93.
2. Broadway, "Is It Not the Communion?," 403.

et charitatem (That the Lord's Supper is the external sign of the communion of Christ, and of the faithful amongst themselves by faith and love)."[3] This brief statement is closer to the Reformed position rather than the Zwinglian understanding. The term "sign of the communion" is typically Calvinist. This description of the Lord's Supper emphasizes that at the heart of this practice is communion (*communionis*) with Christ and one's brothers and sisters.

The second *Short Confession of Faith*, compiled in 1610 and signed by John Smyth and forty-one members of his group, speaks of the Lord's Supper and water baptism as sacraments. It is confirmed not only by the use of that term but also by the implication that something happens when these visible signs are performed: "These are outward visible handlings and tokens, setting before our eyes, on God's side, the inward spiritual handling which God, through Christ, by the cooperation of the Holy Ghost, setteth forth the justification in the penitent faithful soul" (article 28).[4] The Lord's Supper is something more than merely a mental process of recollection – it is a real sacrament, an event of encounter with the grace that produces "the inward spiritual handling."

Further, the text of this confession explains in article 32 that the Eucharist is a "spiritual supper, which the believing soul, feeding and [missing word] the soul with spiritual food."[5] This statement clearly reveals the sacramental nature of the holy meal, which differs from the Catholic understanding in that it only "witnesseth and signifyeth," that is, plays the role of a sign representing Christ's ministry, life, and death on the cross. Smyth hardly ever refers to the Lord's Supper as a commemoration in any of his confessions. In his view, the Lord's Supper is presented as a spiritual act that Christ performs in the repentant soul of the partaker. This description unmistakably alludes to the Calvinist view of the Supper as a spiritual meeting with Christ that attempts to avoid the notion of Christ's materialized, visible presence but, at the same time, clearly indicates his invisible presence in the Eucharist.

Having returned to England, the Baptist movement, as we know, began to spread in two forms: General (Arminian) and Particular (Calvinist) Baptists. Their views on the Lord's Supper differed, but not fundamentally. For example, in an important General Baptists' document, *The Orthodox Creed* of 1678, the Lord's Supper and water baptism are called both sacraments and ordinances. "Those two sacraments, viz. Baptism, and the Lord's-supper, are ordinances of

---

3. Lumpkin, *Baptist Confessions of Faith*, 101.
4. McGlothlin, *Baptist Confessions of Faith*, 61.
5. McGlothlin, 62.

positive, sovereign, and holy institution, appointed by the Lord Jesus Christ."[6] For seventeenth-century Baptists, these concepts, though synonymous, carried different meanings. The word *sacrament* was used to emphasize the fellowship with Christ and his spiritual support. In contrast, the word *ordinance* was more often used to describe procedural matters, stressing the way in which the believers should have submitted to and obeyed the one who instituted the Eucharist.

The second part of Article XXXIII outlines the proper order of the Lord's Supper's celebration, displaying an absolutely sacramental attitude towards the eucharistic elements:

> And the outward elements of bread and wine, after they are set apart by the hand of the minister, from common use, and blessed, or consecrated, by the word of God and prayer, the bread being broken, and wine poured forth, signify to the faithful, the body and blood of Christ, or holdeth forth Christ, and him crucified.[7]

It is important to note how the text speaks of the bread and wine becoming blessed and separated from common, profane use after the consecratory prayer. This language must look very unusual in the eyes of modern Baptists.

From the outset, Particular Baptists had a sacramental view of the Lord's Supper that goes back to Calvin. It was due to the fact that their Eucharistic doctrines were formed mainly in England, under the influence of the Puritan Separatists, and were close to the wording used in the *Westminster Confession of Faith*. The Lord's Supper is dealt with in the extensive chapter 30 of the so-called *Second London Confession of Faith* of 1677.[8] The document says that the Eucharist was instituted "for perpetual remembrance and shewing forth the sacrifice in his death confirmation of the faith of believers in all the benefits thereof their spiritual nourishment, and growth in him, their further engagement in, and to, all duties which they owe unto him."[9] Here, the Supper is presented not only as an instrument of remembering Christ and proclaiming his death, but as a means of spiritual nourishment and growth in Christ. It is also a bond and pledge of fellowship with Christ and one another.

---

6. McGlothlin, 144.

7. McGlothlin, 148.

8. The full title reads: *Confession of Faith put Forth by the Elders and Brethren of Many Congregations of Christians (Baptized upon Profession of their Faith) in London and the Country*. Although the *Second London Confession* was compiled in 1677, its official preface refers to it as the "Baptist Confession of Faith of 1689."

9. McGlothlin, *Baptist Confessions of Faith*, 270.

Both the *Orthodox Creed* and the *London Confession* highlight an important truth that is lost in Zwinglian theology. After the prayer of consecration, the bread and wine are separated from the profane use. Their essence does not change. They remain bread and wine, but their purpose does change. Therefore, in describing the Supper, the *Orthodox Creed* refers to the bread and the cup as "holy and divine mysteries,"[10] emphasizing the holiness of the eucharistic elements. The text of the *London Confession* makes it quite clear that the elements are in some mysterious way related to the person of Christ. It is, therefore, permissible to call the bread and wine of the Supper the body and blood of Christ, but such a name should only be applied *figuratively* or metaphorically.

> The outward Elements in this Ordinance, duely set apart to the uses ordained by Christ, have such relation to him crucified, as that truely, although in terms used figuratively, they are sometimes called by the name of the things they represent, to wit body and Blood of Christ; albeit in substance, and nature, they still remain truly, and only Bread, and Wine, as they were before.[11]

A comparison of the *Second London Confession* and the *Westminster Confession* and their teachings about the Eucharist easily demonstrates that the texts match each other almost verbally, except for the word *figuratively*. The original Westminster text has the word *sacramentally* instead.

Thus, it is beyond dispute that the early Baptist texts dealing with the Lord's Supper employ the sacramental language and speak about the sacramental spiritual presence of Christ. It is despite the fact that the *Second London Confession* never mentions the term *sacrament*, and all verbatim quotations from the *Westminster Confession*, where the word *sacrament* occurs in the original, have it replaced with *ordinance*. This is perhaps the only major difference with the Westminster original. Why did the English Particular Baptists drop the word *sacrament* and substitute it with *ordinance*? It is difficult to explain. After all, almost the same year, the English General Baptists also used the *Westminster Confession* to formulate their doctrine of the Eucharist. But they retained the term *sacrament* as a synonym for *ordinance*, without copying the Westminster

---

10. A fuller quote: "this holy ordinance ought to be often celebrated among the faithful, with examination of themselves, viz. of their faith, and love, and knowledge of these holy and divine mysteries." McGlothlin, 149.

11. McGlothlin, 271.

text the way the Particular Baptists did.[12] It is possible that the Particular Baptists wanted to avoid word-for-word duplication in their text. Furthermore, by that time, *ordinance* had already become a commonly used word in their vocabulary along with *sacrament*. Whatever the case, this shift in terminology had far-reaching consequences that surfaced in later generations as Baptists began their drift away from sacramentalism and toward Zwinglian theology.

The General Baptists' *Orthodox Creed* and the Particular Baptists' *Second London Confession* were the most comprehensive and influential seventeenth-century Baptist expressions of faith. There were other confessions in addition to these, but they tended to have a primarily local and not very lasting influence. Almost all early Baptist confessions – both of Particular and General Baptists – consistently use sacramental language that speaks of *spiritual nourishment* and *inward benefit from outward use*. They almost always allude to the dialectical relationship of the outward and the inward, which is reminiscent of the typical language of Reformed theology of the period.

The situation began to change in the eighteenth century with the arrival of the Enlightenment and its emphasis on the triumph of Reason. The era of Pietist piety and individualism arrived. In this context, a change of emphasis in Baptist eucharistic theology began to take place, as well: there was a movement away from a Reformed view of Holy Communion toward a Zwinglian one, which, in fact, had always been present in Baptist thinking.

The most vivid expression of the Zwinglian view on the Lord's Supper can be found in a treatise by John Sutcliff, an influential Baptist church pastor in Olney, Buckinghamshire. He was one of the founders of the *Baptist Missionary Society* and a close friend of William Carey. Sutcliff wrote: "Our remembrance of him implies his absence. Once he was an inhabitant of our world, but he is gone into heaven. We remember events that are past, or persons who are absent."[13] Sutcliffe explains that one can only remember someone who is absent, not present, and Christ, according to the faithful statement of Scripture, is absent on earth after his ascension and present only in heaven. Thus, the Lord's Supper becomes a mere memorial.

This understanding reemerged in the second quarter of the eighteenth century and then began to spread widely and freely in the nineteenth century.

---

12. "Those two sacraments, viz. Baptism, and the Lord's-supper, are ordinances of positive, sovereign, and holy institution, appointed by the Lord Jesus Christ." McGlothlin, 144.

13. Sutcliff, "The Ordinance of the Supper Considered." The year 1803 was chosen by this Association as the year of the Lord's Supper, so this encyclical letter to the churches was devoted entirely to the Eucharist.

Many scholars emphasize that the underlying factor that set this tendency in motion was the new faith in science and the vogue for rational explanations.[14] Another significant factor, as Michael Walker has convincingly shown, was the theological influence of a revitalized English Catholicism and the Baptist opposition to the Tractarian (Oxford) movement.[15]

American baptism, at first, was theologically dependent on English baptism and adhered mainly to the *Second London Confession*. By the mid-nineteenth century, however, there was clear evidence of an exclusively commemorative approach to the Eucharist. It is most clearly demonstrated by the Free Will Baptists' *Treatise on the Faith* of 1834 and the Calvinistic Baptist ministers' *New Hampshire Confession of Faith* of 1833. Both documents present a purely memorial approach but speak of *commemoration* rather than *remembrance*.

The *Southern Baptist Convention*, the largest Baptist association comprising churches in every state, outlines its beliefs in the *Baptist Faith and Message* document, which many churches use as their official statement of doctrine. The first version was adopted in 1925. Revised versions appeared in 1963 and 2000. The Lord's Supper is viewed in all of these redactions exclusively from the standpoint of Zwinglian theology as a symbol and act of remembrance. Thus, the *Baptist Faith and Message* obviously uses the wording of the *New Hampshire Confession*. But, in comparison with the latter, any hint of sacramentality has been removed, the word *sacred* has disappeared, and there is no mention of the participant's prior introspection. Another peculiar feature of this document is the replacement of the word *wine*, which was present in all early Baptist confessions, with *the fruit of the vine*.[16] It seems to be a more biblical expression but actually reflects a procedural change that occurred in American churches when they replaced the eucharistic wine with grape juice. The 2000 version of this document has not undergone any changes with regard to the Lord's Supper.[17]

English Baptist community had passed through the memorial phase of eucharistic theology, and at the end of the nineteenth century, there began a return to sacramental theology. While at the beginning of the twentieth century, only a few theologians spoke of sacramentalism,[18] in 1951, the *Principals'*

---

14. See *Introduction* in Cross and Thompson, *Baptist Sacramentalism*.

15. Walker, *Baptists at the Table*, 84–120.

16. The story of the substitution of *wine* for *the fruit of the vine* and the debate over it is discussed in Smith, *The Making of the 1963 Baptist*, 151–52.

17. See SBC, "Baptist Faith and Message 2000."

18. H. Wheeler Robinson, Neville Clark, G. R. Beasley-Murray, R. E. O. White, and others.

Conference, which consisted of tutors of the eight Baptist Theological Colleges in the United Kingdom, approved the following statement:

> The Communion Service is more than a commemoration of the Last Supper and a showing forth "of the Lord's death until He come." Here the grace of God is offered and is received in faith; here the real presence of Christ is manifest in the joy and peace both of the believing soul and of the community; here we are in communion, not only with our fellow-members in the church, not only with the Church militant on earth and triumphant in heaven, but also with our risen and glorified Lord.[19]

This definition brings back the holistic view of the Lord's Supper. It emphasizes that this event means more than just remembering and proclaiming Christ's death.

During the same period, a renewed interest emerged in theological reflection about the Lord's Supper in the American Baptist tradition. A number of articles appeared that advocated a return to a broader understanding of this commandment.[20] In 1969, the leading Baptist journal *Review & Expositor* devoted an entire issue to the Lord's Supper,[21] focusing on the return of a sacramental approach. Rust of Southern Baptist Seminary presented a theological perspective on the topic. He suggested that it was time to reconsider the conception of the Eucharist as something secondary and akin to a memorial meal. Rust insisted on a broader view of the Lord's Supper.

The Baptist theologian McClendon, Jr., was particularly influential and instrumental in the emergence of the Baptist Sacramentalist movement in the late twentieth century. He considered the Supper a performative sign producing a certain action. He wrote: "The power of the acted sign Christians call Lord's Supper (or Eucharist, or covenant meal, or Holy Communion) lies especially in its nearness to the person of Christ."[22] Thus, the Lord's Supper is again seen in Baptist theology as a broad and multifaceted event of real encounter with Christ, which cannot be reduced to an empty symbol and mere commemoration of Christ's death.

---

19. Child, ed., *The Lord's Supper*, 9.

20. Miller, "Reducing the Reality,"; Trent, "Ourselves and the Ordinances,"; Bender, "A Theological and Functional Understanding."

21. *Review & Expositor*, Volume 66.

22. McClendon Jr., *Doctrine: Systematic Theology*, 400.

The Lord's Supper in the Eastern European Context

As is well known, the earliest form of the Baptist movement in Eastern Europe was Stundism, which was a national version of German Pietism. Stundism emerged in the Ukrainian lands in the mid-nineteenth century as a native God-seeking movement,[23] but from the very beginning, its representatives found like-minded people among the German colonies, undergoing a Pietist revival at that time. Pietism, with rare exceptions, did not create separate ecclesiastical bodies but tended to remain within the framework of the mother church. The situation in the Russian Empire was different. The Russian Orthodox Church, using the state machinery at its disposal, began to persecute the Stundists, primarily physically. In a way, it pushed the new movement out of the cradle of Orthodox Christianity[24] and forced it to create its own ecclesiastical structures. This accounts for the very short period of existence of Stundism per se and rapid adoption of Baptist identity.

Johannes Dyck, in his dissertation and articles, analyzes in detail this transition from Stundism to the organized Baptist movement and underscores the high pace of this process.[25] For example, Mikhail Ratushny from the village of Osnova, Odesa district, was baptized on 8 June 1871, and on 28 November of the same year, he had already notified his archbishop of his defection from the Orthodox Church.[26] At the beginning of August of 1873, Ratushny reported in a letter to the clerk of the chancellery Nikolai Lyashkov that they had fully completed the formation of their church and elected a presbyter, to whom the community had granted the right to "baptize, celebrate the Lord's Supper, wed, bury, and [do] everything that belongs to the Church."[27] Thus, in the seventies of the nineteenth century, there emerged national Baptist congregations, which independently administered baptism and the Lord's Supper and had a clear understanding of their essence.

The ecclesiological views of these congregations undoubtedly underwent strong influence from the Mennonite Brethren. Lawrence Klippenstein pub-

---

23. See Reshetnikov and Sannikov, *Obzor Istorii Evangel'sko-Baptistskogo (A Survey of the History of Evangelical-Baptist)*, 59ff.

24. The German Pietists who preached in their countrymen's colonies in the 50s-60s of the nineteeth century (Eduard Wüst, Johann and Karl Bonekemper, and others) did not recommend Russian and Ukrainian adherents leave Eastern Orthodoxy, but the hostile attitude of the Orthodox clergy forced them to do so. Savinskiy, *Istoriya Evangel'skikh (A History of Evangelical Christians-Baptists)*, 59.

25. Dyck, *U Kolybeli Bratstva: Iogann Vieler (At the Brotherhood's Cradle: Johannes Wieler)*.

26. Dyck, "Fresh Skins for New Wine," 122–23.

27. Dorodnitsyn, *Materialy Dlya Istorii Religiozno-Ratsionalisticheskogo (Materials for the History of Religious-Rationalist Movement)*, 189.

lished in 1987 a document he obtained from the archives of Colonel Pashkov, written by the Mennonite teacher Johannes Wieler. In it, he says that in January 1870,[28] he, Mikhail Ratushny, and other brothers composed the *Rules of the Confession of Faith of the Newly Converted Russian Brotherhood*, which were discussed in all Stundist groups.[29] Based on these *Rules*, Ratushny and other Stundists baptized new converts and ministered in churches. The *Hamburg Confession* strongly influenced this text. This influence was mediated through Wieler, who was in Hamburg in the late 1860s and had close fellowship with Gerhard Oncken.

This document refers to the Eucharist as a sacrament and communion. Although this terminology is borrowed from the Eastern Orthodox tradition, it was consistent with the views of the early Baptists, who were not afraid to dismiss and vigorously oppose other Orthodox terms that did not fit their understanding of the biblical text. One should also remember that this text was compiled under the direction of the Mennonite Wieler, who had no penchant for Orthodoxy.

The fourth paragraph of the *Rules* concerns the essence of the Eucharist:

> The Holy Mysteries have this meaning: as we are all partakers of one bread, so we are all members of the body of Christ, which is the community of saints, and as we drink from one cup, we all are witnesses of His blood, which cleanses us from our sins.... We receive the Mysteries of Christ in remembrance of Christ's suffering and death, as a sign of communion with Christ and as a sign of communion of the faithful with each other.[30]

The nature of the Lord's Supper is to commemorate Christ's suffering and death and have fellowship with Christ and one another.

In other words, the text articulates not only the commemorative aspect of the Eucharist but also the idea of communion, which exists in the community that receives the bread and the cup as a sign of fellowship. This text intuitively, on a purely biblical basis, but very unequivocally expresses an idea reminiscent of James McClendon's notion of the conjoining role of the eucharistic signs. What McClendon expressed through the wordplay of *re-membering* and *remembering*, the authors of the *Rules* have framed in terms of the reception

---

28. The St. Petersburg Archive's documents indicate that it was not 1870, but 1871. See Zhabotinskiy, "Prosheniye Ivana Ryaboshapki (Ivan Ryaboshapka's Plea)," 130.

29. Klippenstein, "Johann Wieler (1839–1889)," 49–50.

30. Zhabotinskiy, "Prosheniye Ivana Ryaboshapki (Ivan Ryaboshapka's Plea)," 143.

of the Lord's Supper constituting a sign of communion with one another. The same sentence hints cautiously at the connection between the reception of the Eucharist and one's purification from sin. The authors were careful: they connected the forgiveness of sins with the blood of Christ, not the Eucharistic wine.

The last quarter of the nineteenth century was marked by the active growth of so-called sectarian groups. The Ukrainian lands and the Caucasus had good ties with the Mennonites and German Baptists, and the congregations there had a large percentage of Germans, Latvians, and Estonians.[31] Therefore, they were connected to the world Baptist movement, and their views on church polity and the Lord's Supper in this region were strongly influenced by Gerhard Oncken, Hamburg seminary, and the theology of the Mennonite Brethren. All this eventually resulted in the formation of classical Baptist communities here.

In St. Petersburg, the evangelical revival began with the arrival of Lord Granville Redstock in 1874, who was a flamboyant preacher of the Holiness movement (the Keswick movement). As a result of his preaching, a congregation emerged among the St. Petersburg aristocracy, which, after Redstock's expulsion from Russia, was led by Colonel Vasily Pashkov. It was a typical Pietist community that sought personal holiness and did not have a clear ecclesiology, being rather loosely structured. New people accepted to the community based not on their conscious baptism, but on having a life-changing faith. Therefore, this movement did not pay much attention to church regulations: they recognized infant baptism, and when they started performing eucharistic services, they adhered to the practice of open table. When Ivan Prokhanov, with his Baptist background, assumed leadership in the congregation, the situation began to change, but differences of opinion regarding church practices persisted for a long time. The Northern Revival became known under the name of Evangelical Christianity. This group developed relatively independently and did not always have friendly relations with the Baptists, although attempts to unite these groups were made repeatedly.

The Lord's Supper has been interpreted differently by Baptists and Evangelical Christians. The Baptist understanding was directly influenced by the *Hamburg Confession* of 1847, which V. G. Pavlov translated for the Baptist community in Tiflis (Tbilisi) in 1876. Pavlov's translation was often copied by hand and used in various Ukrainian and Transcaucasian congregations. In 1906, Pavlov published a revised translation of the *Hamburg Confession* in the form

---

31. Kucheryavyy, "Obzor Ucheniya o Vechere Gospodnei (An Overview of the Doctrine)," 153.

of a pamphlet entitled *The Beliefs of the Russian Evangelical Christians-Baptists*.[32] The Lord's Supper is mentioned there in paragraphs 6 and 9. Paragraph 6 states that there is a certain order of the means of grace God uses to draw sinners to Himself and give them salvation. This order is unchangeable. It begins

> (a) with the Word of God and water baptism, through which new converts are joined to the Church of Christ, followed in second place by the Eucharist.
>
> (b) the Holy Supper to proclaim the atoning sacrifice of Jesus Christ and to have the most intimate fellowship with Him.[33]

One immediately notes how this text follows the eucharistic theology outlined by the Particular Baptists of the seventeenth and early eighteenth centuries and uses sacramental language. The Supper is called holy, that is, separated from profane use. It is the second most important means of grace after the word and baptism, not merely a conventional symbol of remembrance. In other words, it somehow becomes a channel the Lord uses to transmit his grace and impart it to the participant.

Paragraph 9 is entitled "On the Holy Supper" and gives its detailed explanation, linking twice the commandment to break bread together with the bestowal of God's grace and referring to it as a gracious ordinance and means of grace. *The Beliefs* insist that the Lord's Supper should be celebrated frequently, and church members are to partake of it under both kinds. It is qualified as a proclamation and commemoration of Christ, and the reader's attention is drawn to the missional component – the Supper should proclaim Christ's death until his second coming. The second part of the statement focuses on the spiritual nourishment that takes place during the Supper:

> We believe that in this holy sign, Christ grants to the faithful to taste in a spiritual way His Body and His Blood. The communion of the Body and Blood of Christ should be unto the believer a divine pledge, by which the sense of his participation in Christ and in His sacrifice is elevated and strengthened, and through which

---

32. *Veroucheniye Russkikh Evangel'skikh Khristian-Baptistov* (*The Beliefs of the Russian Evangelical Christians-Baptists*). This text was republished with minor stylistic changes in the *Baptist* journal in 1907–1908, and as a separate edition published by N. Odintsov in 1928, and later by others.

33. *Veroucheniye russkikh*, (*The Beliefs of the Russian*), 5.

the forgiveness of sins received by faith is declared and assured to him once again.[34]

By speaking of spiritual nourishment that happens through the reception of the eucharistic elements, the text employs the concepts used earlier in the *Westminster* and *Second London Confessions*. As a result of this partaking of Christ's body and blood, the participants obtain a pledge, are confirmed in their abiding in Christ, and renew their awareness of the forgiveness of their sins they had received by faith in the cleansing blood of Christ. All of this shows a broad, deep, and undeniably sacramental understanding of the Eucharist, although the text mentions neither sacrament nor mystery.

The St. Petersburg Evangelical Christian movement was composed mainly of high-ranking, well-educated people with a broad-minded and often critical attitude toward church structures. They saw too many negative examples in the Eastern Orthodox and Roman Catholic churches. Therefore, Redstock's ideas about personal holiness found a fertile ground among these people and helped them form rather scant regard toward water baptism and the Eucharist. No special explanation of the meaning of the Supper was given by any of the early leaders of the community. Judging from the memoirs of some of its members, one can legitimately assume that it was interpreted mainly as a commemoration.

I. S. Prokhanov compiled the first systematic confession of faith of evangelical Christians in 1909.[35] The Lord's Supper is covered in the chapter entitled "On the Ecclesial Ordinances." From the outset, Prokhanov emphasizes that both baptism and the Lord's Supper are God's binding commandments. Thus, they are taken out of the sphere of man's liberty, and any failure to obey them is interpreted as disregarding God's direct command. It must have sounded like a pretty stringent statement to a rather liberal community of evangelical Christians. Henceforth, both conscious baptism of adults and participation in the breaking of the bread become necessary elements of evangelical Christians' church life and membership in this community. Moreover, the *Confession* unequivocally insisted on the closed-table practice, which was difficult for many evangelical Christians to accept.

Prokhanov describes the nature of the Eucharist as consisting of six components. First and foremost, he emphasizes the memorial understanding of the

---

34. *Veroucheniye russkikh*, (*The Beliefs of the Russian*), 8–9.
35. *Bratskiy listok*, a supplement to the *Khristianin (Christian)* journal 9, 1.

Eucharist. Then follows the spiritual communion with Christ, which should clearly be taken as a statement about the believer's encounter with Jesus.

In 1913, Ivan Veniaminovich Kargel', who had been the leader of the evangelical Christians in St. Petersburg after the forced departure of Pashkov, wrote *A Brief Exposition of the Evangelical Christians' Beliefs* and published it on behalf of the Second Congregation of Petersburg where he served. Kargel's doctrine was Arminian but retained many formulations that would also satisfy Calvinistic Baptists.[36] This balanced approach made it very popular among the various evangelical groups, and after their unification into a single All-Union Council of Evangelical Christians-Baptists (AUCECB) in 1944, its leadership adopted this statement of doctrine as its official creed.[37]

Baptism and the Lord's Supper are the topic of article 7, "On the Ordinances of Christ for the Church." It reads:

> The Lord's Supper is given by the Lord Himself for the remembrance of Him (Lk. 22:19; 1 Cor. 11:24–25), namely of His suffering and death as a ransom price (1 Cor. 11:26; 1 Pet. 1:18–19), His love reaching its limit (Jn. 15:13; 13:1; Rom. 5:8), and His giving of Himself not only for us but also to us as spiritual, heavenly food (Jn. 6:51; 1 Cor. 10:16). Received with a living faith, it makes us partakers of fellowship both with Him and with all the members of His Church (1 Cor. 10:16–17).[38]

This description, like that found in Prokhanov's *Confession*, combines both memorial and sacramental views, and in this case, it is hard to say which is favored more. In addition to the documents mentioned above, there existed several other confessions of faith, but their discussion of the Lord's Supper and

---

36. One should bear in mind that Kargel' was baptized by Ivan Voronin in the Baptist congregation of Tiflis and spent his youth there. Later, he studied theology in Germany where his teacher was for some time G. Oncken. Therefore, Calvinist theology undoubtedly had a great influence on him.

37. Kargel''s *Brief Exposition* was the official confession of faith for the Baptist Union of USSR from 1966 to 1985. It was approved by one of the Union's Congresses, yet with some amendments. Thus, the paragraph about the inadmissibility of second marriage was removed. Later, and one of the reasons it was replaced by a new confession of faith was that it had an excessively detailed eschatological section, reflecting strict premillennialist and pretribulationalist views.

38. Ivan Kargel', *Kratkoye Izlozheniye Veroucheniya Evangel'skikh Khristian (Brief Exposition of the Evangelical Christians' Beliefs)*, 8.

theological emphases do not differ fundamentally from the positions already presented.[39]

Thus, an analysis of the confessional documents of both Baptists and evangelical Christians in the pre-revolutionary period clearly shows that at that time, the concept of the Lord's Supper as a remembrance was dominant in neither group. Both Baptists and evangelical Christians noticeably display the language of sacramental theology, although the word *sacrament* occurs in none of the documents we analyzed. Still, almost all of them highlight the significance of the Eucharist as spiritual nourishment, as a way of being fed with Christ himself, which in no way matches the idea of a symbol. Furthermore, almost all confessional texts of that time emphasize that celebrating the Lord's Supper brings about communion and, hence, an encounter with the lord himself that the participants regard as real. In both their statements of doctrine and in their sermons and articles, Baptists clearly affirm that the Supper is a means of grace[40] that exists and functions in an ecclesial framework, while evangelical Christians view it primarily christologically as a means and expression of participation in Christ.

After the October Revolution (1917), the new Soviet period of the history of the Eastern European Baptist movement began. It brought pressure from atheistic ideology, the physical extermination of many leaders of both Baptists and evangelical Christians, and the dissolution of all evangelical church unions. The theological development came to a halt. Some relief came during the difficult years of World War II when, in 1944, a single church association comprising various evangelical groups[41] was formed under the name of the All-Union Council of Evangelical Christians-Baptists (AUCECB). During this entire period, up to the end of the twentieth century, there was little, if any, theological discussion of the Lord's Supper.

The official publication of the AUCECB, the *Bratskiy Vestnik* (*Brotherly Herald*), often published articles on the Lord's Supper. But their main emphasis was either on this institution's historical aspects and Old Testament origins or

---

39. For a detailed comparative analysis of the Baptist confessions, see Savinskiy, *Istoriya Evangel'skikh Khristian-Baptistov (A History of Evangelical Christians-Baptists)*, 323.

40. The anonymous author of an article in the *Baptist* journal writes: "certainly the Supper is a means of grace, but not a means of stirring up faith when it is not yet there; rather, it is a means of strengthening it when it is already there." N.a., "Kto Mozhet Pristupit' k sv. Vechere? ("Who Can Partake of the Holy Supper?)," 11.

41. This Union initially comprised Baptists and evangelical Christians. Later, they were joined by various pentecostal groups, Free Christians (Darbists), Christians in the Apostles' Spirit (unitarians), Evangelical Christians-Teetotalers, and Mennonites.

on the observance of this commandment. At the same time, the sacramental understanding of the Lord's Supper receded into the background while its purely memorial aspect came to the fore.

A. Karyev, one of the first chairmen of the AUCECB, wrote: "The bread and the cup of wine should revive in our memory Christ, His sufferings, His death, [and] His blood."[42] No sacramental connotations surface in his account of the Eucharist. His main emphasis is on the proclamation of Christ's death and the commemorative meaning of the Lord's Supper. The same may be said of other articles in the *Bratskiy Vestnik* of this period.

A certain exception is M. J. Zhidkov's paper presented at the 41st Congress of Soviet Baptists in December 1974. In it, he gives a brief but rather profound analysis of the theological meaning of the Eucharist. He points to the main theological components of this ordinance, beginning with thanksgiving (*eucharistio*), stressing the unity it creates (*communio*), moving on to proclamation and eschatological hope, and reminding about introspection. Zhidkov emphasizes that "the Lord's Supper is a sacrament of remembrance."[43] Later, explicating this notion of sacramental remembrance, he adds,

> Participation in the Lord's Supper ends with one more act on our part: the renewal of our commitment. The word *sacramentum* has a double meaning: a sacrament and an oath of allegiance. Something similar should happen to us: we need to renew our commitment to the One with whom we have a personal encounter in fulfilling His commandment.[44]

M. Zhidkov explicitly calls the Supper a sacrament and even uses the word *sacramentum*, referring his readers to Tertullian's works. It is especially noteworthy that M. Zhidkov points to the Eucharistic encounter when speaking of a person's meeting with Christ during the Eucharistic celebration. It suggests pretty obviously the sacramental practice of the Lord's Supper even though the theology articulated is that of the Zwinglian memorial approach.

The memorial component dominates the official *Beliefs* of the Evangelical Christians and Baptists Union, adopted at the 43rd Baptist Congress in 1985. The main emphasis is on remembrance and proclamation, while the Eucharistic

---

42. Karyev, "Vecherya Gospodnya" ("The Lord's Supper"), 20.

43. Zhidkov, "Vodnoye Kreshcheniye i Vecherya Gospodnya (Water baptism and the Lord's Supper)," 59.

44. Zhidkov, 59.

signs are said to simply "point to the Body and Blood of Jesus Christ."[45] After the establishment of the Ukrainian Baptist Union and its separation from the former AUCECB in 1990, the 21st Congress of the *Ukrainian Union of Evangelical Christians-Baptists* approved its official statement of doctrine. The section on the Lord's Supper practically repeats the text of the 43rd Baptist Congress (1985) *Beliefs* but somewhat expands it. It emphasizes that a participant enters into a spiritual union with Christ by partaking of the eucharistic signs.[46]

Until 2000, discussions about the various interpretations of the eucharist were practically non-existent. The main focus of sermons and articles of the period was on liturgical aspects.[47] Since the 1990s, a stream of popular theological literature has flooded Eastern Europe. It presented the Supper mainly as a symbol and remembrance of Christ's death. At the same time, rare articles by national authors attempted to give a broader picture of this ordinance.[48] This double tendency has produced an extremely diversified view of the Lord's Supper. Northeastern Baptist groups, preserving the tradition of evangelical Christians, have more often emphasized the importance of the Lord's Supper as a commemoration and proclamation of Christ's death,[49] while the heirs of the traditional Baptist approach have usually focused on the mystical component.[50] This difference began to create theological tensions, especially after 2000, when sacramental theology began to return to Eastern Europe, even though Baptist authors have been careful to avoid the word *sacrament*.

A significant marker of the development of Baptist sacramentalism was Oleg Turlac's master's thesis entitled "The Eucharist and Ecclesiology," published in the Moscow Theological Seminary's journal *Put' Bogopoznaniya (Path to Theological Knowledge)*. The author provides an in-depth theological analysis of the Supper from a sacramental perspective. Turlac views the Eucharist as a sacrament of unity, the sacrament of remembrance, and the sacrament of

---

45. "Veroucheniye Evangel'skikh Khristian-Baptistov" ("Beliefs of Evangelical Christians-Baptists"), 46.

46. Ukrainian Union of Evangelical Christians-Baptists, 'Virovchennya (Confession of Faith)', 1990, Section 5:4 https://www.baptyst.com/virovchennya/.

47. See Matviyiv, *Svyashchennodiyi Pastora (The Pastor's Sacred Acts)*, 52–69; Kolesnikov, "Tserkovnyie Svyashchennodeystviya Evangel'skikh Khristian-Baptistov" ("Church Sacred Acts of Evangelical Christians-Baptists"); Romanyuk, *Tserkovne Slyzhinnya (Church Ministry)*, 39–44.

48. Koval'chuk, "Shcho Bibliya kazhe pro Gospodnyu Vecheryu" ("What Bible says about the Lord's Supper"), 23.

49. "We believe that the Lord's Supper (Breaking of the Bread) is Jesus Christ's commandment to remember and proclaim His sufferings and death on the cross." *Veroucheniye YeKhB (Beliefs of Evangelical Christians-Baptists)*, "O Vechere Gospodnyey (On the Lord's Supper)."

50. Sipko, "Kreshcheniye i Vecherya (Baptism and the Lord's Supper)."

thanksgiving. He concludes his discussion by pointing to Christ's spiritual presence and saying: "The Eucharist is not only a symbolic remembrance but also the spiritual presence of Christ in the midst of the Church."[51] The appearance of such works[52] points to a burgeoning theological potential within contemporary Eastern European evangelicalism.

The Eucharist in the Old and New Testaments

Although the Lord's Supper was instituted in the New Testament,[53] its roots obviously go back as early as the prophecies and images of the Old Testament. They were, in Paul's words, "a shadow of the things that were to come" (Col 2:17, NIV, compare with Heb 10:1).

Identifying the prototypes (*typoses*) of the Lord's Supper in the Old Testament presupposes the presence in these texts of what is sometimes called, following the Jewish sages, the "mysteries of the Torah," as Joseph Ratzinger noted.[54] In other words, in addition to the literal, historical-grammatical meaning, each complete passage of Scripture contains a hidden, mysterious meaning that one can extract using a specific methodology. A Christological approach that reads the Old Testament texts focusing on Christ's messianic dignity, person, and work reveals this meaning most vividly.[55] This approach analyzes the prototypes based on their subsequent actualization (or interpretation) in Jesus rather than on a reconstruction of the text in its most ancient form.

---

51. Turlac, "Yevkharistiya i Ekkleziologiya (The Eucharist and Ecclesiology)," 147.

52. At present, there is an influx of serious research papers appearing in various theological schools of Eastern Europe. See, for example, Vitaly Gura's master's thesis: "Pryroda Dukhovnogo Vplyvu Vecheri Gospodnyoyi na Khrystyyanyna" ("The Nature of the Spiritual Influence of the Lord's Supper on the Christian").

53. A significant number of contemporary researchers, one of the most prominent of them being Paul F. Bradshaw, believe that Christ did not institute the Eucharist. Bradshaw writes that the life of early Christian communities revolved around regular communal meals, reflecting, in his view, Christ's primary mission. In these poor communities, "the bread and wine of the meal might have been thought of as simply 'spiritual food and drink' (as in the *Didache*), or as the flesh and blood of Jesus. . . . Someone, however, possibly even St Paul himself, did begin to associate the sayings of Jesus with the supper that took place on the night before he died, and interpreted them as referring to the sacrifice of his body and blood and to the new covenant that would be made through his death." Bradshaw, *Reconstructing Early Christian Worship*, 26. This is how, according to these researchers, the eucharistic liturgy began to take shape.

54. Ratzinger, *Joseph Ratzinger Collected Works*, 196–97.

55. For the reasoning behind this typological reading of the Old Testament through the lens of Jesus Christ, see, Ratzinger, *Collected Works*, 234.

The entire sacrificial system of the Old Testament was not self-sufficient in the theological sense. It pointed prophetically to the future sacrifice of Christ on the cross. But, importantly, in most cases, the sacrifice was also connected with eating the sacrificial meat. This link between sacrifice and food represents a rather loud echo of the Lord's Supper in the Old Testament.

An allusion to the Eucharist is found in all sin offerings, guilt offerings (Lev 4–6, compared with Heb 9:12; 12:24), thankfulness or fellowship offerings (Lev 7:11–35), and especially in the Passover meal (Exod 12:3–13 compared with 1 Cor 5:7).

The sacrifices had both an intrinsic spiritual meaning and an extrinsic ritual accompanied by specific material actions. The spiritual component of the sin offering was forgiveness and restoration. Certainly, "[i]t is impossible for the blood of bulls and goats to take away sins" (Heb 10:4), but the Old Testament sacrifices pointed to the true sacrifice of Christ. One's partaking of the sacrificial meal visibly signaled the acceptance of the sacrifice, whereas the satisfaction from the eating reflected the satisfaction of divine justice, and the peaceful and festive mood testified to the restoration of previously broken wholeness. In other words, the fact of communion of sacrificers and the spiritual result of the sacrifice visibly took place through the communal consumption of sacrificial meals.

Sergius Bulgakov suggests that the connection between the spiritual meaning of the sacrifice and its eating has universal bearing. He even goes as far as to call participation in the sacrificial meal "deification" (*theosis*) and states that it has occurred not only in Christianity but also in the Old Testament offerings and even in pagan idolatry. He writes:

> The basic idea of sacrifice consists, in the first place, in offering a gift to God in the form of specific things expressly selected in thanksgiving to God. Second, it consists in liberation from guilt or sin by an offering as a ransom in their place via the death of the animal sacrificed. And third, it consists in a kind of deification through union with the Divine in the communion of the sacrificial flesh, which is made holy after immolation.[56]

If we understand deification as our communion with the deity, then the eating of the sacrificial meat is indeed a sign of union with the god to whom the sacrifice is offered, although the substance of the sacrifice does not ontologically become sacred. *Deification* becomes a spiritual process that happens

---

56. Bulgakov, *Yevkharistia* (*The Eucharistic Sacrifice*), 4.

when the material food is united with the spiritual phenomenon resulting from the partakers' attitude toward the sacrifice. It is why apostle Paul says that food sacrificed to idols is nothing in itself (1 Cor 10:19–20) but becomes something when the worshipers bestow divine properties on their idol. It is why participation in "idol feasts" is prohibited (1 Cor 10:28–29). In the same vein, when eating the Old Testament sacrifices, their participants prefigured and prototypically shared in the sacrifice of Christ.

One of the most distinct echoes of the Lord's Supper in the Old Testament is the idea of the covenant and the related notion of covenant renewal that accords with Christ's words at the Last Supper (Matt 26:28). Christ stands as the testator of eternal life, salvation, and the gracious work of the Holy Spirit for all who accept the terms of his covenant and enter into it. This is analogous to the legal procedures that regulate one's entry into a material inheritance. The sacrifices that Noah, Abraham, and Moses made when they entered the covenant with God were the prototypes of Christ's death. The testator in all these cases was God through the mediator Jesus Christ, but in the pre-Christian covenants, the sacrificial animals served as the pointer to Christ's sacrificial death. Jesus established the New Covenant at Calvary but had referred to it earlier at the Last Supper, commanding his disciples to remember it and celebrate the eucharistic meal until his second coming. Thus, the Lord's Supper is the ratification of Christ's covenant with his disciples. As the authors of "Re-Envisioning Baptist Identity: A Manifesto for Baptist Communities in North America" write, "In the Lord's Supper the Spirit thus signifies and seals the covenant that makes us one with Christ and one in Christ with one another."[57]

The New Testament accounts of the Lord's Supper speak both directly and indirectly, implicitly, of this ordinance. The explicit narratives are, first of all, those of the synoptic evangelists (Matt 26:26–29; Mark 14:22–25; Luke 22:15–20) and instruction Paul gives to the Corinthian congregation in 1 Corinthians 11:23–25, as well as the explanation he provides regarding the nature of the Lord's Supper in 1 Corinthians 10:16–17. The indirect accounts usually include John's narrative of Jesus's Last Supper before the Passover (John 13:1–38)[58] and his account of Jesus's teaching in the synagogue in Capernaum (John 6:53–58). Also, one can add to that the numerous prototypes of the Lord's Supper.

An analysis of the New Testament narratives of the Lord's Supper shows that the Matthew-Mark narrative emphasizes a priestly discourse focused on

---

57. Broadway et al., "Re-Envisioning Baptist Identity."

58. Some scholars regard John's account in 13:1–38 as a controversial description and deny its association with the Last Supper.

sacrifices and strict legalism. In contrast, the Luke-Paul narrative espouses a primarily prophetic approach, highlighting the priority of internal spiritual processes over external ritualism.

Apostle Paul's discussion of the Lord's Supper in 1 Corinthians 10 is textually related to the issue of "idol feasts" and, thus, provides insight not so much into the eucharistic liturgy as into its sacramental character. Paul draws from the image of Israel coming out of Egypt and reaching Canaan with great difficulty in spite of God's unparalleled care for this nation. Building on this historical example, Paul shows the necessity for Christians to be fed constantly with the spiritual bread of the Eucharist and living water that comes from "the spiritual rock that followed them," which is Christ. In contrasting the Lord's meal with the idolatrous one, Paul suggests a somewhat flexible position that depends on the attitude, understanding, and intentions of those who participate in the meal.

Speaking of the link between the material and the spiritual, Paul points to the breaking of the bread, which is "a sharing in the body of Christ," and the cup of blessing, which is "a sharing in the blood of Christ" (1 Cor 10:16, NRSV). Thus, he unveils the spiritual connection between the material objects, the bread and the wine, and the spiritual entity, the body and blood of Christ. This connection is actualized through the intentionality of faith, just as in the case of eating the food sacrificed to idols and depends only on the participant's focused attention. It is this intentional act, not the substantial change of the eucharistic elements (transubstantiation), that gives meaning to the action.

Christ's shocking monologue in the Capernaum synagogue (John 6:25–71) employs the perechoretic language of the mutual indwelling of the Father in the Son, and the Son in the Father. Christ has the same kind of relationship with those who, by faith, accept his challenge to eat his flesh and drink his blood.

Another eucharistic text from John's gospel gives an implicit, tacit description of the Lord's Supper. It is John 13:1–38. This account has many easily identifiable overlaps with the synoptics' narratives but lacks important historical details that would allow this narrative to be explicitly equated with the Last Supper of other evangelists. Clearly, John articulates a covenantal rather than cultic tradition and conceptualizes the events of Jesus's Last Supper theologically rather than historically. This is why this narrative's central theme is "love to the end."

John shows how this love particularly manifests itself in Jesus's self-humiliating act of washing his disciples' feet. This act later resulted in a heated debate between advocates of a literal versus symbolic interpretation of Jesus's example. Yet, the literal washing of feet and turning it into a sacrament most often overrides its spiritual meaning because it is not prompted by a real need to humble oneself and serve one's neighbor. But this is precisely what Christ teaches us to do with his own example. The contemporary foot-washing ritual can, at best, only remind us of humility but not generate it. Christ's example is about serving the people whose status is lower than ours.

Love to the end, in John's description, was manifested not only in Jesus's washing his disciples' feet but much more powerfully in his kenosis, vulnerable self-giving to people utterly unworthy of his love. This love, being an ontological characteristic of God himself, has the amazing quality of depending only on the one who loves, not on the beloved, and is characterized by a radical and complete self-giving that repudiates all partiality and half-measures.

The Character and Dating of the Last Supper

The debate surrounding Christ's Last Supper has stemmed mainly from the inconsistencies between the Gospel narratives, many indubitable stipulations of the Jewish tradition, and the contradictions between the synoptic gospels and the Gospel of John. The first three evangelists plainly indicate that Jesus celebrated the Last Supper with his disciples the night the Passover lambs were slaughtered and portray it as a traditional Passover meal (Matt 26:17; Mark 14:12; Luke 22:7–8). All three evangelists seem to agree that the Supper took place on Thursday and that Jesus was taken into custody on Thursday night, tried early Friday morning, and crucified at noon. However, reading John the evangelist's account gives the impression that Jesus and his disciples ate the meal the day before the Passover because, according to his testimony, Jesus was tried and crucified the next day, which was Friday. "Now it was the day of Preparation for the Passover; and it was about noon" (John 19:14, NRSV; compare with 19:31). John also reports that the high priests and Sadducees did not enter the Praetorium, "so as to avoid ritual defilement and to be able to eat the Passover" (John 18:28). In other words, John seems to say that the Passover was on Saturday but, according to the synoptics, it was on Friday.

Theologians have been struggling with the conflation of these records for centuries. Some scholars declare this contradiction irresolvable; others consider the synoptics's testimony erroneous; still others are inclined to believe that John is mistaken.[59] Also, many theologians believe that both the synoptics

---

59. Donald Carson, in his commentary on John 13:1–30, demonstrates the arguments of authors who hold each of the mentioned positions. Carson, *The Gospel According to John*, 455–56.

and John are equally correct and offer more or less convincing explanations that seek to reconcile these two accounts.[60]

One of the simplest ways out of this New Testament conundrum is to stop treating Jesus's Last Supper as a Jewish Passover meal.[61] In such a case, the clear testimony of the synoptics is declared to be either an error, a theological supplement, or even a later Christian interpretation. But that would go against well-documented research by Joachim Jeremias, who has comprehensively analyzed all gospel texts and proved that the Last Supper was indeed a Passover meal.[62] But then, what date and on what day did Jesus and the disciples have that meal? What day of the week was 14 Nisan, the year of Christ's crucifixion?

Another method of reconciling the synoptics and John is based on the presence in Second Temple Judaism of various calendars and rival religious groups that defined the cycles of Jewish festivals differently.[63] The theory of two calendars was at the core of a dissertation that Annie Jaubert, a professor at the University of Paris, wrote in the early 1950s.[64] Jaubert developed a theory mainly using the pseudepigraphic *Book of Jubilees* and the Qumran Scrolls, but also finding some corroboration for it in patristic literature.

Jaubert began by scrutinizing the *Book of Jubilees* as a second-century BC document, possibly written in the Essene community, that provides the most comprehensive information about alternative calendar systems of the Second Temple Judaism. In the *Jubilees'* calendar, all feasts and "holy days" always fall on the same day of the week. For example, while in the official calendar, the first day of Passover changes with shifting lunar cycles, the *Jubilees'* calendar has it always on Tuesday, 14 Nisan.

Jaubert and her followers believe that Jesus fulfilled the Passover with his disciples as described by the synoptics on the Tuesday evening of Holy Week, which, according to the Essenes's calendar, was the evening of 14 Nisan. But Sadducees and Pharisees celebrated the Passover following the official temple calendar, according to which the day of 14 Nisan fell on Friday, the year of Christ's crucifixion. That means that John describes Jesus's Last Supper from the perspective of the official calendar, while the synoptics look at it through the lens of the Essenes's calendar.

---

60. For more details, see Marshall, *Last Supper and Lord's Supper*, 67.
61. For example, see McKnight, *Jesus and His Death*; Klawans, "Was Jesus' Last Supper?," 24–33.
62. Jeremias, *The Eucharistic Words of Jesus*, 41–62.
63. Prat, *Jésus Christ: Sa Vie, Sa Doctrine*, 515.
64. Jaubert, *The Date of the Last Supper*.

However, this interpretation raises many questions. If, as the two-calendar theory suggests, Jesus ate the Passover lamb on Tuesday, a few days earlier than the official date of 14 Nisan, how could the official Jewish leaders have allowed the Essenes into the temple, and who could have performed the lamb slaughter for them if the priestly families completely controlled the Temple? Joachim Gnilka writes:

> And if one attempted to assume that Jesus wanted to celebrate the Passover on Tuesday, it would not have been possible for him to secure a lamb that has been slaughtered in the temple in keeping with the regulations. Yet this must be absolutely presupposed for this festival. The assertion that the Essenes had permission to slaughter lambs in the temple on their date is pure invention.[65]

It is obviously the most significant difficulty for the theory of two calendars that we are rejecting the clear evidence of the synoptics and, in addition, have to explain the possibility of slaughtering the Passover lambs a few days earlier, either in the temple or another place. Both of these options would have been hardly feasible for the scrupulously law-observant Essenes.

A fairly large group of theologians insists that there is no contradiction between the Passover narratives of the synoptics and John. Instead of following the two-calendar theory, they suggest that, for some reason, the slaughtering of the lambs and the following celebration of Passover lasted two days instead of one, in the year of Christ's crucifixion. This approach holds that the day of preparation, 14 Nisan, fell on a Friday, and the first day of Passover was on Saturday, 15 Nisan, but Christ and the apostles ate the Passover on Thursday, 13 Nisan. In this case, there is no calendar problem; the gospel accounts harmonize well; Jesus's Last Supper is a Passover *seder*. But there arises the question: why and how the offering of the Passover lambs could have taken place on Thursday, 13 Nisan, instead of 14 Nisan? There is a wide range of possible explanations, all of which have to do with varying rabbinic traditions and contradicting views on interpreting the Torah.

According to Paul Billerbeck, who meticulously cataloged and analyzed different rabbinic sources, during the Second Temple period the two most powerful groups were the Sadducees (Boethusians),[66] who controlled the

---

65. Gnilka, *Jesus of Nazareth*, 280.

66. Boethus's family came to control the temple and the Sanhedrin since the time of Herod the Great, who married Boethus's daughter and appointed him high priest. From this time on, the Talmud makes no distinction between the Sadducees and the Boethusians. "Saddukeyi" ("Sadducees"), in *Kratkaya Evreyskaya Entsyklopediya (Concise Hebrew Encyclopedia)*, 587–8.

Temple, and the Pharisees. These two factions had different opinions about when the month of Nisan began.[67] The Sadducees calculated it in such a way as to make 14 Nisan fall on Friday and the Pentecost on Sunday (see Acts 2:1). The Pharisees considered this method to be a fabrication and began the month of Nisan a day earlier, with 14 Nisan falling on Thursday. The compromise, however, was that the Boethusian Sadducees, controlling the Temple and the sacrifices, agreed to slaughter the lambs the Pharisees brought on Thursday while they slew their lambs on Friday.[68] With this conflict in the background, one can see how Christ, together with his disciples and a part of the Jewish population, could eat the Passover on Thursday, 13 Nisan according to the official temple calendar (but 14 Nisan according to the Pharisaic calendar, which they considered to be authentic), while the rest of the people celebrated the Passover on Friday (14 Nisan for the Sadducees) when the true Passover lamb was crucified on the cross. Joachim Jeremias and many other conservative evangelical theologians[69] find this theory quite satisfactory.

One of the most interesting proposals seeking to resolve the calendar quandary was made by the famous historian and Hebraist Daniel Chwolson[70] (1819–1911), who translated most of the Old Testament books into Russian. Chwolson points out that although the synoptics believe that the Last Supper was a Passover meal that took place on Thursday, the next day, Friday, could not have been the first Passover day because the gospel-writers describe human activities that indicate that that day was an ordinary weekday (Jesus's arrest, Jesus's trial, temple guard wielding weapons, Simon of Cyrene coming from the field, etc.). Given that the evangelists (especially Matthew) were writing in a Jewish context, it is hard to imagine them overlooking this contradiction. Consequently, all four evangelists unanimously say that the Friday when Jesus was crucified was not the first day of Passover but the day of preparation, 14 Nisan. This means that Passover (15 Nisan) for the year of Christ's crucifixion fell on Saturday, and he and his disciples ate the Passover lamb on Thursday, 13 Nisan.

Chwolson explains that when the first day of Passover, 15 Nisan, fell on the Sabbath, there arose a contradiction between the careful adherence to all

---

67. Strack and Billerbeck, *Kommentar zum neuen Testament*, 847–50.

68. Practically the same position is held by Lagrange, the founder of École biblique in Jerusalem. Lagrange, *L'Evangile de Jésus Christ*, 494–96.

69. Marshall tentatively accepts this theory and regards Billerbeck's theory as "the most plausible." Marshall, *Last Supper and Lord's Supper*, 74.

70. Chwolson, *Das letzte Passamahl Christi und der Tag seines Todes*.

the regulations surrounding the Passover feast and the strict observance of the Sabbath. In particular, there were two major inconsistencies.

The first had to do with the slaughter of the Passover lambs. According to the ancient rules, clearly stated in the Torah, the Passover sacrifice was to be slain in the evening, after sunset (Exod 12:6). But in this case, the Passover eve would coincide with the beginning of the Sabbath, when no one was allowed to work or cook (Exod 35:2). The solution to this situation was twofold: it was possible either to move the slaughter a few hours earlier so that it would take place during the evening sacrifice (between 3 and 5 p.m.)[71] or to move it even further to the evening of the day before, to comply with the letter of the law. Joseph Lvovich Klausner, a writer, Zionist activist, and excellent expert on Judaism, in his *Jesus of Nazareth*,[72] specifies:

> According to the ruling which was newly promulgated by the Pharisees in Hillel's time, the Passover was regarded as a public sacrifice . . . they used to argue that, like every public sacrifice, 'the Passover abrogates the Sabbath rules.' According, however, to an earlier ruling, which held good among the priestly party almost to the close of the period of the Second Temple, the Passover was regarded as a private sacrifice and one which might not abrogate the Sabbath rules.[73]

Consequently, if Nisan 15 fell on the Sabbath, one group (the Pharisees) considered it permissible to disregard the Sabbath regulations and make the sacrifice on Friday evening or to move it to Friday afternoon so as not to violate the Sabbath, while the other group, extolling the holiness of both the Sabbath and the Day of Preparation, argued for the need to move all these preparatory activities to a day earlier, to Thursday, Nisan 13.

Another inconsistency results from the tension the two divine commands create in this case. On the one hand, the Torah prescribes: "Do not light a fire in any of your dwellings on the Sabbath day" (Exod 35:3), but, on the other hand, it also says regarding the Passover lamb that "if some is left till morning, you must burn it" (Exod 12:10). When the Passover and Sabbath eves coincide, these two commandments become incompatible. Therefore, the easiest solution for the stricter, "conservative" group was to move the lamb slaughter

---

71. Josephus says that in his time this is how it was done. *Jewish War* VI, 9:4.

72. Jeremias believes that Chwolson relies on Klausner in his work. They do explain the chronology of Jesus's life consonantly, but in fact it is Klausner who often refers to Chwolson, not the other way around, *The Eucharistic Words of Jesus*, 22.

73. Klausner, *Jesus of Nazareth*, 326.

and Passover meal one day earlier. However, the more lenient, "liberal" group believed that the Passover "supplants the Sabbath;" therefore, one could ignore some of the Sabbath regulations for the sake of proper Passover celebration.

Chwolson writes that when Passover coincides with the Sabbath, "the later rabbis give a precise answer by saying: 'the Passover sacrifice supersedes the Sabbath,' i.e., the Sabbath observance in this case ceases and all ordinarily forbidden works are permitted as long as they are necessary for the offering of the Passover lamb."[74] But he goes on to say that there are compelling reasons to assert that "the ruling regarding the offering of the Passover lamb on the Sabbath was an *innovation* that was previously unknown" (italics in original).[75] It is also the point that other scholars who have examined the customs of the Karaites and Samaritans make.

Chwolson, unlike Klausner, believes that these difficulties led the Jewish authorities, the year of Christ's death, to move the slaughter of the Passover lambs for all Israelites one day earlier, from the 14th to the 13th of Nisan. Thus, the temple Passover sacrifice took place on one day only, Thursday, but the Passover meal as a private affair was celebrated in homes rather than in the temple. Therefore, some Jews held the meal immediately after the slaughter, on Thursday evening, while others did so on Friday evening, as the Passover regulations dictated. According to Chwolson and his followers, this situation is reflected in the gospel narratives.

Another approach suggests an astronomical solution to the problem of Passover dating. Colin Humphreys and Graeme Waddington proposed an updated version of this solution.[76] Their calculations pointed to Friday, 3 April AD 33 as the date of Christ's death, which coincides with 14 Nisan.[77]

In addition, textual solutions to the dating problem are also known. They emphasize that the strict distinction between the Passover and the Feast of Unleavened Bread existed only in official vocabulary, not in common usage, where they often functioned as synonyms. This has allowed Brant Pitre and other scholars to conclude that "the Gospel of John begins its account of the

---

74. See Chwolson, "Poslednyaya Pashalnaya Vecherya Iisusa Hrista i Den Ego Smerti (The Last Passover Supper of Jesus Christ and the Day of His Death)," 468. Here, Chwolson cites the Mishnah (Pesach, 5:3 and 6:1–5) and the Talmud (Pesach, 65b–66a.) as an innovation dating from Hillel's time.

75. Chwolson, 469.

76. Humphreys and Waddington, "Dating the Crucifixion," 743–46.

77. See also Humphreys and Waddington, "Astronomy and the Date of the Crucifixion," 165–81. Later Humphreys developed his views further in *The Mystery of the Last Supper Jesus*, 39–60.

Last Supper on the same afternoon as the Synoptics: the afternoon of 14 Nisan, 'just before the feast of Passover,' the night when the lambs would be eaten,"[78] that is, before the Passover meal.

Theological Reflections on the Lord's Supper

From the perspective of a holistic theological approach that seeks to incorporate various doctrinal constructs, the Lord's Supper represents *the encounter between the partaker of the meal and the divine presence that occurs in the context of the Christian community*. One can summarize the essence of Holy Communion in a relatively simple theological statement – it is an encounter with Christ. The subsequent analysis simply unpacks this succinct assertion and highlights different aspects of the sacramental event it speaks of.

When Jesus was instituting the Eucharist, he stated about the bread and wine, "This is my body" and "This is my blood" (Matt 26:26–28; Luke 22:19–20). By doing this, he pointed to the most essential features he had as a human being. "Body and blood" is a metaphor for a living creature, a figurative expression describing a real, fully living person, and a phrase that, in poetic language, has always served to point to man per se. Having said that, Christ went on to tell his disciples of his coming death and his abiding with them "to the very end of the age" (Matt 28:20). It follows that the Eucharist, which is celebrated in remembrance of him (Luke 22:19) and thus points to his death, can and must, simultaneously be an event of a real encounter with a living person, the risen Jesus.

If there is no real encounter with Christ, the Lord's Supper – no matter how properly and solemnly celebrated – turns into an ordinary meal devoid of any spiritual component. In such a case, it is a usual dinner of friends who mentally recall their master, a kind of wake for the deceased teacher. In other words, if Christ is neither met during the Supper nor participates in the event, its essence vanishes. All that is left is the name and appearance of the Lord's Supper, its prop, simulacrum, a combination of some unimportant accidents that do not constitute the integrity of the event that Christ established. That is why it is so important not to lose sight of the encounter as its integral element when analyzing the individual doctrinal components of the Eucharist.

How can one conceptualize the encounter with the divine presence in the Eucharistic event theologically? Perhaps the best way is to start off with a few definitions. In this study, I distinguish seven essential characteristics or

---

78. Pitre, *Jesus and the Last Supper*, 340.

interpretations of the meaning of the Lord's Supper, each of which reflects a particular facet of this integral phenomenon. It is important to remember that the number seven is provisional and is used only to facilitate the examination of a complex question. In fact, the number of such descriptive definitions may be different. They all exist objectively in the Lord's Supper, but their identification and suggested number may vary depending on the researcher.

The Lord's Supper as Remembrance

The straightforward and literal meaning of the Lord's Supper is the remembrance of Jesus Christ. When the Lord gave the disciples the bread and the cup, he said, "Do this in remembrance of me" (Luke 22:19). The apostle Paul repeats the same word ἀνάμνησις (anamnesis) in his instruction on the Lord's Supper to the Corinthians (1 Cor 11:24–25). The gospel narrative contains no further explanation or specification as to the semantic content of the Eucharist that Christ himself would have given. For this reason, this institution is understood primarily as a memorial in the Baptist tradition, which has historically relied on common-sense hermeneutics rather than theological-historical analysis.

This emphasis is due to the fact that Baptist theology has been formed in opposition to the historic churches' views. As a result, Baptist eucharistic thought has inevitably sought a different language for expressing the essence of the Lord's Supper. In Catholicism and Eastern Orthodoxy, the primary focus was on analyzing the reality of Christ's presence in the eucharistic substance and justifying the unconditional and efficient operation of grace on those participating in the sacrament. In contrast to this view, Baptists shifted their theological lens to the aspect of the Supper that had been scarcely explored in other traditions. This has led to emphasizing, and often overemphasizing, the idea of remembrance and, even more narrowly, the commemoration of Christ's death and suffering.

The biblical understanding of "remembrance-anamnesis" differs from the modern European use of the term. To the contemporary mind, remembering is the process of returning to the past, reconstructing it in the cognitive images, experiencing it emotionally (either positively or negatively), replaying it in one's mind, making sense of the past, revisiting it, and even conversing with it. Yet, Ray Carlton Jones notes: "The biblical concept of anamnesis is not an abstract concept or mere recollection, but in the Old Testament it is always closely bound up with an action and with the cult – with a feast, a sacrifice, an offering, and the like."[79] Similarly, in his classic work on Israel and its culture, Johannes Pedersen adds:

> What we call objective, that is to say inactive, theoretical thinking without further implications, does not exist in the case of the Israelite. . . . When the soul remembers something, it does not mean that it has an objective memory image of some thing or event, but that this image is called forth in the soul and assists in determining its direction, its action. When man remembers God, he lets his being and his actions be determined by him.[80]

In other words, the Jewish notion of *remembering* is active rather than purely mental. It means more than merely imagining something, namely, acting or at least being galvanized to action.

Scripture says that God remembers his covenant with Abraham and his descendants (Exod 2:24; 6:5; Lev 26:42, 45, etc.); remembers his people (Num 10:9; Ps 9:12, etc.); remembers the land he promised to Abraham's descendants (Lev 26:42). For their part, the Jews had to remember the exodus from Egypt and God's miracles that he had performed there (Deut 7:18; 16:3, etc.), and all of God's commands and statutes (Num 15:39–40; Ps 119:52), especially those concerning the Sabbath (Exod 20:8). Thus, the concept of "remembering, recalling, and bringing to memory" applies to both God and people. It implies the need to do something, not just to replay pictures of the past in one's head.

Brevard Childs draws the following theological conclusion from his analysis of the biblical texts speaking of remembering. He believes that to remember means to actualize the past. "Actualization occurs when the worshipper experiences an identification with the original events. This happens when he is transported back to the original historical events. He bridges the gap of historical time and participates in the original history."[81] Thus, in biblical discourse, *remembrance is an action in the present, drawing on and using the experience of the past to prepare for the future.*

It means that Jesus invited his followers to remember him not so much mentally as actually. He was pointing to his real, ontological presence, which obliges them to act, obey his words and commands, and live under his rule.

---

79. Jones Jr., "The Lord's Supper," 434–35.
80. Pedersen, *Israel: Its Life and Culture*, 106.
81. Childs, *Memory and Tradition*, 82.

In this sense, remembrance is an encounter with Christ in the present. Joseph Ratzinger says it "is essentially a 'remembrance' that creates presence."[82]

The act of recollection at the Lord's Supper transforms the event of the breaking of bread into a symbolic representation of the past that is used to evaluate the present in anticipation of the future. Put differently, the Supper as a memorial is not and should not be turned only to the past. Recollection should become a chain linking past, present, and future. It needs to reflect Christ himself, who is not bound by time but *is* a continuity of time, a link between the times. He was, is, and always will be.

Historically, Baptist theology has most commonly defined the Lord's Supper as remembrance. Madison Grace concludes his analysis of early English Baptist confessions of the seventeenth century: "The remembrance of Christ in the Supper is a central theme for the Baptists since they do not perceive of a corporeal communion with Christ."[83] This is an accurate observation, but it should be noted that virtually none of the early Baptist confessions speak of the Lord's Supper solely as a remembrance of Christ's suffering. These texts do place the remembrance first, but after it, they always mention other aspects of the Supper.

For example, Article XXXIII of the so-called *Orthodox Creed* of 1678 states that the Lord's Supper is intended "for the perpetual remembrance, and showing forth the sacrifice of himself in his death; and for the confirmation of the faithful believers in all the benefits of his death and resurrection, and spiritual nourishment and growth in him; sealing unto them their continuance in the covenant of grace."[84] The same point can be made regarding Eastern European Baptists' views at the early stages of their history. The *Rules of the Confession of Faith of the Newly Converted Russian Brotherhood*, found during the police raid in Ratushny's house in 1873 that he had transcribed by hand, read: "We accept the mysteries of Christ in remembrance of Christ's suffering and death, as a sign of communion with Christ, and as a sign of communion among believers."[85] This statement explicitly points to at least two essential features of the Lord's Supper: first and foremost, "remembrance," and then, "communion" with Christ and other members of the congregation.

In the doctrinal statement Kargel' drafted in 1913, section "On Christ's Institutions for the Church" reads,

---

82. Ratzinger, *Joseph Ratzinger Collected Works*, 234.
83. Grace, "Early English Baptists' View," 178.
84. Lumpkin, *Baptist Confessions of Faith*, 321.
85. Dorodnitsyn, *Materialy Dlya Istorii (Materials for the History)*, 480.

> The Lord's Supper is given by the Lord Himself for the remembrance of Him (Lk. 22:12; 1 Cor. 11:24–25), namely of His suffering and death as the ransom [for us] (1 Pet. 1:18–19; 1 Cor. 11:26), His love reaching its limit (Jn. 13:1; 15:13; Rom. 5:8), and His giving of Himself not only for us, but also to us as spiritual, heavenly food (Jn. 6:51; 1 Cor. 10:16).[86]

This confession, that became the first official expression of doctrine of the AUCECB in 1966, also emphasizes the paramount importance of "remembrance" but does not stop there. It expands the meaning of the Lord's Supper to include the idea of "spiritual, heavenly food," which is noticeably inconsistent with a purely Zwinglian understanding of the Eucharist. However, as we have already mentioned, by the 1970s, the AUCECB official documents and sermons came to stress more and more that the Supper was merely a remembrance of Christ's suffering and death. From that time, the idea of *remembrance-anamnesis* as the main content of the Lord's Supper began to gain ground in Baptist church consciousness.

This relatively narrow view of the Eucharist has become particularly widespread among Baptists in the United States, who have come to reduce the essence of the Eucharist almost exclusively to remembrance. Broadway notes in his study: "United States Baptists, caught up in nativist anti-Catholicism and debates with Campbellism, reacted by shifting further toward a narrow 'memorialist' position that grew to be widely accepted in the twentieth century throughout most of North America."[87] This trend started to reverse only toward the end of the twentieth century when the Baptist sacramentalist movement began gaining popularity, first in Great Britain and then in North America. The memorial aspect of the Supper should indeed occupy a central place in the theological understanding of this ordinance. Yet, it must be properly understood and practiced.

First, one should note that the act of eucharistic recollection has Christ himself as its object, not just his suffering and death. In two different passages, the Scripture unequivocally presents Christ's words concerning the institution of the Eucharist: "Do this in remembrance of me" (Luke 22:19; 1 Cor

---

86. Kargel', *Kratkoye Izlozheniye Veroucheniya (Brief Exposition of the Evangelical Christians')*, 8.

87. Broadway, "Is It Not the Communion?," 407.

11:24–25). Remembering Christ does not mean speaking only of his suffering. As McClendon Jr. wrote, it is

> a meal "in memory of me" that is, of Jesus himself, and thus of the longer story that frames his life: the divine-human story of creation, and the election of Israel, and its existence as a people, and the birth of Messiah Jesus, his life and ministry, and the great signs from God that have followed.[88]

So, to remember Christ means to recall his birth, his ministry, his work, his instructions, his sermons, his parables, especially his sacrifice on the cross, and, of course, his resurrection! To remember Christ during the Lord's Supper is to speak of the meetings of the risen one with his disciples, the joy of eternal life, the victory over hell and death, and much more. In other words, we should remember the *whole Christ*, not just the climax of his mission on Calvary.

Second, we should pay attention to the fact that the remembrance of Christ is not a wake for the deceased leader, nor is it a mourning for the master who passed away in the prime of life. It is a celebration of the encounter with the risen lord of glory, who continues to dwell in his church. He is alive, and he is here! This is the main difference between the eucharistic commemoration and the ordinary memorial dinner. As we know, the Jewish tradition used to practice a "feast of mourning" in memory of a deceased relative or friend, which was held with the breaking of bread ("food to comfort") and "a drink to console." The prophet Jeremiah alludes to this practice when he speaks of the ruin of the land of Judah (Jer 16:5–7).

Christ's actions as he broke the bread and gave the disciples the cup of wine looked as if he celebrated the feast of mourning, but in this case, Christ used the familiar practice to convey a new meaning. The old form served as a contrast to the new creation; it highlighted even more sharply the peculiarity of remembering Christ, who died but is alive. This is why the church often regards the Lord's Supper as a celebration. If one turns the Lord's Supper into a wake, it will be a "feast of mourning" rather than a "celebration of life."

There are two distinct ways how we remember the absent person. One mode of remembering implies that we recall someone who has passed away forever; the other suggests that we remember someone who has gone away for now but promised to come back later. Christ wanted us to remember him in the latter sense because he firmly promised his followers that he would return

---

88. McClendon Jr., *Doctrine: Systematic Theology*, 404.

in a visible way and take his own from the earth (Matt 24:30–31), "to be with me where I am," as Christ says (John 17:24).

It explains why the day early Christians and later evangelicals designated for celebrating the Lord's Supper was not Friday, the day Christ died, but Sunday, when he came back to life. It unequivocally demonstrated that the disciples understood the master's commandment correctly and remembered him risen, not dead. In a liturgical sense, it means that the sorrow and grief over Christ's death should not receive undue emphasis. It is proper on this day to use solemn and festive hymns to praise the Lord, to dress in festive rather than mourning garments, to offer prayers of praise rather than lamentations, etc.

Often, those participating in the Lord's Supper reduce it to a funeral service on behalf of the departed Christ, or worse, turn it into an empty symbol. Donald Hustad wryly quotes the words of some American Baptist pastors before the breaking of the bread: "Now remember that this is not a sacrament as some believe; this is an ordinance, and we do not expect that it will make us more holy or bring us any particular grace."[89] It is clear that such an introduction to the Lord's Supper does not do much for those who participate. Moreover, according to Hustad, it has the potential to make the Supper look hollow, having the appearance of a powerful means of grace but actually having no effect. He compares this attitude toward the Lord's Supper to a placebo. Unfortunately, the Eucharist can lose its gracious effect if the faith of the communicants is not cultivated but destroyed, and the breaking of bread becomes a kind of a requiem mass, or an empty symbol intended to have a merely psychological effect.

Third, it is essential to emphasize that remembrance should be a commemoration, not a mental act. Even early Baptist theologians of the seventeenth century stressed this point. Thomas Grantham, who published the first Baptist systematic theology textbook in 1678 in London, writes in the second part of the second book, "[o]f the Holy Table of the Lord, or the Lord's Supper celebrated in Bread and Wine, for a perpetual Commemoration of the Death of Jesus Christ, till his second coming."[90] When discussing the Eucharist with representatives of other traditions, Grantham constantly emphasizes that the Supper is not a simple but a special act of remembrance, which he calls the "solemn Memorial."

Interestingly, when referring to the Lord's Supper, seventeenth-century Baptists used the term *commemoration* much more often than *remembrance*.

---

89. Hustad, "The Lord's Supper," 180–81.
90. Quoted in Grace II, "Early English Baptists' View," 166.

It suggests that they understood it not as a mental act of recollection (remembrance) but as an event designed to commemorate someone or something solemnly in the here and now. The Eucharist must be about commemorating, that is, in some sense *celebrating* Christ, and not merely remembering him as a teacher who lived in the past. Commemorating Christ is different from remembering, which amounts to a mere representation of the events of Christ's life. Commemoration causes the participants of the meal to reevaluate their personal condition.

There is also a second, equally important feature of remembrance as commemoration, which is forming a communal identity based on Christ's life, suffering, and death. The Lord's Supper, filled with commemorative meaning, plays a crucial role in bringing the community together and shaping its identity. During the celebration of the Lord's Supper, the congregation members realize themselves to be both members of the universal church of Christ and members of a particular local church with its traditions, experiences, history, and unique ethos. That is why, for Eastern European evangelicals, the "breaking of the bread" Sunday service is the most important liturgical event. It is the day when the whole congregation is gathered, and announcements concerning all church members are made.

The Lord's Supper is thus both an individual and collective commemoration.[91] The whole congregation participates in this commemorative act. This engagement with the collective Christian memory becomes both a means of each participant's self-identification and a way of identifying the congregation as a whole. In other words, as a historical memory of Christ, the Eucharist identifies the individual Christian and the local church as being in and with Christ.

Thus, we can say that the commemoration of Christ at the Lord's Supper is a conscious act of communicating worldview-shaping information about him and his work of redemption to the participants. Certain expressions of the collective memory accompany this act. Through them, the events of Christ's life are "reconstructed" and actualized in the realm of memory so that those present at the liturgy can perceive them.

The Lord's Supper as Proclamation of Christ's Death

Scripture points to another highly significant theological aspect of the Lord's Supper, which in Baptist consciousness almost merges with the memorial aspect. It is the proclamation of Christ's death. Explaining the nature of the

---

91. On the notion of collective memory, see Halbwachs, *On Collective Memory*.

Supper to the members of the Corinthian churches, Paul wrote: "For whenever you eat this bread and drink this cup, you proclaim the Lord's death until he comes" (1 Cor 11:26). The Eucharist is a remembrance of Christ and, furthermore, a proclamation of his death.

Baptist texts often underscore this aspect of the Eucharist. For example, one of the earliest Baptist confessions (*A Short Confession of Faith*, 1610), signed by Smyth and forty-six members of his congregation, says concerning the Lord's Supper: "The whole dealing in the outward visible supper, setteth before the eye, witnesseth and signifyeth, that Christ's body was broken upon the cross and his holy blood spilt for the remission of our sins."[92] This definition emphasizes that when a minister administers the Eucharist, his words and actions unfold before the minds of those receiving the bread and wine, a picture of Jesus's suffering and death, which occurred in the distant past. The *Second London Confession* states that the Lord's Supper should be celebrated "unto the end of the world, for the perpetual remembrance and shewing forth the sacrifice in his death."[93] Note that the role of the Supper is to show "forth the sacrifice in his death." In other words, the Baptist tradition considers it very important to show the whole universe the death of Christ and its significance. It is especially evident in the liturgical elements of the Baptist eucharistic celebration: in sermons, prayers, and communal singing.

In all evangelical Christians' and Baptists' hymnals that have been published in Eastern Europe, the section devoted to the Lord's Supper mainly contains hymns and songs that vividly and often sentimentally describe Christ's death on the cross. Typically, they have from ten to twenty hymns, the bulk of which were written or translated by Ivan Prokhanov and published from 1862 to 1927 in the following collections: *Prinosheniye Pravoslavnym Khristianam (An Offering to Eastern-Orthodox Christians)*, 1862–1872; *Golos Very (The voice of faith)*, 1882; *Gusli (The Harp)*, 1903; *Desyatisbornik (Ten Collections)*, 1927. Later generations considerably expanded this section, but its fundamental thrust has not changed.

The Eucharist, as the proclamation of Christ's death, has a twofold meaning: it says something to the community and the world. For the Christian community, it is a reminder of the price of salvation; for the world outside, it is a missional statement.

When Christ left earth, he told his followers to be his witnesses (Acts 1:8), not missionaries working for a large missionary organization. The witnesses

---

92. Lumpkin, *Baptist Confessions of Faith*, 110.
93. Lumpkin, 291.

are supposed to personally experience the encounter with the kingdom. Only then can they proclaim their experience to the world and demonstrate its effect on their lives. The sequence is precisely that of entering the kingdom, represented by the church in the present age, and only then submitting oneself to the work of God's mission that requires the church's "coming out" into the external post-secular world.

According to this understanding, the life of the church is thoroughly permeated by and, hence, becomes a mission. Therefore, the desire of modern missiologists to show the "poverty of sacramentalism" and to replace Christian witness with prophetic ministry is too radical. It is impossible to agree with Joshua Searle, who, in his *Theology After Christendom*,[94] contrasts the kingdom and the church way too intensely and radically. He believes that "it is difficult to see any connection between *Missio Dei* and the eucharist. For instance, how does the consumption of bread and wine by Christians in church buildings empower or enhance the church witness in the world?"[95] Such a statement indicates an inattentive approach to both eucharistic and missionary practices. Of course, if one only sees the Lord's Supper in terms of a passive indoor mission, which the representatives of the historic churches often advocate (calling it the "temple mission"), such criticism is understandable and commendable. The concept of temple mission views the church's liturgy and, especially, the Eucharist as the climatic expression of its ongoing mission.

The New Testament teaching and, in particular, Paul's instructions to the Corinthians regarding the Lord's Supper reveal a broader understanding of the missional aspect than that allowed by the temple mission of presence. Paul's words in 1 Corinthians 11:26 directly link one's partaking of the eucharistic meal to the missionary dimension.

It is well known that to proclaim (καταγγέλλετε) means to speak openly and loudly, announce to the public, or preach. This is the sense in which the word is used in all eighteen New Testament passages where it occurs. In Paul's mind, participation in the Lord's Supper means proclamation. What does this mean? The preaching of, and at the Lord's Supper has two effects: direct and indirect.

The direct effect amounts to the straightforward proclamation of Christ's death during the eucharistic services aimed primarily at church visitors and neophytes. It is an evangelistic sermon focusing on the meaning and significance of Christ's suffering and death for all people. It speaks about and proclaims the major event of universal proportions that changed the course of

---

94. Searle, *Theology after Christendom*.
95. Searle, 161.

world history. Typically, this is the kind of sermon heard in traditional Eastern European evangelical churches during eucharistic services, often referred to by this name: *Remembering Christ's death and suffering*.

Unfortunately, in many young people's churches, or what is now called modern evangelical churches, a sermon about Christ's death during the administration of the Lord's Supper seems optional. The preacher may speak on an entirely detached ethical or dogmatic topic. It is hardly in line with Paul's understanding. He believed that the congregation while participating in the Eucharist, should proclaim, preach, and point purposefully to the death of Jesus Christ. If this is an indispensable element of the Lord's Supper, how can we deny the missional role this sacramental action plays?

The indirect effect of preaching Christ's death during the eucharistic service is to inspire and encourage believers to participate in the meal administered by Christ himself. He is invisibly but actually present at the table, guiding the participants in their missionary endeavors. Unless there is a real connection with Christ, the church mission becomes a mere business project.

It is this empowering and motivating aspect of the Lord's Supper that *Faith and Order*, the famous document of the World Council of Churches, points to in paragraph 26:

> the eucharist brings into the present age a new reality which transforms Christians into the image of Christ and therefore makes them his effective witnesses. . . . The eucharistic community is nourished and strengthened for confessing by word and action the Lord Jesus Christ who gave his life for the salvation of the world.[96]

The text indicates that the Lord's Supper does something to the partakers of the meal: it causes them to become more active missionaries. That is, it equips them for the mission. Before one can go into the world, one must be clothed in Christ and the power of the Holy Spirit. Therefore, the authors of the *Lima Statement* emphasize the indirect rather than direct contribution of the Eucharist to Christian missions.

These two essential aspects of the Eucharist, namely direct proclamation and equipping for ministry, are both rooted in the gospel and intended to renew and enhance Christ's presence in the life of the communicant. Indeed, it is Christ's presence and guidance in believers' lives that is the most important – in fact, the only – factor in their full-fledged involvement in the *Missio Dei* (John 20:21). Searle believes that the *Missio Dei* "takes its point of departure not from

---

96. World Council of Churches Commission on Faith, *Baptism, Eucharist and Ministry*, 13.

church sacraments, but from the kingdom of God in the world."[97] But it is the other way around. Christian mission begins with the church and is carried out by its ordinary members who need the spiritual nourishment and encouragement only Christ provides. Participating in congregational life, including the Eucharist and other church ordinances, provides Christians with the spiritual guidance they need. Otherwise, present-day calls to establish the kingdom of God as opposed to establishing the church lead to humanistic activism that invites Christians to participate actively in projects seeking justice, poor relief, social welfare, etc. All this is in itself very important and absolutely necessary. However, by severing the ties with church, this approach undermines genuine spiritual life and says nothing about the discernment of God's will that is necessary for one's involvement in the *Missio Dei*.

Almost a century ago, Barth noted how vital the harmony of preaching and church ritual is. The *Barmen Declaration of Faith* he composed states that the church's commission is "to extend through word and sacrament the message of the free grace of God to all people."[98] The document emphasizes both forms of the gospel message, word, and sacrament, referring primarily to the preaching and the Lord's Supper. In Barth's view, both modes of Christian witness have the same power.

Thus, the proclamation of Christ's suffering and death reveals the mission dimension of the Lord's Supper. This event brings about the participant's encounter with Christ, who sends each member of his church on a mission, accompanies them through the Holy Spirit, and incorporates them into God's plan they help to fulfill.

The Lord's Supper as the Partaking of the Body and Blood of Christ

When the apostle Paul explained to the Corinthians why they were not allowed to partake of idolatrous meals, he argued that these meals implied a real and profound involvement with the spiritual powers standing behind the idols. To prove his point, he drew an analogy with the Eucharist, considering the validity of his argument to be self-evident. He wrote:

> I speak to sensible people; judge for yourselves what I say. Is not the cup of thanksgiving for which we give thanks a participation in the blood of Christ? And is not the bread that we break a par-

---

97. Searle, *Theology after Christendom*, 162.
98. Leith, *Creeds of the Churches*, 522.

ticipation in the body of Christ? Because there is one loaf, we, who are many, are one body, for we all share the one loaf. Consider the people of Israel: Do not those who eat the sacrifices participate in the altar?" (1 Cor 10:15–18).

The main point of this passage is that physical action (eating) entails participation in a spiritual reality. By partaking of the wine and the bread, the Christian is partaking of the blood and body of Christ. This is the participation or communion (κοινωνία) Paul talks about. The Christian partakes (μετέχομεν) and, hence, is made part of Jesus himself. In fact, the expression, "The body (flesh) and blood of Christ," point to Christ himself.

How is it possible? Can one partake, μετέχομεν, of the material elements (bread and wine) so as to have a share or participation in Jesus Christ's divine-human nature? This is precisely the meaning the apostle pinpoints in the word *participation*, κοινωνία. For him, it does not mean a standard, friendly fellowship but a much more profound one – a fellowship in which everything – or almost everything – is shared. This word sometimes denotes even the intimacy that exists between spouses in marriage. But Paul deepens this idea even further by saying that we all "share (μετέχομεν)" the same bread. The notion of μετέχομεν means something beyond having a small portion of something; it implies sharing one's life or destiny with others, being equal in all rights and duties with someone else, and sharing everything one has. Such a deep communion between those who receive the eucharistic meal and Christ inevitably raises many questions: how is this communion possible through the reception and consumption of material elements? Do these elements somehow contribute to the communion, or are they simply vestiges of primitive ritualism?

The Baptist tradition, especially in its earliest form (the seventeenth to eighteenth centuries and, for Eastern Europe, the nineteenth century), when speaking of participating in the Eucharist, clearly and unequivocally emphasized that this sacramental act brought one into a unique communion with Christ (different from the communion that occurred during prayer or Bible reading), saturated human soul, and imparted to the communicants something from Christ's spiritual treasury. In other words, partaking in the bread and wine entails a tangible result, a benefit of sorts, as many confessions of faith suggest.

The early confessions, especially those of calvinistic Baptist groups, clearly expressed the conviction that the eucharistic elements served as a kind of mediator. They were believed to convey the benefits and goods Christ wanted to bestow upon the participants. In this sense, the believers entered into communion with Christ through these material tokens. The Separatists' *True Confession* of 1596[99] says about the eucharistic elements that,

> they are in the ordinance of God signes and seales of Gods euerlasting couenant, representing and offring to all the receiuers, but exhibiting only to the true believers the Lord Jesus Christ and all his benefits vnto righteousnes, sanctification and eternal life, through faith in his name to the glorie and prayse of God.[100]

This statement makes it clear that it is through the bread and wine that true believers (the faith factor is crucial) receive spiritual benefits and advantages. The benefits are truly substantial and include righteousness, sanctification, and eternal life.

Ratushny's *Rules of the Confession of Faith of the Newly Converted Russian Brotherhood* (1873) says: "The Holy Communion has this meaning: as we are all partakers of one bread, so we are all members of the Body of Christ, which is the company of the saints, and as we drink from one cup, we are all witnesses of His blood, which cleanses us from our sins."[101] Note how the Eucharist is considered to bear witness to the cleansing of sins by the blood of Christ. It goes without saying that Ratushny does not think that the wine of the Lord's Supper cleanses from sin; it only testifies to the cleansing that takes place in spiritual reality when material signs are eaten.

Kargel''s *Brief Exposition* (1913) also stresses that the Lord's Supper, apart from remembrance, is given "to us as spiritual, heavenly food (Jn. 6:51; 1 Cor.10:16). Received with a living faith, it makes us partakers of fellowship both with Him and with all the members of His Church (1 Cor. 10:16–17)."[102] This statement even more explicitly links the reception of the eucharistic bread and wine with spiritual food and points to its most important effect, the fellowship (*koinonia*, communion) with Christ and with other brothers and sisters.

The confession of faith the Baptist wing of the Eastern European Evangelical Christian-Baptist movement adopted under the leadership of Pavlov is even more emphatic about the Lord's Supper being a means of grace. It contains the following phrase: "This is a gracious ordinance which the Lord gave to His Church, which we consider an unappreciated means of grace, and which we

---

99. These Separatists formed the first Baptist congregation in 1609.

100. Lumpkin, *Baptist Confessions of Faith*, 93.

101. Dorodnitsyn, *Materialy dlya Istorii Religiozno-Ratsionalisticheskogo (Materials for the History of Religious-Rationalist Movement)*, 480.

102. Kargel', *Kratkoye Izlozheniye (Brief Exposition)*, 8.

ought to use frequently (Acts 2:42, 46; 20:7)."[103] While analyzing early Baptist documents, Fiddes observes:

> Both General and Particular Baptist theologies in the first two centuries of Baptist life witness to the Supper as an occasion for 'communion' with Christ, for receiving the 'benefits' of his atoning work on the cross, and for spiritual feeding and nourishment of the soul. In some sense they all regard the meal as a 'means of grace,' and lack the intense suspicion of this phrase that was generated in the debates of the nineteenth century.[104]

Thus, the Baptist interpretation of the Lord's Supper definitely includes the idea of communion, which implies that by eating the bread and drinking the wine, the true believer enters into a close fellowship with Jesus – meets him – and receives spiritual reinforcement and nourishment for his soul from him. It is as if he were *eating Christ*, or as Spurgeon put it in one of his sermons:

> The Lord's supper represents the giving of the whole body of Christ to us, to enter into us for food; surely, if we enter into its true meaning, we may expect to be revived and vitalized; for we have here more than a mere touch of the hand, it is the whole Christ that enters into us spiritually, and so comes into contact with our innermost being. I believe in "the real presence": do not you?[105]

As Calvin observed, eating Christ is a spiritual metaphor that is completely beyond reason's capacity to comprehend,[106] but it is very difficult to describe the process in other terms. Thus, while cautiously accepting the idea that believers are nourished by Christ, including during the Lord's Supper, Baptist theology generally does not go further, seeking an answer to the question: what is accomplished in the Eucharist, and how does this nourishment take place?

In answering this question, Christian theology, by and large, constantly oscillates between the poles of spiritual symbolism and material realism. At one pole is Gnosticism or Docetism, which separates the spiritual and the material by practically rejecting matter altogether. At the other pole stands crude materialism, which degenerates into magical thinking, reducing spiritual processes to physicalism and ritualism.

---

103. Sannikov, ed., *Istoriya Baptizma (The History of the Baptist Movement)*, 427.
104. Fiddes, *Tracks and Traces*, 159–60.
105. Spurgeon, *Till He Come*, 353.
106. Calvin, *Institutes*, b. 4, §17:1d.

Bulgakov believes that the eucharistic controversy began with the works of the French scholastic Berengar of Tours. Bulgakov and his later follower, the Russian Orthodox theologian Alexei Zaitsev, mercilessly criticize "eucharistic realism, which seeks to completely objectify the sacrament, [and] to look at it through the eyes of this world."[107] These are the words Bulgakov employs to describe the scholastic idea of *transubstantiation*, which explains the process of eating Christ's flesh and blood in the Eucharist through the notion of physical change in the elements.

Catholic theology finally approved the concept of transubstantiation in the canons of the Council of Trent (1545–1563). Chapter 4 of the "Decree Concerning the Most Holy Sacrament of the Eucharist," adopted on 11 October 1551, repeatedly affirms: "[B]y the consecration of the bread and of the wine, a conversion is made of the whole substance of the bread into the substance of the body of Christ our Lord, and of the whole substance of the wine into the substance of His blood."[108] Furthermore, these substantive changes occur, according to the document's authors, not only when the communicants receive the bread and the wine but immediately after the consecration and before their reception: "[I]n the Eucharist, before being used, there is the Author Himself of sanctity."[109] This is how the ultimate embodiment or objectification of the glorified God-man Jesus in the Eucharist reaches its climax.

In the fourteenth and fifteenth centuries, at the time of active interaction, long discussions, and short-lived unions between the Orthodox East and the Catholic West, the concept of transubstantiation entered the Eastern Orthodox theological vocabulary. The term came to be used widely after the approval of Peter Mohyla's *Orthodox Confession* in the 1640s. There, it appears several times as a synonym for the typical Eastern Orthodox term *conversion (pryelozheniye)*. The Peter Mohyla's text affirms that

> in the holy Supper, the same Son of God, God and man, is present on Earth *by a change of Substance*, for the *Substance* of the *Bread* is changed into the *Substance* of his most *holy Body*, and the *Substance* of the *wine* into the *substance* of his most precious *blood*.[110]

---

107. Bulgakov, *Yevkharistia (The Eucharistic Sacrifice)*, 142 (appendix unavailable in the English translation by Roosien).

108. Waterworth, trans., *The Canons and Decrees*, 79.

109. Waterworth, 78.

110. Mohyla (Mogila), *The Orthodox Confession*, 50 (Question 56), italics in the text.

Originally written in Greek, this confession was translated into Russian in the nineteenth century and widely disseminated.

By denying transubstantiation, sixteenth- and seventeenth-century Protestantism modified the language of sacramental theology and moved the discussion from ontology to semantics. This was especially true of Reformed (Calvinist) theology. Neither Zwingli nor Calvin nor their followers wanted to engage in a dialog with Catholic theology using the language of ontotheology. Perhaps it was due to the generally negative attitude toward scholasticism (and Aristotle) among the Renaissance humanists, from whose circles virtually all the leaders of the Reformation came. But it is more likely that the rationale behind this linguistic turn stems from philosophical contradictions the theory of transubstantiation engenders. For example, it is possible to explain Christ's real, tangible presence in many places across the globe at once (when the Eucharist is celebrated) only in terms of action and not in terms of localized presence, as Catholic doctrine insists.

For Calvin, this was the main argument for denying transubstantiation: the material substance of the body of Christ cannot be in different locations at the same time. Furthermore, from a theological and philosophical point of view, it is very difficult to explain how the bread's substance is absent while its accidents are still present after transubstantiation. Transubstantiation presupposes that accidents (external manifestations) can exist without the substance in which they normally inhere. It means that the substantial essence of Christ replaces the ontological essence of the bread, but the bread's external characteristics continue. It is also difficult to understand what makes the bread and wine present after the consecration (epiclesis) if their substance has been replaced by the substance of Christ's body and blood. Are the partakers of the meal dealing with a material illusion? Or do the bread and wine acquire some miraculous properties that allow them to be present when they are really absent? The proponents of transubstantiation typically dismiss these philosophical questions by claiming that God can perform any miracle and, consequently, he can make accidents exist without their substance.

The rejection of transubstantiation was also often based on common sense arguments. For example, John Wycliffe debunks this theory using the Ten Commandments as the basis for his criticism. The First Commandment forbids worshipping anyone or anything other than the one God, but the belief in the conversion of bread into the actual body of Christ leads to an adoration of the consecrated bread, which is unacceptable. Luther rejects the idea of substantial change in the eucharistic elements simply because, for him, this notion is a "monstrous absurdity" and an attempt to rationalize the mystery of Christ's presence. Nevertheless, by denying the old sacramental theology, one encounters the need to create a new one.

The main thrust of the Reformers' positive theological interpretation of the Eucharist, as well as any other sacrament, involved a shift in the language. They began using a vocabulary introduced as early as Augustine and based on the concept of *sign*. In the first chapters of his *On Christian Doctrine*, Augustine gives a theological analysis of this category and describes it as follows: "A sign, after all, is a thing, which besides the impression (*species*) it conveys to the senses, also has the effect of making something else come to mind."[111] Next, he emphasizes the central role of words as a sign system and develops his thinking in this direction.

Calvin picks up this understanding of signs and, citing Augustine, applies it to the doctrine of sacraments. For him, the sacraments are God's grace manifested through some external signs. Calvin regards a sacrament as a "testimony of the divine favour toward us, confirmed by an external sign, with a corresponding attestation of our faith towards Him."[112] Later, he adds that a sacrament is also a seal of God's favor toward men. In fact, Calvin moves the conversation about the essence of the sacraments into the realm of semiotic discourse. In his discussion with Luther, Zwingli also steers away from ontological realities and embraces the language of commemorative practices, treating the Eucharist as merely a remembrance.

From the nineteenth century onwards, Baptist theology developed in opposition with Anglicanism and Roman Catholicism. Thus, it has been built on negating and overcoming the doctrine of transubstantiation, often dismissing even the idea of grace conveyed and received in the Lord's Supper. Therefore, while leaning toward the Zwinglian approach, it often found itself at the opposite end of the *materialism-spiritualism* axis. Baptist thinking shunned materialism and, as a result, sometimes fell into a Gnostic tendency to divorce the material from the spiritual and to reduce all eucharistic processes to spiritual activity. Note how Peter Gentry, a Southern Baptist and professor at Phoenix Seminary, explains the *Southern Baptist Convention*'s current confession of faith. Regarding the Lord's Supper, he says:

> no idea [is] presented that by a physical participation of the bread and the wine a person receives saving grace from God. We receive saving grace by faith, by putting our trust in Jesus Christ. John

---

111. Augustine, *Teaching Christianity (De Doctrina Christiana)*, 133.
112. Calvin, *Institutes*, b. 4, §14:1, 491.

wrote his Gospel that we might believe, and that by believing we might have life (John 20:31).[113]

Comparing early and late United States Baptist documents in his dissertation, Harland Cason III concludes that "early confessions use language speaking of the communicants eating the spiritual body of Christ and gaining spiritual blessing or nutrition. In later confessions, the notion of feeding on Christ is totally removed."[114]

He goes on to point out that in later confessions, the emphasis shifts from the individual event (what happens to the participant when they eat) to the community that performs certain *acts*. In other words, these Baptist documents emphasize that all the participants remember something, celebrate together, have communion, and so on. The biblical passages cited in the sections dealing with the Lord's Supper reflect this tendency. For instance, later Baptist confessions tend to omit the reference to John 6:53. It leads one to conclude that a hermeneutical shift has taken place in the Anglo-American Baptist tradition.[115] The Eastern European Baptist movement saw these changes coming in the early 1990s.

First Eastern European Baptists readily accepted the idea of eating bread and wine during the Supper as a means of conveying and sustaining grace. Evangelical Christians were more reluctant to subscribe to the view but embraced it, nevertheless. This belief began to disappear from the Baptist dogmatic statements at the beginning of the third millennium but is still firmly in place in practical church life. The vast majority of Baptist congregations treat the eucharistic bread and wine with reverence as a sacred object. The leftovers are never thrown away after the Supper but are shared among the participants and consumed down to the last crumb. However, the situation is different in the younger congregations that emerged either under the influence of Western missionaries or due to rampant anti-traditionalism. Their members often interpret the eating of bread and drinking of wine at the Lord's Supper solely as a symbolic, conventional act.

---

113. Gentry, "The Lord's Supper," 27.
114. Cason III, "The Gathered Community," 72.
115. Cason III, 72–73.

Symbol or Sign?

Categorically rejecting Christ's physical presence in the eucharistic substance, Baptists have divergent views of the nature of the bread and wine of the Eucharist. Some see them as signs connected with a spiritual reality, while others consider them conditional, empty, and easily replaceable symbols. Interpreting them as signs results in the insight that Christ is really present in the Eucharist, while symbolic understanding implies his real absence.

Both in the West and the East, in sermons and catechisms, the bread and wine of the Eucharist are often referred to as symbols of Christ's body and blood. For example, Viktor Schlonkin, in his popular work *The Sacraments of Evangelical Christians-Baptists*, emphasizes symbolism as follows: "The eating of bread and wine, which symbolize the Savior's Body and Blood, has become a symbol of the New Covenant that Jesus makes with His disciples."[116] However, the Baptist confessions of faith, especially the earliest ones, present the bread and wine as signs rather than symbols.

For example, the earliest Baptist confessional document, the *Short Confession* (1609), reads: "The Lord's Supper is the external sign of the communion of Christ."[117] Ratushny's *Rules* (1873) states that the Supper is received "as a sign of communion with Christ and as a sign of the communion of believers among themselves."[118] Pavlov's *Beliefs* of 1880 explicitly call the bread and wine holy signs: "We believe that in this holy sign, Christ gives to the faithful to taste spiritually His body and His blood."[119] The current Ukrainian Baptist Union's *Confession of Faith* declares: "The bread and wine point to the body and blood of Jesus Christ, and by receiving these signs, the believer has spiritual communion with Him (Mt. 26:26–28)."[120] Is there a difference between a symbol and a sign, and if the answer is positive, how does this affect our understanding of the Lord's Supper?

Unfortunately, many people, among laypeople and academics, have frequently confused these concepts. In everyday language, the words *sign*, and *symbol*, often function as complete or partial synonyms. For instance, a circle may appear as a symbol of the sun and simultaneously be called a solar sign,

---

116. Schlonkin, "Tainstva Yevangel'skikh Khristian-Baptistov" ("The Sacraments of Evangelical Christians-Baptists").

117. Lumpkin, *Baptist Confessions of Faith*, 101.

118. Dorodnitsyn, *Materialy dlya Istorii Religiozno-Ratsionalisticheskogo (Materials for the History of Religious-Rationalist Movement)*, 480.

119. *Veroucheniye Russkikh (The Beliefs of the Russian)*, 8.

120. Uchbova Rada, *Vyznannia Viry Yevangel's'kykh (The Confession of Faith of Evangelical)*, 25.

or the image of the all-seeing eye is sometimes called a Masonic symbol and sometimes a Masonic sign. However, even dictionaries suggest a difference between these concepts. They define a *sign* as "an external feature indicating something else,"[121] while a *symbol* is described as "a conventional sign, a conventional designation of a concept or phenomenon."[122] Thus, according to contemporary word usage, a symbol differs from a sign precisely by its conventionality, unrelatedness to the denotate (denoted object), and, in fact, represents a special, higher, and more abstract class of signs.

The symbol is a product of consciousness, linked to consciousness itself. It reflects and reduces (in the phenomenological sense of the word) objects, phenomena, and things, "purging" and abstracting them from reality by fixing the focus on itself. At the same time, the sign reflects a reality in one's consciousness and is directly connected with that reality. A sign, to put it simply, is something that really exists but represents a reality different from itself. For example, smoke is a sign of fire, although both smoke and fire exist independently of each other as separate realities. Similarly, symptoms of illness indicate to the doctor the illness itself while being its signs. The signs of this type are pointers.

In a simplified form, one may describe the different types of signs using Charles Sanders Peirce's topology.[123] In his effort to systematize the theory of signs, he introduced trichotomy: *icons* (or likenesses), *indices*, and *symbols*. Peirce's symbols have a conventional, contingent, and synthetic meaning; the index functions as an indicator or pointer that points to the signified; icons are somehow – in a sense ontologically – related to the signified objects "in virtue of some shared quality."[124]

For example, a photograph of an object and someone's unique fingerprint are iconic signs (copies, reflections); a traffic sign that gives orders, warns, or informs may be an example of an indexical sign (indicator, pointer); words are a typical instance of symbolic signs. The word *dog* does not resemble a real dog at all because it generalizes a set of phenomena or objects and functions as their conventional symbol. At the same time, a sign always constitutes the

---

121. Merriam-Webster Dictionary, "Sign" – entries 6a,b. https://www.merriam-webster.com/dictionary/sign.

122. Merriam-Webster Dictionary, "Symbol" – entries 2,3. https://www.merriam-webster.com/dictionary/symbol#nearby-entries

123. The first and simplest variant of his classification was offered in 1867 and published in *The Proceedings of the American Academy of Arts and Sciences* 7 (May 1867): 187–298. Later, Pierce elaborated his theory further and came to talk about ten classes of signs.

124. Atkin, "Peirce's Theory of Signs".

unity of the signifier and the signified, referring the observer to an object different from itself.

A symbol never refers to a specific object or phenomenon but denotes a generalized idea. For example, the scales are the symbol of justice. But the connection between the represented notion and its symbolic representation is contingent, dependent on the coincidence of properties or relations that the human consciousness singles out. There is no physical similarity between the symbol and the symbolized.

Using the approach of Merab Mamardashvili and Aleksandr Piatigorsky, we can say that the human consciousness shapes symbolic dualism. In contrast, sign dualism is formed by and rooted in the object itself. Consciousness produces the symbol based on the process of consciousness itself, while the sign emerges within consciousness due to the connection between the sign and reality. Mamardashvili and Piatigorsky write: "We think of symbols as representations not of objects and events but of conscious assumptions and results of consciousness." They go on to say:

> Objectless signs do not exist and in principle cannot exist, but symbols can be viewed as objectless. . . . When we say "the snake in Hinduism symbolizes the creative power of the feminine" or "the snake in Gnosticism symbolizes contemplative wisdom," the things symbolized here are not things but imaginary objects of mental life and consciousness.[125]

Schmemann correctly notes: "The word 'symbol' ceased to designate something *real* and became in fact the antithesis of reality. In other words, where one is concerned with 'reality' there is no need for a symbol and, conversely, where there is symbol there is no reality."[126] Thus, the sign, particularly the iconic sign, is closely, firmly, and, as a rule, unambiguously linked to the signified reality, while the symbol denotes an abstract, categorical reality. Moreover, the richer the symbol, the less it is linked to reality. Religious philosophers often underestimate this point.[127]

---

125. Mamardashvili and Piatigorsky, *Simvol i Soznanie (Symbol and Consciousness)*, 99 and 200.

126. Schmemann, *The Eucharist: Sacrament of the Kingdom*, 30.

127. Such prominent figures as P. Florensky, A. Losev, and A. Schmemann seek to prove in their works the ontological interrelatedness of the symbol and reality, especially with regard to the bread and wine of the Eucharist, although the very idea of symbol precludes such interrelatedness. They basically follow pseudo-Dionysius the Areopagite, who, as Bychkov has shown, turns the notion of symbol into a generalizing category, the one that absorbs such concepts

The bread and wine of the Lord's Supper do connect the material and the spiritual, but this bond is iconic, not symbolic. Therefore, if we speak of the eucharistic elements being really linked to the body and blood of Christ, these elements should be considered iconic signs, not symbols of spiritual reality. It is through iconic signs that the image of an object is revealed or, as some say, shimmers. This type of sign bears a resemblance to the object they reflect and is related to its essence, whereas symbols are polysemous and objectless.

A typical example of conventionality is mathematical symbols. They have been chosen by convention, and it is often the case that different symbols refer to the same mathematical reality. In doing so, they are called symbols rather than signs. Still, there are quite a few examples of signs (rather than symbols) that have not conventional but unambiguous and very stable ontological connection with reality. A typical case would be money. No one would ever call banknotes monetary symbols. They are signs that accurately reflect some value and, therefore, have a definite worth, while the symbol of gold used in the periodic table has no connection with the actual value of this metal and will never be called a banknote or bill.

Banknotes are linked to the real world of material values by some kind of social consensus and supreme state regulation that assigns them a certain value. They do not represent the abstract world of symbols, ideas, and images, like the chemical symbol of gold or the golden calf. The symbols help one to perceive reality indirectly, as any image does. By virtue of their iconic nature, banknotes have become a reality, and transactions involving them are absolutely equivalent to transactions involving gold or other valuables. At the same time, no symbol of gold can be used to perform an actual transaction.

Schmemann explains that the original ancient meaning of the *symbol* was completely opposite to the modern one:

> The purpose and function of the symbol is *not* to illustrate (this would presume the *absence* of what is illustrated) but rather to *manifest* and to *communicate* what is manifested. We might say that the symbol does not so much "resemble" the reality that it symbolizes as it participates in it, and therefore it is capable of communicating it in reality.[128]

---

as icon, sign, image, and name and even incorporates the objects and phenomena of real life. Bychkov, *Malaya Istoriya (A Brief History)*, 84.

128. Schmemann, *The Eucharist*, 38.

This was indeed the case in the ancient world, where the word *symbol* (from the Greek σύμβολον, συμβαλλω: "to join," "hold together") designated a material sign that had a secret meaning for a particular group of people. When parting, people took with them a clay fragment or half of a coin, leaving the other fragment to those with whom ties of friendship or companionship bound them. When they met again, the matching parts proved that they belonged to each other. These parts were called *symballon*, the matching shards of the whole. But the modern understanding of *symbols* is quite different. It treats the symbol as a sign of something else, which is not in the symbol itself, as, according to Schmemann, there is no water in its chemical symbol. Similarly, the chemical symbol of gold (*Au* from the Latin *aurum*), unlike banknotes, has nothing to do with financial reality. Therefore, by calling the Lord's Supper a symbol, theologians deny the real presence of Christ and give it a conditional, conventional meaning.

Thus, we can firmly and confidently state that the bread and wine of the Eucharist are not symbols of spiritual reality but rather iconic signs that unequivocally and ontologically link the material and spiritual worlds. The bread and wine point to and manifest Christ without replacing him. They represent a material reality that is indisputably connected to a spiritual reality analogous to the connection that exists between the sign and the signified in the case of banknotes. The person who receives the bread and wine becomes a communicant or partaker (μετέχομεν) of the body and blood of Christ, not in the physical but in the real spiritual sense.

Such an understanding allows us to discard the Gnostic separation of the material from the spiritual and to justice to the wholeness of being, which both the symbolic and materialistic interpretations of the Lord's Supper tear apart. Therefore, the insights of the early Baptist confessions seem very true. They conceive of the Eucharist in terms of signs rather than symbols, calling the bread and wine the signs of Christ. In the same vein, virtually all representatives of modern Baptist sacramentalism refer to the Lord's Supper as signs rather than symbols. In his three-volume *Systematic Theology*, James McClendon calls it a *remembering sign*[129] and distinguishes it from other signs of salvation. Therefore, eating the eucharistic signs creates a space for a real encounter with the Lord, which takes place through the faith of those involved. Hence, it becomes a real communion with Christ.

---

129. McClendon Jr, *Doctrine: Systematic Theology*, 382.

The Lord's Supper as Communion

St. Paul writes: "Because there is one bread, we who are many are one body, for we all partake of the one bread" (1 Cor 10:17, NRSV). When it comes to communion with the lord's body and blood, it is mainly the individual aspect of the Eucharist that is discussed in detail. But Paul speaks here of the broader context. He writes not of an individual church member per se but of *us* as the body of Christ, "for we all partake (μετέχομεν) of the one bread." "We" refers to the community, the congregation. In Paul's view, one does not eat the eucharistic bread alone, as an isolated individual, but receives it as a member of the group representing the collective body of Christ.

As noted above, when Paul uses μετέχομεν or its more generic synonym κοινωνία (1 Cor 10:16), he has in mind a profound commonality, shared communion. This communion has two dimensions: fellowship with Christ and fellowship with the brothers and sisters who, together with the communicant, constitute the body of Christ.

A whole cluster of biblical terms concerns the notion of community and communion. They are especially numerous in the New Testament and are derived from the Greek κοινός (common). This word is used in various contexts and may describe one's relationship with God as well as the relationships people have with one another. For example, *koinonia* often refers to the Eucharist in the traditional church vocabulary because the concept of communion with Christ and communion with one another has merged in the church's consciousness over time. Therefore, some authors suggest that the best way to understand what *koinonia* means is to think of it in terms of *living together* because "κοινωνία involves all of 'life,' not just the 'fellowship hour' after worship or the activities that take place in the 'fellowship hall.' 'Life together' happens before, during, and after worship; on Monday through Saturday; in homes and workplaces."[130]

Koinonia implies more than a passing conversation or a protracted business meeting. It suggests equal rights and duties, a sense of belonging, and shared experience. Therefore, it is sometimes interpreted as *something that belongs to and is shared by all*. One should keep in mind that the word *koinonia* came from secular Greek, where it was used in business settings and referred primarily to the funds or property the business partners shared. Also, it could describe a close marital relationship.[131] Even colloquial Greek of the Mediterranean ports and market squares was often called *koine*, the language common to all.

---

130. Kloha, "Koinonia and Life Together," 23.
131. Lillie, "Koinonia in the New Testament," 55.

There can be many kinds of communion with God and other people. Some are of a profound koinonic nature, while others may be superficial and transient. One can experience deep communion with God and people while praying or reading the Bible. The apostle John writes: "so that you also may have fellowship (κοινωνίαν) with us. And our fellowship (κοινωνία) is with the Father and with his Son, Jesus Christ" (1 John 1:3). But the Lord's Supper is *koinonia*-communion in the fullest sense of the word because it presents the possibility of a true, profound, and recurrent encounter with Christ through the reception of bread and wine and a simultaneous encounter with other members of Christ's body in the church premises. This encounter is not only enriching but also purifying. While living in human society, a Christian cannot help but interact with the world of sin and iniquity. They can even find themselves deeply engaged in this fellowship with the fallen world. Therefore, Paul warns, "Do not be yoked together with unbelievers. For what do righteousness and wickedness have in common (κοινωνία)? Or what fellowship (κοινωνία) can light have with darkness?" (2 Cor 6:14; 1 Tim 5:22). The Lord's Supper is one of the venues that can help the Christian acknowledge his koinonia with sin and be cleansed from it.

John even considers koinonia as a condition of cleansing by the blood of Christ. "But if we walk in the light, as he is in the light, we have fellowship (κοινωνίαν) with one another, and the blood of Jesus, his son, purifies us from all sin" (1 John 1:7). It is important to note that this Johannine text is somewhat ambiguous. John does not unequivocally specify with whom we have fellowship. The context suggests that it is communion with God, but Cleon Rogers argues for a different conclusion. He writes, "John's general use indicates that he takes the fellowship of Christians as a visible sign of fellowship w[ith] God (Westcott; Schnackenburg) αἷμα blood."[132] So, it looks like the Scripture intentionally retains the ambiguity in order to emphasize the profound nature of *koinonia*. The real communion happens both horizontally, with other believers, and vertically, with God.

The *koinonia* of the Lord's Supper points to a communal way of life and revitalizes the church as a community of saints. It helps the church to be more than an assembly where the word of God is proclaimed, and each person is individually responsible for receiving and practicing it.

In the classical Baptist understanding, a congregation is a gathering of people who have entered the covenant with Christ and taken responsibility for one another. The Lord's Supper, as understood from the covenantal perspec-

---

132. Rogers, *The New Linguistic*, 592.

tive, strengthens and sustains the local Christian community. When Christ said at the Last Supper, "This is my body" (Matt 26:26), he was undoubtedly pointing to the bread, but he could well have been pointing also to the disciples gathered at the table. Together with all subsequent generations of God's faithful children, they constituted his body, the church (Rom 12:5; 1 Cor 12:13, etc.).

In other words, the eucharistic body of Christ (the bread) and the localized body of Christ (the ecclesial community) are different signs pointing to the real universal "church, which is his body, the fullness of him who fills everything in every way" (Eph 1:22–23). As Andrew Hamilton notes, contemporary theology is returning to the early Christian idea of the body of Christ's threefold image. He writes: "When early Christians spoke of the body of Christ, they moved easily between the body of Jesus who lived, died and rose again, the body of Christ in the Eucharist, and the communal body of Christ which he makes up of those who are his members."[133] In later times, theology focused mainly on the differences between these manifestations, but in the twenty-first century, a holistic view of the body of Christ is once again returning to the center of theological attention.

The connection between Christ's body as manifested in the eucharistic bread and Christ's body as revealed in the community of living persons was explored by many scholars as early as the first half of the twentieth century, from the Eastern Orthodox liturgist Afanasiev to the Baptist theologian Paul Fiddes. The latter writes:

> In some way, sharing in the Lord's Supper deepens not only the relationship of Christ with the individual believer, but the presence of Christ in his gathered people.... Baptist writings on the Lord's Supper commonly slide from the meaning "communion with Christ" to "communion with each other," and the term "fellowship" works in the same way.[134]

As evidence, Fiddes cites many early Baptist confessions of faith. For example, the British General Baptists' *Orthodox Creed* (1678) in Article XXXIII emphasizes that for believers, the Lord Jesus's Supper is "to be a bond and pledge of their communion with him and with each other."[135] Fiddes stresses that the word *communion* in Baptist documents often has a double meaning

---

133. Hamilton, "Eucharist in Retreat," 110.
134. Fiddes, *Tracks and Traces*, 168.
135. Lumpkin, *Baptist Confessions of Faith*, 321. The same phrases are repeated, almost verbatim, in Chapter XXX of the Second London Confession of 1677 and 1688, see Fiddes, 291.

and incorporates the concept of *koinonia* since it links the presence of Christ in the congregation with the presence of Christ in the eucharistic elements.

This connection of communion with Christ to communion with one another in the Eucharist is underlined in *The Beliefs* Nikolai Odintsov published in 1928. Here, the Lord's Supper is called a means of grace "for the proclamation of Christ's death and closer communion with Him (Jn. 6.56). At the same time, the Holy Supper is [also] the highest expression of the fellowship of saints (1 Cor. 10.17)."[136]

As is evident from these statements, sharing in the Lord's Supper creates the most intimate communion with Christ and helps to express the communion the members of the congregation have with each other. It was this connection that was so important to early Baptist theologians. They emphasized that the Lord's Supper played the most crucial role in the life of local congregations because it enhanced brotherly love among its members. In their view, the Eucharist created and fostered the *koinonia*-communion. As stated in the 1611 *Declaration of Faith of English People in Holland*, "The Lords Supper is the outward manifestacion off the Spiritual communion between Christ and the faithful mutuallie to declare his death vntil he come."[137]

With this approach, one's reflections about the broken body of Christ at Calvary during the Lord's Supper naturally interlock with the pictures of the suffering body of Christ in modern society. The church *qua* the body of Christ endures suffering and distress in this world, continuing to bear Christ's wounds and afflictions (Col 1:24). Therefore, each celebration of the Lord's Supper is a reminder of the ongoing suffering of God's children and a call to action, an invitation to do something to alleviate this suffering.

The community's compassion is expressed in the prayers of intercession during the eucharistic service for those who find themselves broken by sin and illness. These actions *koinonically* integrate the memory of the suffering Christ, on the one hand, and love in action on behalf of the afflicted members of the body of Christ, on the other. The vertical and horizontal components of *koinonia* overlap. But the church needs to deepen and broaden this connection even further, remembering that each Eucharist points not only to the broken body of Christ on the cross but also to the suffering body of Christ in the world of evil and sin.

Communality is the most important asset in the Baptist tradition's treasury, and this quality is in grave danger in an age of individualism and social

---

136. Sannikov, ed., *Istoriya Baptizma (The History of the Baptist Movement)*, 427.
137. Lumpkin, *Baptist Confessions of Faith*, 120–21.

distancing. This danger has increased in the age of the COVID-19 pandemic and of wars that destroy what once was common and push people back to what is private and individual. Many Baptist theologians have, therefore, begun to turn their attention to the loss of communality. In 1997, a group of North American Baptist theologians produced a document called "Re-Envisioning Baptist Identity."[138] In it, they articulated the need to revisit Baptist individualism and restore the vanishing communality.

The document calls for faithful discipleship, emphasizing communality as a core baptistic value. The text of the Manifesto shows that linking individual freedom with communal life avoids the danger of slipping into the excesses of individualism. One's personal freedom should be tied to serving others in a spirit of love. The document states: "In the Lord's Supper the Spirit thus signifies and seals the covenant that makes us one with Christ and one in Christ with one another."[139] Unity with Christ and unity with one another manifest themselves in the community's eucharistic gathering.

Thus, the Lord's Supper as communion presupposes a profound *koinonic* fellowship, which occurs both as an encounter with Christ in the eucharistic signs of his body and blood and as an encounter with his body-church as represented by the community of the faithful. Christ, who once suffered on the cross of Calvary, suffers no less today through his body-church, and each Supper reminds us of this.

The Lord's Supper as Thanksgiving

The first thing Christ did when instituting the New Testament holy meal was to offer a prayer of thanksgiving. Paul confirms it by saying, "The Lord Jesus, on the night he was betrayed, took bread, and when he had given thanks, he broke it and said, 'This is my body, which is for you; do this in remembrance of me'" (1 Cor 11:23–24, NIV; compare with Luke 22:17).

The New Testament narrative makes it clear that the breaking of bread begins with thanksgiving, εὐχαριστία. In ancient times, significant events, books, and procedures were often named by their first word. Therefore, it was natural that the word *eucharist*, meaning "thanksgiving," came to refer to the Lord's Supper in the earliest period of the Christian era. One of the ancient Christian documents, the *Didache*, employs this name to refer to the entire event of the Lord's Supper as well as to describe the eucharistic substance:

---

138. Broadway et al., "Re-Envisioning Baptist Identity," 303–10.
139. Broadway et al., 307.

"Now this is how you should engage in giving thanks, bless God in this way" (*Did.* 9:1) and further, "Only let those who have been baptized in the name of the Lord eat and drink at your Eucharists" (*Did.* 9:5).[140] Obviously, the word *eucharist* had a rather broad meaning in early Christian practice, as the name for the bread and wine of the Lord's Supper and as a designation for the many prayers of thanksgiving.

The Lord's Supper is a special time when the faithful can focus on thankfulness and gratitude. The New Testament encourages giving thanks for everything. This plea sounds like an imperative, more of a commandment than a recommendation. A crucial Bible passage reads: "Rejoice always, pray continually, give thanks in all circumstances; for this is God's will for you in Christ Jesus" (1 Thess 5:16–18). Yet, in practice, it is not so simple. To give thanks properly, one should meet two conditions: one must have a thankful heart and be able to discern the gift received.

Only born-again people are capable of giving thanks because at the moment of their conversion, their inner self, which until then had been centered only on themselves, opens up and undergoes radical transformation. The heart opens wide to let Christ in. As a result, it wants and learns to give thanks, that is, to return the good gift it has received from the outside. *This is gratitude, in a nutshell: a grateful response in return for a good gift that the person has received and acknowledged.*

Sin cannot give thanks. It is by definition ungrateful because it is associated with pride, which puts itself above everyone else. Therefore, the proud person thanks no one but himself. Humility, on the other hand, gives thanks to everyone because it regards itself as inferior to everyone else. The child of God who has experienced spiritual regeneration knows how to give thanks but does not always do so. Pride creeps up on every Christian, and sometimes, thanksgiving becomes lip service rather than heartfelt motivation. The Christians need to wrestle with ungratefulness throughout their whole life. Ingratitude arises in people's hearts when they fail to accept the circumstances in which they find themselves and when they are envious of, or tempted by the gifts the Lord has given others. Ingratitude may skillfully disguise itself as discontent or complacency, as criticism or self-humiliation, but its root is the falling away from love. Therefore, the Eucharist gives every Christian an opportunity to test the sincerity of their gratitude, remembering that it is thankfulness that rebukes both sinners and Satan who do not know how to give thanks.

---

140. O'Loughlin, *The Didache*, 166..

The participants is the Lord's table begin to realize that everything around them is a gift from the most perfect love, and this understanding always produces gratitude. No one can repay the giver for the overwhelmingly great gift of life and salvation (when one acknowledges it for what it is) because of its immense magnificence. It is too grandiose to be placed among the ordinary gifts that we exchange with one another. There is nothing believers can give in return for the divine gift of Christ and, in him, the whole universe. Nothing can repay for the infinite grace!

Can we cultivate a sense of gratitude? Although every cultural community teaches appreciation, unfeigned gratitude to God arises naturally in the born-again person touched by grace. In such a case, a person may give thanks even before they discern what the gift is. Sometimes, the divine gift is wrapped up in sorrow and grief; only its outer shells are visible as if they were the gift's garments. They may be coarse and prickly. One must have great courage to give thanks for the gift without seeing it but believing that a blessing awaits behind the thorns. It is why many saints called gratitude a gesture of courage. Indeed, the Lord often sends tests and trials our way, and we are reluctant to thank him for them. It is only later, after many days or even years, that we come to understand God's plan. This is the first condition for thanksgiving.

The second condition is the ability to discern and acknowledge the gift we have received. Unfortunately, Christians throughout history were prone to overlook divine gifts. People simply fail to notice both small and large manifestations of God's mercy. Out of ten lepers Jesus healed, only one came back to thank him, and even that one was a foreigner (Luke 17:12–19). Our flesh often overshadows our sense of gratitude. Without Christ's help, even Christians cannot properly give thanks to God. Therefore, the pneumatological aspect of the Eucharist – the sustaining and guiding work of the Holy Spirit – is so important.

The Lord's Supper teaches us to understand the reality around us as a gift because it represents the giver. Bread and wine, being simple physical foods, signal more than just the utilitarian function of food to satiate the flesh. They serve as signs referring to their giver. Any physical food points to a person's dependence on God and his gifts, but people often need a considerable amount of time and unique circumstances to realize this.

A grateful person encounters the world around them as a gift, not as a given. All creatures and events around them, such as people, time, and circumstances, are the greatest gift from God. Thankfulness allows the believer to experience what Schmemann called "the Church's experience of paradise,"[141] the blending of earthly and heavenly liturgy.

The Lord's Supper vividly demonstrates the connection between the material and the spiritual, between food and the word. Thanksgiving is a spiritual act, but it often involves material objects and, oddly enough, food. This is how it developed in both the Jewish and Christian traditions. The eating of bread as a daily meal in Judaism has always been associated with thanksgiving. Christians also say grace before every meal. McClendon places the Thanksgiving Day celebration, with its associated dinner, in the same tradition. In his opinion, it "is the model nearest to hand"[142] of the connection between food and thanksgiving. The table talks and fellowship that evangelical Christians of the Eastern European tradition often held after the Lord's Supper also fall into the same category. Furthermore, McClendon considers the Eucharist a new thanksgiving and notes: "This thanks giving meal is inseparable from *awed gratitude*."[143]

Human cultures regard food as a meal, not just physical satiation. It has a somewhat sacramental character because it can and should be experienced as giftedness, although this is not always the case. In many cases, the food is taken as a *given* rather than a *gift*, that is, something that God is somehow "obligated" to give. But when one comes to realize that it is a gift, genuine gratitude takes root in the human heart. The ultimate case of acknowledging the gift and showing gratitude is participation in the Eucharist. Perceiving the eucharistic bread as an inconceivably great gift causes the *awed gratitude* that McClendon mentions.

Gratitude is, by its very nature, liturgical and communal. A human being is transformed through a doxological life lived in a community of praise and abundant grace. But this transformation happens only in the fellowship with others and in the presence of the triune God. As Gregory Beale has convincingly argued in his monograph, "We become what we worship."[144]

Thus, thanksgiving permeates all elements of the Lord's Supper, from the sermon and the words of the institution to the direct participation in this sacred meal to the closing prayer. It is fundamental to the event of encounter with Christ.

---

141. Schmemann, *The Eucharist*, 175.
142. McClendon Jr., *Doctrine: Systematic Theology*, 404.
143. McClendon Jr., 405.
144. Beale, *We Become What We Worship*, 308–10.

The Lord's Supper as Sanctification

The believers' encounter with the Lord during the Supper inevitably leads to their sanctification as long as it is a genuine encounter with a holy God. "*Sanctus Dominus Deus Sabaoth!* Holy is the lord of hosts!" the seraphim cried out (see Isa 6:3). This song entered all of the ancient Christian liturgies of both the Western and Eastern rites and is often sung during solemn Baptist worship services in Eastern Europe. In describing his encounter with God, the prophet Isaiah comments that he would have perished if seraphim had not taken away his sin and iniquity. No flesh can endure the encounter with genuine holiness unless the Lord cleanses and purifies it.

The Eucharistic encounter with the body and blood of Christ, whatever one's interpretation of these concepts, necessarily leads to sanctification because Christ is not only the redemption but also the sanctification of believers (1 Cor 1:30). Eastern Orthodox culture has always known the sanctifying effect of the Eucharist, but many people mistakenly take it to happen in a way automatically, *ex opere operato*. On the other hand, members of contemporary evangelical youth communities often deny or have little thought about the Eucharist's sanctifying effect, considering any institutionalized church practices as backward and outmoded traditionalism. For them, sanctification is a purely spiritual process that has nothing to do with material things. As a consequence, they do not associate examining themselves and confessing their shortcomings with the material signs of the Eucharist.

Paul, concluding his instruction on the proper administration of the Lord's Supper, says: "So then, whoever eats the bread or drinks the cup of the Lord in an unworthy manner will be guilty of sinning against the body and blood of the Lord. Everyone ought to examine themselves before they eat of the bread and drink from the cup" (1 Cor 11:27–28).

The apostle draws attention to the fact that the Lord's Supper is a profoundly important and even dangerous sacred act. The main idea of his eucharistic discourse is crystal clear. Paul wants to show that the Lord's Supper has an impact on those who partake of it, be they worthy or unworthy.

The theme of judgment, as Taras Dyatlik points out, dominates Paul's reasoning here:

> In the First Epistle to the Corinthians, the section on the [Holy] Communion, we find six words whose root is *-judg-*: judgment (κρίμα); without discerning (διακρίνων); more discerning with regard to ourselves (διεκρίνομεν); we would not be judged

ἐκρινόμεθα); we are judged (κρινόμενοι); we will not be finally condemned with the world (κατακριθῶμεν).[145]

Nevertheless, although the apostle refers to judgment and a few derivative concepts, he does not dwell on the topic. He does not proclaim, like the Old Testament prophets, the formidable *Dies Irae* but seeks to promote the spiritual growth of the partakers of the eucharistic meal and encourage their sanctification.

Sanctification occurs first of all through the communicants' self-examination and self-condemnation. If they fail to do so, they should prepare themselves for the manifestation of God's judgment on them. Paul shows that wrong self-assessment and wrong "discernment" of the body of Christ results in one's guilt and condemnation, followed by divine punishment in the form of weakness and sickness, all of which are the consequences of people's unworthy participation in the Supper (1 Cor 11:29–30). Paul suggests avoiding such guilt by worthy participation that involves careful self-examination (1 Cor 11:31–32). What constitutes worthy and unworthy participation in Holy Communion?

Any adequate consideration of the inescapable eucharistic impact begins with the thesis: *eating and drinking unworthily leads to culpability*. The key element of this thesis is the adverb ἀναξίως, the opposite of "worthily" or "in a worthy manner." The question arises: does the phrase "whoever eats the bread or drinks the cup of the Lord in an unworthy manner" concern the *person* receiving the Eucharist (who is unworthy to eat and drink this meal?) or the actual process of eating (how does one eat and drink unworthily)?

Most often, the concept of *participating unworthily* refers to the one who partakes of the meal and implies the question: do they have the right spiritual condition? This approach has been particularly prevalent in the Christian East since patristic times. Here, it is customary to think that a person who is in a state of sin, who is not reconciled to God, and who has not repented participates unworthily despite his being formally a Christian. John Chrysostom frames this idea like this: "For he that hath fallen into sin and draws nigh, is worse than one possessed with a devil. For they, because they are possessed are not punished, but those, when they draw nigh unworthily, are delivered over to undying punishment."[146] According to this approach, people who live in sin and participate in the Lord's Supper condemn themselves to eternal damnation and are deprived of the possibility of forgiveness.

---

145. Dyatlik, "Bogoslovsko-Ekzegeticheskiy Analiz (A Theological-Exegetical Analysis)", 103.

146. Chrysostom, *Homilies on the Gospel*, LXXXII.6.

Of course, not all Eastern European Christians subscribe to such a radical view. But, in general, the idea that, first, unworthy participation means that the communicant has unconfessed sins and, second, such participation is unacceptable is almost the standard view that many practicing ministers embrace. In Eastern European Baptist churches, one's – worthy or unworthy – participation is largely a question of whether one is at peace with God and people. Most often, a grave, unconfessed sin or bitter conflict with one's neighbor that a person discovers during his self-examination would be a sufficient reason for one's decision to refrain from participation in the Eucharist. The indicator of worthy participation is repentance, which leads to the cleansing of one's personal sin. The authoritative minister of the Council of Baptist Churches, D. Minyakov, writes:

> The Lord's Supper is the most holy commandment, and to participate in it unworthily is to dishonor the Lord and become guilty against the Lord's Body and Blood (1 Cor. 11:27). . . . Where sin occurs, there is no Christ, no broken Body and shed blood; what remains is bread and wine, and eating [and drinking] them no longer means participating in the death and suffering of Christ and His shed blood.[147]

In other words, worthy or unworthy participation is reduced to the involved person's spiritual (self-)evaluation, not their actions and attitudes.

However, this view raises many questions from a soteriological perspective. Classical Protestantism has laid bare the problem of human unworthiness, stressing it to such an extent that it makes no sense to speak of anyone being worthy. "[F]or all have sinned and fall short of the glory of God" (Rom 3:23), as Paul asserts. Luther elaborated on this in his *Large Catechism*, saying, "I, indeed, desire to be worthy; but I come not upon any worthiness, but upon thy Word, because thou hast commanded it, and I desire to be thy disciple, no matter what becomes of my worthiness."[148] Thus, although worthy participation is certainly connected with a person's spiritual condition, Paul is *not* talking about worthy and unworthy participants since everyone is truly unworthy of reaching out to the eucharistic bread and wine. Rather, he speaks about the *unworthy participant's worthy or unworthy participation*. As both the NIV and NRSV put it, the problem has to do with people's eating and drinking "in an unworthy manner."

---

147. Minyakov, "O Vechere Gospodney (On the Lord's Supper)," 8.
148. Luther, *The Large Catechism*, 110.

When the unworthy participant is conscious of, and acknowledges his unworthiness by coming to Christ with a contrite heart, Jesus's righteousness embraces him and makes him worthy. The remorse with which each participant approaches the Lord's Supper consists not so much in an awareness of one's specific transgressions – although this is undoubtedly necessary – but in realizing one's sinful nature as a whole. This understanding is unrelated to one's neighbor but rooted solely in one's own self.

Yet, when speaking of worthy or unworthy participation in the Lord's Supper, Paul does not focus on the communicants' spiritual condition but rather on their attitude toward the meal. How can we verify that the communicant participates in a worthy manner? Or how can we avoid participating in the Eucharist in an unworthy manner?

David Garland, author of an extensive exegetical commentary on 1 Corinthians, believes that the apostle offers several key tests to determine whether one eats the Lord's Supper in a worthy manner. The first test implies self-examination. The communicants "are to test (δοκιμαζέτω, dokimazetō) their genuineness before God does."[149] What does it mean to verify one's genuineness? Garland understands it as the absence of arrogance and the recognition of social and spiritual equality: "The genuine Christian recognizes that there are no class divisions at the Lord's table."[150] Taking Paul's words as his starting point, Garland develops the idea of unworthy participation as social or class pride. In his view, the central idea of the apostle's instruction is that the Lord's Supper, as a communal meal for all members of the congregation, probably associated with the so-called *agape* meals, was meant to remove social disparities. The more influential and wealthy members of the church were to share their supper with the poor, and for some, it was probably their only opportunity to have a meal that day. The Corinthian church's practice distorted this essential element of the Supper (1 Cor 11:21–22). Paul attempts to correct this and explains that such a situation is totally unacceptable and makes the violators of social equality blameworthy and accountable before God, whose punishment would follow.

From this perspective, unworthy participation is basically reduced to exalting oneself before the socially disadvantaged. Despising these people amounts to despising Christ himself. This is certainly a correct but rather narrow understanding. Paul hardly reduces the Eucharist to the love feast (*agape*) because he concludes by saying, "Anyone who is hungry should eat something at home"

---

149. Garland, *First Corinthians*, 551.
150. Garland, 551.

(1 Cor 11:34). This statement shows that the purpose of the Eucharist is not to share food with the poor. Taras Dyatlik, in his exegetical analysis of this pericope, rightly expands the concept of self-examination. He writes: "Trying to understand the use of the verb δοκιμαζέτω in this context, we can trace the following three main vectors: the believer is to test (1) his attitude toward the church and other believers; (2) his conscience and spiritual condition; (3) his attitude toward the Lord's Supper."[151] It is clear that self-examination is not only about class equality and the lack of arrogance of the haves over the have-nots. It also has to do with one's inner state and the right attitude toward the Lord's Supper itself, not only toward its partakers. The Eucharist is neither a simple Greek dinner of like-minded people, the *dypnon*, nor a Jewish party of *habour* friends. It is an intimate encounter with Christ and his body, which should be distinguished from an ordinary get-together between friends. Such a view much more accurately reflects the meaning of the apostle's admonition to examine ourselves.

Another test, according to Garland, is expressed in Paul's words: "For those who eat and drink without discerning the body of Christ eat and drink judgment on themselves" (1 Cor 11:29). It means that one may fail to care about the body of Christ while participating in the Eucharist, and that will entail divine condemnation.

The key notion here is that of *discerning* (διακρίνω). It occurs twice in this passage in verses 29 and 31 and, according to all leading Bible scholars,[152] literally means to *divide (into its constituents), detect, distinguish, differentiate, make a difference, estimate rightly, judge,* or *judge rightly.* Strong's Concordance, entry 1252, explains that "diakrínō" may mean "to separate thoroughly, i.e. to withdraw from, or oppose; figuratively, to discriminate, or hesitate." The KJV translates διακρίνων as "discerning" in verse 29 and "we judged" in verse 31, while the NIV renders it "discerning" in both verses.

Clearly, the chief meaning of this word, as Anthony Thiselton comments,[153] is to recognize and separate one phenomenon or event from another. To act with discernment means to analyze an object or situation, make correct judgments about it, and act in accordance with them. Conversely, acting without discernment means acting rashly without prior reflection and careful analysis of the situation. That is why some people are called reckless.

---

151. Dyatlik, "Bogoslovsko-Ekzegeticheskiy Analiz (A Theological-Exegetical Analysis)," 106.

152. Thiselton, *The First Epistle to the Corinthians*, 892.

153. Thiselton, 892.

It is the careless, thoughtless, superficial, inconsiderate, unreflective, and basically wrong attitude toward the body of Christ that the apostle reproaches in 1 Corinthians 11. Still, the interpreter faces the difficulty of trying to understand what this frivolous, thoughtless, and inappropriate attitude toward the body of Christ means in practice and how exactly the receiver fails to discern what the body of Christ is and what that body is not.

Thiselton, Garland, and other contemporary experts on the New Testament Greek text give at least three different readings of 1 Corinthians 11:29. The first one goes like this: "A venerable view going back to Justin and Augustine and reflected in some modern commentators (Godet 1887: 167; Weiss 1910: 291; Lietzmann 1949: 59; Héring 1962: 120) thinks that it refers to distinguishing the sacramental presence of Christ in the eucharistic elements from the ordinary bread on the table."[154] The well-known Bible commentator Matthew Henry puts it this way: "The Corinthians came to the Lord's table as to a common feast, not discerning the Lord's body, not making a difference or distinction between that and common food, but setting both on a level."[155]

In other words, the unworthy celebration of the Lord's Supper, in this view, consists of an improper attitude toward the eucharistic meal, which is treated as if it were ordinary food. Most modern interpreters, especially those in the evangelical tradition, do not accept this view, arguing that it detracts from the main idea and context of the passage. Garland points out that Paul "accuses the Corinthians of despising and humiliating their impoverished brothers and sisters at their supper, not profaning the elements."[156] However, this objection loses its force if we understand Paul's admonition not only as a correction of the Corinthian distortions in the administration of the Lord's Supper but also as an opportunity to explain the theological meaning of the Eucharist using the "story within a story" technique.

The second view, prevalent among evangelical theologians, suggests that Paul is referring to the Corinthians' failure to recognize the church as the body of Christ, that is, to discern Christ's presence among his people. Thiselton quotes Günther Bornkamm,[157] who believes that Paul alludes here to "the mystical body of Christ . . . the 'body' of the congregation."[158] Hence, a failure

---

154. Garland, *First Corinthians*, 552.
155. Henry, *An Exposition*, 445.
156. Garland, *First Corinthians*, 552.
157. Bornkamm, "Lord's Supper and Church," 123–60.
158. Bornkamm, "Lord's Supper and Church," 148–49, quoted in Thiselton, *The First Epistle*, 892.

to *discern the body of Christ* on this approach means that some Corinthians took the assembly of the saints lightly, making no distinction between a Christian congregation, on the one hand, and a secular voluntary association or an average civic gathering, on the other. Garland summarizes this view: "What they were doing accentuated the social and economic differences between the 'haves' and the 'have-nots' and showed a flagrant disregard for the body. Mistreating fellow members in this way at the Lord's Supper becomes an offense against Christ."[159]

This position looks appealing but seems to impose on the apostle a preoccupation exclusively with socio-economic rather than spiritual aspects of church life. Furthermore, it does not correspond well to the basic meaning of the verb "to discern" (διαχρίνω) and, most importantly, reduces the concept of the body of Christ to a local congregation. The New Testament portrays the body of Christ much more broadly than a single, say, Corinthian community.

The third view focuses neither on the elements that represent, and for some are, Christ's body and blood (first position) nor on Christ's body-church (second position) but on the suffering body of Christ on the cross. In this view, the participants of the eucharistic meal should recognize the uniqueness of Christ as distinct from all other human beings. His body that suffered on the cross is the atonement for the sins of all humankind. He is set apart in the sense that he gave himself to suffer for the sake of others, and the Lord's Supper emphasizes the uniqueness of Christ *qua* the suffering God.

In other words, the cross and Christ's suffering body constitute the focal point of proper participation in the Lord's Supper. The loss of this focus, that is, a careless attitude toward Holy Communion, lighthearted participation in it as if it were a typical meal, and failure to realize what the body of Christ on the cross is, translated into eating and drinking in an unworthy manner and entail imminent punishment. Thus, as Thiselton observes,[160] the cross of Christ is a form of double sentence: it signifies both "guilty" and "justified." When reflecting on it, the communicants examine their genuineness. One's focusing on Christ's sacrifice, understanding and appreciating his suffering, and reflecting on and thinking about the Lord enables God to render a favorable verdict, proclaiming the person justified. Conversely, when one approaches the Eucharist as a mere custom and participates in it out of habit, without considering Christ's sacrifice and reflecting on it, it amounts to unworthy participation and entails condemnation.

---

159. Garland, *First Corinthians*, 552.
160. Thiselton, *The First Epistle*, 894.

This is the interpretation of the phrase "without discerning the body of Christ" that is most common among Eastern European Baptists. Here is how Ivanov, the leading theologian of the Russian Baptist Union, explains the difference between worthy and unworthy participation in the Lord's Supper in his systematic theology textbook: "Unworthy participation in the Lord's Supper, without proper consideration of this rite's spiritual essence, offends God and can lead to serious punishment. . . . Those participating in the Lord's Supper should intently reflect on Christ's sufferings and His sacrifice on Calvary."[161] A senior elder of the Leningrad Baptist Church (1966–1980) earlier wrote:

> To discern the body of the Lord is to have a correct understanding of the following: That Christ here on earth was in the likeness of the flesh (Jn. 1:14; Phil. 2:7; Heb. 5:7); He experienced the physical world in the same way as we do; He was tired (Jn. 4:4–6; Lk. 8:22–23); He felt hunger and thirst (Mt. 21:17–18; Jn. 19:28–29); He could weep (Jn. 11:35; Lk. 19:41); And in His broken body we have sanctification (Heb. 10:10); and perfection (Heb. 10:14).[162]

To discern the Lord's body, then, is to receive the Eucharist properly, recognizing, sharing, appreciating, and correctly evaluating the body of Christ.

Practically, it may mean the following:

- One should be able to distinguish the bread and cup at the Lord's Supper from ordinary food, seeing the sacramental value of the eucharistic elements. It does not oblige people to believe in transubstantiation. One can speak either of the co-presence, or of the sign presence of Christ's body and blood in the bread and cup. A crucial mark of sacramental understanding is the conviction that the eucharistic substance is to be treated with awe and reverence, that is, differently from ordinary material objects, even though it is hard to explain its mystery.
- One should be able to recognize the church as the body of Christ in one's brothers and sisters, that is, to discern Christ's presence among his people and to learn to distinguish the church community from the secular assembly. The eucharistic gathering is – and should be seen as – a reflection of Christ's universal body-church. In practice, it means that when celebrating the Lord's Supper, it is forbidden to

---

161. Ivanov, *Osnovy Sistematicheskogo Bogosloviya (Basics of Systematic Theology)*, 52.
162. Fadyukhin, "O Tserkvi" ("On the Church"), 67–68.

show any disregard on the grounds of social inequality, envy, pride, or other negative attitudes toward other communicants.
- One is expected to contemplate the suffering body of Christ on the cross during Communion and come to understand its meaning, realizing that it is the sacrifice for the sins of all humankind. In fact, perceiving the often repeated and familiar truths about Jesus's broken body in a new, fresh, and profound way is an art. The communicant is to ponder intently and "consider him who endured such opposition from sinners, so that you will not grow weary and lose heart" (Heb 12:3).

These are the three interrelated directions one might take and the threefold interpretation of Paul's invitation to discern the body of the Lord that we offer here. Such a holistic interpretation broadens the horizon and helps us to look at the concept of sanctification through the lens of worthy or unworthy participation in the Eucharist.

The effect of Christians' participation in the Lord's Supper is outlined in the next part of Paul's eucharistic discourse. He writes:

That is why many among you are weak and sick, and a number of you have fallen asleep. But if we were more discerning with regard to ourselves, we would not come under such judgment. Nevertheless, when we are judged in this way by the Lord, we are being disciplined so that we will not be finally condemned with the world (1 Cor 11:30–32).

Here, the theme of judgment reaches its greatest intensity and goes beyond itself as Paul speaks of judgment as the highest expression of love.

It is quite possible that Paul had heard of the deaths and severe illnesses of some of the Corinthian brethren from his friends, who also informed him about divisions and other troubles in that community. In any case, he connected this mischievous state of affairs with the wrong attitude toward the Lord's Supper. Cases of sickness and death among Christians have various causes. They may be the consequence of sin (Matt 9:2), or a compromised lifestyle. Often, they serve as a testing of one's faith (Job 2:5–8) or a manifestation of God's glory (John 11:4). However, in this case, the apostle unequivocally identifies the cause-and-effect relationship between the unworthy participation in the Lord's Supper and some members of the congregation's death (1 Cor 11:30).

Such a bold statement is not easy to explain, given that the apostle does not always hold that sickness is a consequence of sin (2 Tim 4:20). Gordon Fee thinks that, in this case, Paul had a prophetic, spiritual revelation concerning the situation in Corinth.[163] Whatever the apostle's motives, it is clear that, from his point of view, the manner of one's participation in the Eucharist can be either a great blessing or a threatening condemnation. The Eucharist is like a double-edged sword, one side of which brings justification and life, the other side judgment and death. It is why the patristic tradition,[164] following Ignatius of Antioch,[165] called this sacrament "the medicine of life" (φάρμακον ζωῆς), playing with the meaning of the word φάρμακον which means both medicine and poison. Therefore, the medicine of life can easily turn into the poison of death (φάρμακον θάνατος).

Thiselton suggests that Paul alludes to the ancient Israelite law concerning jealousy and marital unfaithfulness (Num 5:12–29).[166] This law functioned as an ordeal (the judgment of God) for a potentially unfaithful wife. If a husband suspected that his wife committed adultery but had no proof of that, he could resort to the public procedure of testing her fidelity at the entrance to the Tabernacle. After a grain offering had been made and a priest had performed some necessary acts, the wife was given so-called "bitter water," which had no effect if she was innocent but caused severe sickness if she was indeed guilty.

Although some view this action as a mere placebo, Paul quite straightforwardly says that the eucharistic substance plays a role in believers' self-examination since God himself enters the scene and punishes those who eat and drink in an unworthy manner. In Paul's view, it is not the substance itself that produces the blessing or the sickness, nor is it something the communicants inflict on themselves. Instead, it is the working of divine providence.

It is important to highlight that God does not judge in the sense of punishing people but, rather, seeks to help and *correct* them. The sickness and death that befalls the one guilty of unworthy participation in the Lord's Supper, while causing sorrow in earthly life, preserves the communicant from eternal punishment.

Verse thirty speaks about the infirm (ἄρρωστοι), sick (ἀσθενεῖς), and dying (κοιμῶνται). These terms may have a metaphorical meaning but, according to the most authoritative modern interpreters, are to be taken literally: ἀσθενεῖς are the weak, κοιμῶνται the sleeping. The New Testament's use of these words most

---

163. Fee, *The First Epistle*, 565.

164. See, for example, the article by P. Malkov, who analyzed the patristic theologians' quotations about worthy and unworthy participation in the Lord's Supper. Malkov, "'Ne v Sud ili vo Osuzhdeniye . . .' ('Not into Judgment or Condemnation')," 70–71.

165. In Ephesians 20:2, Ignatius calls the Eucharist φάρμακον ἀθανασίας, "the medicine of immortality." *The Apostolic Fathers*, 198–199.

166. Thiselton, *The First Epistle*, 894–95.

often supports their literal reading and allows one to take them as referring to physical sickness and death, especially in the descriptions of Jesus's healings. Therefore, Garland and Thiselton, in their commentaries, explicitly reject the view of Schneider,[167] who insists on a symbolic understanding of these terms. He reads them as metaphors referring to the "weak in faith," "spiritually sick," and "spiritually asleep." Garland writes:

> This view might appeal to those who do not like to think that sickness can be directly caused by sin or that the Lord's Supper might have numinous properties – mishandling it can lead to death. But Paul has in mind real sickness and real death (see Robertson and Plummer 1914: 253), and his words should be taken at face value (Oster 1995: 285).[168]

The literal meaning corresponds with and stems from God's purposes. If he inflicts sickness and death on some people, this is because he wants to save them from being condemned together with sinners. The use of metaphors would completely invalidate this argument. Spiritual weakness and spiritual sleep can contribute neither to one's sanctification nor to one's correction as rooted in the manner of participation in the Eucharist. This is the view that many Eastern European Baptists endorse.

The Lord's Supper as a Foretaste of What Is to Come

When speaking of the Lord's Supper, Baptists tend to look backward to the past. They stress the importance of remembering the Savior's suffering and death to such an extent that it overshadows both the actual presence of Christ during the Supper and the future encounter with him. As we delve into the past, however, we must remember that it is inextricably bound up not only with the present but also with the future. The past arises out of the immediate present, but the present itself comes from the future, not the past. Moving backward means living in the future. The church's memory of the suffering Christ comes to life through the hope of the imminent encounter with the risen Christ. Therefore, the Eucharist unites past, present, and future.

Remembering the suffering Christ through the reception of the eucharistic bread and wine here and now points to the image of the future kingdom banquet, and also manifests the Christ who is to come. He enters this meeting

---

167. Schneider, "Glaubensmangel in Korinth," 3–19.
168. Garland, *First Corinthians*, 553.

from the future, which for him is present, and we better do our best not to miss this reunion.

During the Last Supper, Jesus Christ said to his disciples: "I tell you, I will not drink from this fruit of the vine from now on until that day when I drink it new with you in my Father's kingdom" (Matt 26:29). He seems to build a bridge whose one pillar rests on holy Thursday and the other on a certain omega point, on which the great and glorious feast, the wedding supper of the Lamb, is expected to take place. Jesus envisions and invites his followers to discern what the prophets saw as if in a blur: "On this mountain the LORD Almighty will prepare a feast of rich food for all peoples, a banquet of aged wine – the best of meats and the finest of wines" (Isa 25:6). The centuries elapse between Isaiah's prophecy and the angel's joyful cry: "Blessed are those who are invited to the wedding supper of the Lamb!" (Rev. 19:9). But Jesus already dwells in the eschatological dimension. At the Last Supper, he left the chronos time, which punctually and methodically counted down day by day, and entered the kairos time, which has no succession of minutes but contains only events.

Sergei Fadyukhin, an elder of the Leningrad Baptist Church, expressed this figuratively in his 1959 article: "Christ's commandment to break bread is the rainbow of the New Testament. One end of the rainbow rests on Golgotha, on the death of Christ, and the other on the eternal mercy at His coming."[169] As a symbol of the covenant, the rainbow not only gives assurance that the flood will never happen again but figuratively connects Calvary, as the true mountain of the transfiguration, with the mountain of the future banquet for all nations.

At the Last Supper, the disciples certainly had no clue as to how long it would take until the glorious celebration in the kingdom of heaven. They wished it were a few days or, at most, a few months. They could hardly believe they would have to wait millennia for the Savior's return. Most likely, the disciples linked Christ's assurance of his imminent coming with the words, "Truly I tell you, this generation will certainly not pass away until all these things have happened" (Matt 24:34). They probably took them as a reference to *their* generation that would witness the Messiah's second coming. Such an interpretation was likely the basis of the "Christian communism" the Jerusalem community practiced after the Pentecost. But by the middle of the first century, it became clear that "the bridegroom was delayed" (Matt 25:5, NRSV), yet this *delay of the parousia* in no way disappointed the early church, as Albert Schweitzer has

---

169. Fadyukhin, "O Tserkvi (On the Church)," 69.

sought to prove.[170] The Christian faith was not based on the expectation of the end of history or the parousia as such but on the fact of Jesus's resurrection and the experience of new life in Christ, as Oscar Cullmann has shown in *Christ and Time*,[171] criticizing Schweitzer's "consistent eschatology."

The second generation of early Christians had already adjusted their eschatological outlook and admitted that it was not for them "to know the times or dates the Father has set by his own authority" (Acts 1:7). Christians focused on preaching and living the gospel as Jesus instructed them. There was no shift in focus but a shift in distance and perspective. It happened because the disciples' love for, and trust in Christ were the reason for their longing for his return, not the other way around. Their faith centered on Christ, not just on his return. Therefore, the fact that Christ did not come during the apostles' lifetime did not destroy but enriched and enhanced the Christian faith.

Early Christians came to realize that there was a serious difference between the future as seen from the past and the future as seen from the future itself. Initially, they supposed that Christ's glorious return of which he spoke much (Matt 24; Mark 13; Luke 21, etc.) should have been a continuation of Jesus's past, earthly life. But the New Testament authors, describing the future advent of Christ, insistently used not the word ἔρχεται but the word παρουσία (Matt 24:3; 27; 37; 39; the epistles of James, Peter, and Paul). *Parousia* literally means someone's arrival and presence. But in all twenty-four occurrences of the word in the New Testament, it denotes not just Christ's coming but a sudden interruption of the sequential, linear time. The *kairotic* – one might say eschatological – revelation, the *parousia*, breaks into and invades the methodical chronos, changing the world once and forever.[172]

As we know, the authors of the New Testament use several different words to describe the future. One can speak of the future as a continuation of what has happened in the past and is happening in the present. It is the future of the past. The biblical text describes it by means of the verb ἔρχομαι (erchomai) and

---

170. See Schweitzer, *The Quest of the Historical Jesus*, and a contemporary overview of this theological trend in Andreev, "The Quest for the Historical Jesus". Many representatives of the *Quest for the Historical Jesus* movement, beginning with Herman Samuel Reimarus (1694–1768), believe that Jesus, approaching his death, mistakenly believed in his imminent return. When his followers realized this error and became disillusioned with the expectation of Christ's second coming, they began to form Christianity as a conventional religious system.

171. Cullmann, *Christ and Time*.

172. Only in Mark 13:26 and Luke 21:27, Christ speaks of the son of man coming on the clouds, employing the word ἐρχόμενον. But in this case, it is not Jesus's self-revelation that is being described but his subsequent action after the *parousia* (he has already revealed himself and is coming to us).

its derivatives (ἔρχεται, ἐρχόμενος, and so on). This is a future that is already coming and completing what is happening in the present. It is an expectation of what is ahead based on what was behind and what is today. Something is about to come because it is already there, and if certain conditions are met, it may happen. For example, Jesus says that temptations "must come, but woe to the person through whom they come (ἔρχεται)!" (Matt 18:7). The temptations are already here, and they may befall someone in the future. This future, when realized, will necessarily become the past by passing through the present.

There is another unpredictable future that cannot be derived from the past and present. It comes suddenly, paradoxically, and unexpectedly. It bursts into the present and "overturns" it. This future comes not from the past through the present but from a different, unknown, and incomprehensible world. It is a παρουσία, the coming as a revelation (Matt 24:3; 27, etc.). While one can foresee the *erchomenon* (future of the present) by watching present trends, the *parousia* or *adventus* (future of the future) is unpredictable. It represents that new future which is neither based on, nor derived from the past. It bursts out of eternity and manifests it. Furthermore, it will never become the past but will always be the present. It is the absolutely new reality that transforms the old by divine intervention, as in the saying, "I am making everything new (καινός, kainos)!" (Rev. 21:5). These are two conceptions of time: linear and chronological, on the one hand, and transcendent, *kairotic*, on the other. Christian thinkers learned to understand and distinguish between the two by the middle of the first century after the bridegroom had slowed down. The New Testament texts written during this period reflect it.

Sometimes, different terms, like *future* and *coming*, signal the distinction between these concepts of time, even though everyday usage treats these words as synonyms. Moltmann observes:

> European languages generally have two possible ways of talking about what is ahead. *Futurum* means what will be; *adventus* means what is coming. The two words go together with two different conceptions of time. Future in the sense of *futurum* develops out of the past and present, inasmuch as these hold within themselves the potentiality of becoming and are "pregnant with future" (Leibniz's phrase) . . . *adventus*, in its turn, is a rendering of the Greek word *Parousia* . . . the language of the prophets and apostles has brought into the word the messianic note of hope."[173]

---

173. Moltmann, *The Coming of God*, 25.

In other words, the *futurum*, or simple future, is the *future of the present* that one can predict by looking at what is happening now, while the *adventus* is the *coming future* that emerges from the future itself. In biblical terms, this distinction can be described as prediction vis-à-vis prophecy. Prediction is grounded in the analysis of the past, while the source of prophecy is revelation.

This understanding of the two *modi operandi* of time completely changed the eschatological horizon of early Christianity. Christian communities came to see that one had to live a full life in the here and now, preaching the kingdom of God come chronologically speaking, and at the same time expecting the kingdom of God to come in the eschatological sense. It could burst into everyday life at any time. The *chronos* and *kairos* point to different dimensions of the Christian life. Both are absolutely real, and the individual Christian may experience either when the father wills it. From that time onward, the Lord's Supper has become a recurring liturgical act, which takes place in a chronological dimension but reflects the *kairotic* event of the wedding feast of the Lamb.

The biblical view of the future leads the participants in the Lord's Supper to turn their gaze to the coming meal in the kingdom of heaven and make every effort to bring this event closer. They might do it in two synergistic ways. First, by active involvement in missions and spreading the gospel worldwide (Matt 24:14), including the rediscovered, old mission fields of Europe and North America. Second, by persistent supplications asking the Lord to hasten the kingdom of God's coming in visible form. As the apostle Peter writes, we "look forward to the day of God and speed its coming" (2 Pet 2:12). This double path implies that we both look forward to the future and work hard and faithfully in the present. As Cullmann observes,

> The situation in redemptive history of the present, which lies between Christ's resurrection and Parousia, is a complex one; it is determined by the noteworthy tension between past and future, between "already fulfilled" and "not yet fulfilled." The world is already ruled by Christ, and yet its present 'form' is passing away (1 Cor. 7:31).[174]

In other words, the kingdom of God is *already, but not yet*.

When understood along these lines, the Lord's Supper is a solemn feast of victory celebrated despite the enemy's visible presence, seeming overpowering and desperate resistance. It is already a feast but not yet a full-fledged celebration. It is no accident that many modern scholars call it the Kingdom

---

174. Cullmann, *Christ and Time*, 212.

Banquet. It lets us glimpse the vision of the coming kingdom, in which the ultimate renewal of the world will take place. A. T. Nikolainen describes it as follows: "Each contemporary Eucharist is in a certain sense the *penultimate* Eucharist, since the next one may be a complete celebration in the Kingdom of God."[175] It might be that the next Lord's Supper will be the banquet about which the Lord spoke to his disciples: "I confer on you a kingdom, just as my Father conferred one on me, so that you may eat and drink at my table in my kingdom . . ." (Luke 22:29–30).

This is why Schmemann defines the Lord's Supper as "the sacrament of the coming of the risen Lord, of our meeting and communion with him 'at his table in his kingdom.'"[176] Although communion with Christ takes place on earth, nonetheless, the participants are already present in the kingdom of God through faith. This communion begins at the moment of one's conversion, reaches completion on the day of their baptism, is renewed in each eucharistic encounter, and, by faith, yearns for the moment of the *parousia* and the Second Coming of Christ in visible form.

Thus, the Lord's Supper evokes and reveals to all those gathered for this feast the dawn of the mysterious, everlasting kingdom of God. It exhorts us to prepare ourselves for this coming kingdom and helps the church to ascend and progress on her way to it. This is precisely the line of thought the apostle Paul takes. He says that Christ's church is to celebrate this meal here on earth "until he comes" (1 Cor 11:26).

Eucharistic Hospitality

One of the difficult practical issues the Baptist ministers in Eastern Europe face is the need to define the boundaries of eucharistic hospitality. The underlying question is simple: who is allowed to participate in this sacred meal? People tend to answer this question subconsciously as their theological views on the Lord's Supper dictate. The question may be rephrased. Is this ordinance an individual or communal act? Or, in traditional Baptist terms, should the Eucharist be an "open" or "closed table?"

---

175. Nikolainen, "Yevkharistiya v Svete Issledovaniy (The Eucharist in the Light of Studies)," 189.

176. Schmemann, *The Eucharist*, 43.

Anthony Clarke, Morgan Patterson, and other scholars[177] have clearly demonstrated that from the earliest days of the Baptist movement, its adherents have, by and large, followed the practice of closed communion. However, some ministers have exceptionally admitted to the Eucharist those baptized by sprinkling or immersion as infants or adults in other churches who were not members of classical Baptist communities.[178] John Bunyan, author of *Pilgrim's Progress*, was a major influence on the idea of open communion. He wrote: "That the church of Christ hath not warrant to keep out of their communion the Christian that is discovered to be a visible saint by the word, the Christian that walketh according to his light with God."[179] Also, the renowned Baptist preacher Spurgeon allowed for an open communion while still advocating closed church membership.

However, regardless of whether the seventeenth- and eighteenth-century Baptists practiced the open or closed table, all Baptist congregations, without exception, have always insisted on the community's right to exercise disciplinary oversight over each communicant. This practice was called the "guarded communion" grounded in the theological assumption that sinful persons could not receive the Eucharist without harming themselves (1 Cor 11:29) and without somehow desecrating the Lord's Supper.[180] Thus, the local church was obligated to prevent anyone whose life did not conform to the Christian moral standards from participating in the Eucharist.

As Patterson writes, the opposite, that is, "'unguarded' or 'mixed communion' usually meant 'indiscriminate participation with profane or unconverted persons, undisciplined persons, and unbaptized persons.'"[181] All Baptist groups agreed that a worthy Christian life was a necessary prerequisite for participating in the Lord's Supper. The main debate concerned the status of water baptism: was it also a precondition for one's participation in the Lord's Supper or not? In William Collins's *Baptist Catechism* of 1693, the question "Who are the proper subjects of this ordinance?" is answered: "They who have been baptized upon a personal profession of their faith in Jesus Christ,

---

177. For a detailed history of this debate among various groups of American Baptists, see W. Morgan Patterson, "Lord's Supper in Baptist History," 32. For the perspective of British Baptists, see Anthony Clarke, "A Feast for All?," 92–93; Winter, "The Lord's Supper," 267–81.
178. See Turner's explanation in Turner, *A Modest Plea*.
179. Bunyan, *Differences in Judgement*, 4.
180. Patterson, "Lord's Supper in Baptist History," 27.
181. Patterson, 27.

and repentance from dead works."[182] Most British and later American Baptists believed that a believer's baptism was a prerequisite for one's partaking in the eucharistic bread and wine.

In the nineteenth century, the situation of the British Baptist movement started to change. More and more pastors began to practice open communion. The influences behind this trend included famous preachers of the time, such as Robert Hall, a Leicester pastor who wrote a tract against the exclusivist approach to the Lord's Supper, Spurgeon, and others. Applying the open table principle caused heated debates and even divisions in the churches, occasionally bringing some cases before the court.[183] Nevertheless, the practice of open communion gained momentum and spread among Baptists.

A similar debate occurred between the representatives of the St. Petersburg Revival (Evangelical Christians) and the Ukrainian-Caucasian Stundists and Baptists in the early days of the Eastern European Baptist movement. The northern group, led by Redstock and Pashkov, believed that only those who had experienced the birth from above and now led a genuinely Christian life were to be admitted to the eucharistic table, while the Ukrainian-Caucasian branch emphasized the additional prerequisite, namely, water baptism.

Pashkov, in correspondence with the editor of the *Church Herald (Tserkovnyi Vestnik)*, archpriest I. L. Yanyshev, wrote:

> I cannot but recognize the sacraments established by the Lord and His apostles, but I also cannot but be convinced by the word of God that all the sacraments are established exclusively for believers, for whom alone they are beneficial, becoming a condemnation for all those who approach them unworthily, i.e., without faith (1 Cor. 11:29).[184]

The belief that the Lord's Supper was intended only *for believers* did not exclude church discipline. It was the conviction of both Pashkov and Kargel', successive pastors of the Evangelical Christian congregation in St. Petersburg. In his *Brief Exposition of the Evangelical Christians' Beliefs*, Kargel' pointed out: "The

---

182. Collins, *The Baptist Catechism*, Question 103. also known as 'Keach's Catechism' on the supposition that Benjamin Keach was its primary author. The oldest known copy of the Baptist Catechism is a 5th edition printed in 1695. The full text is here: https://baptistcatechism.org/.

183. Morgan Patterson relates the case of Baptist pastor George Gould. In 1860, he began practicing open communion, but a part of the congregation protested his decision. They left the church and filed a lawsuit demanding that the church property be handed over to them, but the lawsuit was lost. Patterson, "Lord's Supper in Baptist History," 29.

184. Nikitin, "Perepiska V.A. Pashkova (Correspondence between V.A. Pashkov)," 143.

Church separates [people] from this world (Acts 2:40; 5:13) and, watching over the purity and holiness of its members, removes the unholy from its midst (Acts 5:1–11; 1 Cor. 5:1–13)."[185] This *Exposition*, as well as Pashkov's *Confession*, teaches about baptism and the Lord's Supper, that "they both are entrusted only to the disciples of Christ."[186] The text continues: "Received with a living faith, it [the Lord's Supper] makes us partakers of fellowship both with Him and with all the members of His Church."[187] Yet, the confession says nothing about the necessity of being baptized in order to receive Holy Communion.

The Southern Revival, influenced by Wieler and Pavlov, almost from the outset, insisted on the importance of water baptism as a sign of union with Christ. The early *Confession of Faith* Pavlov penned states: "The Holy Supper is exclusively intended only for those who, through the work of God's regenerating grace, have been made His inheritance and have received holy baptism."[188] In other words, it is not only regeneration that is required of those wanting to receive the eucharistic bread and wine, but also water baptism. Andrei Kucheryavyy, having analyzed the attitudes of different evangelical groups of the Russian Empire to the Lord's Supper, pointed out that none of the members of the Baptist congregations "were allowed to participate in this Sacrament" unless the whole community had previously declared them worthy of it."[189]

When Prokhanov assumed the leadership of the Evangelical Christians' Union, water baptism became an officially recognized necessary prerequisite for people's admittance to the Lord's table. The 1909 *Confession of Faith of Evangelical Christians* states quite unequivocally: "The Lord's Supper may be partaken of only by 1) born-again believers; 2) who have testified to their death with Christ through water baptism (Mt. 28:19–20; Acts 2:41–46; 22:16) and who pursue a Christian way of life (1 Cor. 11:29)."[190] By the time of the official merger of the Evangelical Christian and Baptist movements in October 1944, the practice of the closed communion had become generally accepted and later became mandatory.

Baptist ministers have based their exclusivist understanding of the eucharistic hospitality on several biblical images and allusions. First and foremost,

---

185. Kargel', *Kratkoye Izlozheniye Veroucheniya (A Brief Exposition of the Evangelical)*, 6.

186. Kargel', 7.

187. Kargel', 8.

188. Pavlov, "Kratkoye Veroucheniye Baptistov (A Summary of Baptist Beliefs)," 2.

189. Kucheryavyy, "Obzor Ucheniya o Vechere (An Overview of the Doctrine of the Lord's Supper)," 155.

190. Prokhanov, *Izlozheniye Yevangel'skoy (An Exposition of the Evangelical)*, 64.

Christ's own example suggests this reading. Jesus celebrated the Last Supper in a small circle of disciples. Moreover, Judas, the betrayer, as most biblical scholars believe, left immediately after the Old Testament seder, as John's account makes clear (John 13:30), and did not participate in the institution of the New Testament supper. The same conclusion follows from the analogy with the Jewish Passover, a prototype of the Christian eucharistic meal. The Passover banquet, as we know, was a closed table, and the number of participants was limited. To qualify for it and be allowed to eat the Lord's Passover, one had to belong to the people of God, that is, to stand in covenant with Yahweh or join that covenant through circumcision.

From a theological point of view, the closed table has often been explained in terms of its core essence, which is mainly the communion of the children of God with each other and with Christ. Put differently, the Lord's Supper is an encounter between members of the body of Christ and its head. It goes without saying that to have such communion, one must be a member of the body of Christ, but joining this New Testament community requires being baptized in water and constantly abiding in Christ, which should be corroborated by one's visible life of holiness.

These arguments notwithstanding, by the beginning of the third millennium, many Baptist communities in the English-speaking world had switched to the practice of an open table. North American congregations resisted this tendency the longest, but eventually, they also altered their initial position in the second half of the twentieth century. The authors of *On Being the Church* admit: "Although our earlier practice was predominantly of closed table, amongst current Baptist churches a policy of an open table has become widespread."[191]

The concept of the open table is rooted in the individualistic mentality and the ideas of mission, accessibility, and the theology of love. If we conceive of the Lord's Supper not as communion and fellowship of blood relatives but as a source of grace that sustains the pilgrims on their journey, then an inclusive Eucharist, open to all who wish to experience Christ's love and the touch of his grace, should be our choice. This is precisely the view the proponents of open communion advocate. They emphasize the fact that Jesus had numerous meals with all kinds of people, sharing bread even with tax collectors and sinners (Mark 2:16). These meetings around Jesus's table changed many people's lives. It happened, for example, with Zacchaeus (Luke 19:8) and may happen with sinners today, as the open table advocates claim.

---

191. Haymes, Gouldbourne, and Cross, *On Being the Church*, 137.

Another argument that some contemporary theologians and ministers of the newly formed churches of Eastern Europe accept is this: we should embrace the practice of open communion "since the table is that of the Lord, not the church, and since we cannot put ourselves in the position of turning away any whom Christ has accepted simply because we feel that they have not undergone a particular rite."[192]

Thus, contemporary Baptist churches are gradually changing their theological understanding of the Lord's Supper, focusing on mission, drifting toward individualism, and increasingly practicing a fully open table coupled with open church membership. In this case, the congregation has no control over the communicant's baptism or demonstrable holy living, eschewing any form of church discipline and leaving everything in the hands of God and the individual participant. Eastern European communities, for the most part, still maintain the closed table model, which presupposes both believer's water baptism[193] and visible holiness as prerequisites for one's admittance to the Eucharist, but there is a definite tendency toward more openness and inclusivity in eucharistic practices.

Eucharistic Discipline

The close link between ecclesiology and soteriology that Eastern European Baptist communities tend to draw is manifested not only in their practice of a closed table but also in their use of the Lord's Supper as a tool for disciplinary action. The Eucharist is expected to motivate the wrongdoers to return to the standards of holiness that their community has adopted. The path of coming back to the community represents a return to Christ. In cases of persistent and vehement resistance to disciplining and exhortation, the offender is warned of possible expulsion from the community and, subsequently, excommunicated. This approach is usually grounded in the words of Christ, who granted the church the ultimate right to pass judgment when the offender fails to heed the admonitions and exhortations of the church (Matt 18:17–18). In other words, the persistence in sin of one of the congregation members leads to their expulsion from the community, and this decision, as many ministers believe, has

---

192. Haymes, Gouldbourne, and Cross, *On Being the Church*, 137.

193. For Eastern European Baptists, "conscious" baptism usually refers to the baptism by faith that a person received in any evangelical church, although in some cases, a Baptist congregation might accept as valid the baptism performed in an Eastern Orthodox church upon the condition that a person was baptized of his own will as an adult.

implications both here on earth, in the material world, and in the kingdom of heaven. Therefore, as the traditional practices of Eastern European Baptists present it, preserving one's personal salvation is tied to one's belonging to and presence in the church, which the local congregation represents.

Such a view, as Kenneth Hein has shown,[194] originates from the Jewish practice known as *cherem* (חֵרֶם), literally meaning "the avowed." The word appears nine times in the Old Testament and signifies either something dedicated to God (Lev 27:28–29; Num 18:14; etc.) and, therefore, removed from any profane use or, in the opposite sense, something vile, pagan, or banned (Deut 7:26; Josh 6:17; 7:13; etc.) and, therefore, doomed to utter destruction. In either case, *cherem* is that which is expelled and taken away from society. In later Judaism, the term came to refer to legal disciplinary practices such as excommunication from the community for misconduct that was not punishable according to the letter of the Torah law but was incompatible with the spirit of Judaism.

Christ undoubtedly used the idea of *cherem*, known to his hearers, as a disciplinary measure of exclusion from fellowship in the New Testament context. The metaphorical simile, "treat them as you would a pagan or a tax collector" (Matt 18:17), points to excommunication and the cutting off of all communication, analogous to the way in which the pious Jews avoided interaction with those who violated the Law of Moses. Paul develops this idea of a radical break with the sinner until his complete repentance in his letter to the Corinthian church. He not only recommends that a person who is in the gross sin of shameless sexual immorality be cast out of the midst of the believers but even hands him over to Satan "for the destruction of the flesh, so that his spirit may be saved on the day of the Lord" (1 Cor 5:5).

Here, the apostle identifies the first purpose of the disciplinary practice: to win the sinner back to the community. This is what happened later in the Corinthian congregation (2 Cor 2:5–8). In the same way, he mentions the second objective of his actions, which is to protect the community from the contagious effects of sin. Separating the sinners from the local church and barring them from fellowship automatically entails a prohibition of approaching the Lord's Table. In such a case, Paul recommends expelling the sinner from the Christian fellowship and even forbids sharing meals with him. He commands, "Do not even eat with such people" (1 Cor 5:11). This injunction probably referred to participating in the *agape* meals whose integral part was the breaking of bread, that is, the Eucharist. In cases of minor violations of

---

194. Hein, *Eucharist and Excommunication*, 8–10.

Christian norms, Paul suggests a milder response: "Do not associate with them, in order that they may feel ashamed. Yet do not regard them as an enemy, but warn them as you would a fellow believer" (2 Thess 3:14–15). Thus, he considers it possible to apply the equivalent of *nezif* or *niduyah* to a transgressor – an exhortation with a reprimand, temporary suspension of fellowship, and, hence, exclusion from the Lord's Table. This attitude shows that church discipline, as the early church practiced it, was corrective, not punitive and that exclusion from the Lord's Table was intended to bring the transgressor back into the church as a full and active member.

Taking Jesus's and Paul's words seriously, the early church often used the Eucharist as an instrument of discipline whose purpose was to facilitate the proper spiritual formation of both the individual and the community of believers. It was the approach the pre-Nicene Christianity favored. Glen Zweck distinguishes four phases of formal repentance as practiced during this period: contrition, confession to the bishop, making satisfaction (praying, giving alms to the poor, etc.), and complete reconciliation through prayer.[195] In addition to the act of confession and repentance, these disciplinary measures necessarily included doing everything possible to repair the harm done and performing certain actions, which later came to be called penance.

Protestants, including Baptists, have consistently rejected the medieval understanding of the sacraments in general and the sacrament of penance in particular. Hence, Eastern European evangelical pastors hardly ever use the word *penance* (ecclesiastical Russian *yepitimia*, from Greek ἐπιτίμιον). Yet, penance-like practices are often observed in the actual church life.

Describing early Baptist church policies, T. Dowley notes: "As has been seen, the end of the strict controls on membership was the building up of a pure fellowship of saints. Similarly, discipline was intended to achieve holiness of life and character in the members of the church."[196] He highlights the seventeenth-century distinction between preventive and corrective discipline. The former aimed to maintain individual and collective spiritual health and involved praying together, attending communal services, visitations by ministers, etc. The latter addressed the rebellious and unworthy church members, seeking to rebuke them and correct their behavior. The corrective measures included admonition and exhortation, then suspension from ministry and exclusion from the Eucharist, and, finally, excommunication. Still, importantly,

---

195. Zweck, "Why Did the Issue of Indulgences?," 70.
196. Dowley, "Baptists and Discipline," 157–66.

the need to pray for the sinner and invite them to repent was always emphasized and encouraged in Baptist communities.

Eastern European Baptists have always attached great importance to repentance. They speak much about it and often call not only non-Christians who happen to be at the church, but even long-standing church members to repent, either publicly or privately, and seek the renewal of their spiritual life. However, the disciplinary measures that should follow one's repentance are underdeveloped and need more attention. Baptist radicalism has discarded the historical tradition of penance and fostered pastoral and counseling practices that infrequently offer a simplistic answer to complex spiritual questions: whatever your problem is, repent and believe the gospel. The answer is undoubtedly correct but insufficient. It requires contextualization and adaptation to the specifics of the situation.

Repentance in the broad sense of the word cannot be reduced to penance only. It is not enough to acknowledge one's sin, confess it, and renounce it. The *Catechism of the Catholic Church* aptly observes:

> Many sins wrong our neighbor. One must do what is possible in order to repair the harm (e.g., return stolen goods, restore the reputation of someone slandered, pay compensation for injuries). Simple justice requires as much. But sin also injures and weakens the sinner himself, as well as his relationships with God and neighbor. Absolution takes away sin, but it does not remedy all the disorders sin has caused. Raised up from sin, the sinner must still recover his full spiritual health by doing something more to make amends for the sin: he must "make satisfaction for" or "expiate" his sins. This satisfaction is also called "penance."[197]

Indeed, even after the penitent has received the forgiveness of sin through the blood of our Savior, the traces or stains of sin remain both on the penitent and on those touched by the sin committed. It is sometimes impossible to wipe out and rectify these stains. The Lord forgives the sin, but the conscience continues to reprove the sinner, and his spiritual condition requires a long recovery process. It is precisely the penitential discipline or, simply, penance under the pastor's or Christian counselor's guidance that facilitates speedy spiritual healing and a return to active ministry.

The broader church tradition calls *penitential discipline* the rules and regulations necessary to help one deal with sin and correct the consequences of sins

---

197. *Catechism of the Catholic Church*, Art. 1459.

committed, whether inflicted on the penitent's own soul or the people around them. Paul Sheppy comments:

> Penance opposes the tendency we have to excuse and justify ourselves. It begins by bringing us into contact with another who witnesses our confession and who inhibits swift and easy forgiveness by requiring us to put the past right (insofar as we can). . . . When we make our confession in private by our bedsides, there is no one to check that we are not cheating. If we confess to ourselves (as it were), we may find that we forgive ourselves too quickly: a practice that leads to cheap grace.[198]

More often than not, sin is an offense not only to God but also to men and, invariably, to ourselves. If Christians acknowledge their sins and say, "Forgive us, Lord," they do well but not enough. It is imperative to confess one's sins to another person in order to realize the power of sin and start treading the path of deliverance from it. This other may be a minister, a fellow Christian, or a close friend, as James recommends when one is sick (James 5:16).

The one who forgives themselves, with no witnesses and no subsequent penance, is often left with a sense of guilt, even though God has unconditionally forgiven them. The reluctance to confess sins to others and suffer disciplinary restraint because of what has been done may be the effect of shame one feels and unwillingness to relive the pain or offense one experienced. But even in such a case, it is necessary to submit oneself to penance, not because it guarantees God's forgiveness, but because it alleviates one's guilt, frees one's conscience, strengthens one's faith, and gives one the strength to resist similar temptations in the future.

Discipline imposed by the pastor (penance) often contributes to a speedy recovery. Therefore, sometimes ministers, without announcing it to the congregation or the church board, establish measures of penitential discipline on their own. For example, they might ask the penitent to keep a journal of their prayer life and to regularly meet with the pastor to pray together and give an account of their Scripture reading, personal prayer, and fasting. Sometimes, a person is encouraged to perform certain works of mercy or engage in nonpublic ministry to those in particularly challenging circumstances. In other situations, ministers may suggest self-restraint and self-discipline regarding certain pleasures. In a similar vein, the Lord's Supper also serves as an instrument of spiritual discipline.

---

198. Sheppy, "Penance," 126.

Eucharistic Elements

The Eastern European Baptist tradition attaches great importance to the symbolism of the Lord's Supper. It may have been an attempt by ministers to counterbalance the overemphasis on immaterial spirituality. In many congregations, it is considered important to have only one bread and only one chalice. This was the case in the Landmarkist churches of America,[199] but the growth of their communities and increasing encounters with other traditions have amended this, and outward symbolism has given way to rationality. Most Baptist churches, especially after COVID-19, have switched to disposable cups for the Lord's Supper.

Another highly debated issue is the composition of the eucharistic bread and wine. Theologically, it should not be a subject of discussion at all because the key point of the Lord's Supper is the encounter with Christ, for which the bread and the cup are only the medium. They help the communicant "focus" their faith, fixing their spiritual gaze on Jesus; in this sense, they are, of course, important. However, the encounter by no means depends on the material components of the Supper, just as the meeting of two lovers does not depend on the environment in which it happens. And yet, one can still hear in Baptist churches the echoes of the centuries-old debate between the Catholic and Eastern Orthodox churches that led to the 1054 schism between Christian West and East. It had to do with the use of leavened or unleavened bread in the Eucharist.

The well-known Eastern Orthodox canonist John Erickson has shown that the chroniclers of that period when discussing the schism, refer to the composition of the eucharistic bread as its official cause. He writes: "The earliest such Byzantine reference remarks simply, 'Patriarch Michael Cerularius expunged the Pope from the diptychs on account of the azymes.' On the Latin side, Cardinal Humbert's bull excommunicates Cerularius and his followers as 'prozymite heretics.'"[200]

Eastern European Baptist churches almost universally use leavened bread during the Lord's Supper. The most common philological rationale for this is that whenever the New Testament speaks of the institution of the Eucharist, it uses the word ἄρτος (*artos*, Matt 26:26; Mark 14:22; Luke 22:19; 24:30, 35; 1 Cor 10:16–17 (twice); 11:26–28; etc.) rather than αζύμος (*azymos*, unleavened bread). The word ἄρτος occurs ninety-seven times in the New Testament and, in all these texts, refers to ordinary bread, while *azymos* is used nine times

---

199. Patterson, "Lord's Supper in Baptist History," 33.
200. Erickson, "Leavened and Unleavened," 157.

specifically in the sense of unleavened bread (Matt 26:17; Mark 14:1, 12; Luke 22:1, 7; Acts 12:3, 20:6; 1 Cor 5:7–8). Thus, the Scripture confirms that Christ used leavened bread at the Last Supper and that the Christians of Jerusalem and Corinth continued this practice.

In the West, it is usually emphasized that the Last Supper was a Passover meal and, hence, Jesus could not use leavened bread since the lamb was to be eaten with bread made without yeast (Exod 12:8; Num 9:11). However, if one accepts Daniel Chwolson's dating of the Last Supper, then it looks quite possible that Jesus and the disciples ate the leavened bread. That year, the Passover coincided with the Sabbath; therefore, the slaying of the lambs in the Temple took place one day earlier, on Thursday, 13 Nisan, and the eating of the Passover meal, as a private matter, could have happened on Thursday or Friday evening.[201] The Feast of Unleavened Bread began on Friday, 14 Nisan; therefore, on Thursday, the Jews may well have eaten leavened bread, *artos*.

According to Chwolson, the eating of the Passover lamb and using unleavened bread were not necessarily connected with each other.[202] The halakhic midrash *Mekhilta* that commented on Exodus 12:8 indicated that the lamb meat would be eaten without bitter herbs and without unleavened bread if there were none. It meant that the Jewish teachers of the law[203] could allow having the Passover meal without unleavened bread the year Passover coincided with the Sabbath, since in that case, on Thursday, the Day of Unleavened Bread had not yet come. Therefore, the texts describing the legitimate activities people could engage in during the Passover celebrations sometimes mention neither unleavened bread nor bitter herbs.

Initially, Baptist ministers in the West used leavened bread and fermented wine at the Lord's Supper. James Carter notes that this was the practice in American churches for many years, but now most congregations have switched to unleavened, yeast-free bread and grape juice instead of wine.[204] The reasoning behind this transition rests on the view that the Last Supper was a Jewish *seder* that had no place for yeast, a symbol of vice, although the Scriptural use of the word *leaven* is ambivalent. For example, in Matthew 13:33, the yeast, in Christ's words, symbolically represents the kingdom of heaven.

---

201. For more details, see page 95 above.

202. Chwolson, "Posledniaya Paskhal'naya (Jesus Christ's last Passover)," 418–19.

203. Later, Maimonides took this principle from the *Mekhilta* midrash and integrated into his own set of rules.

204. Carter, "The Lord's Supper," 40.

Currently, Eastern European Baptist communities use leavened bread and wine containing alcohol. Still, both the leavened (fermented) and unleavened (unfermented) substances of the eucharistic elements are commonly accepted as equally valid. The composition of the bread and wine is considered nonessential to the proper administration of the Lord's Supper, although some might disagree.

4

Other Sacraments

The Laying on of Hands

The notion of ἡ ἐπίθεσις τῶν χειρῶν comes from such biblical texts as Luke 4:40, Acts 8:18, 1 Timothy 5:22, 2 Timothy 1:6, and Hebrews 6:2 and is conveyed by several English terms. Contemporary Bible translations often refer to the *laying on of hands*; the KJV mentions the *putting on of hands*, and Catholic translations prefer the *imposition of hands*. These terms are complete and interchangeable synonyms.

The laying on of hands is a ritual action found in many ancient cultures. Donald Baker, along with many other scholars, notes that in the ancient Mediterranean, the gods blessed and healed with the touch of their hands[1] and that hands, in general, played a major role in many rituals.[2] In his dissertation, Rudolf Gonzalez analyzes in great detail the ritual of hand imposition in the ancient Egyptian and ancient Greek cultures. He concludes that often (though not always) the ancient Egyptians "viewed the hands as agents for conveying or transferring a desired thing, benefit, or result not only in day-to-day life, but also in the realm of the spiritual."[3] This understanding is rooted in and linked to the intuitive belief in the continuity between the spiritual and material world, in which spiritual phenomena intersect and interrelate with material ones. In this context, the hands often play the role of concentration points through which the religious faith creates the conditions for an encounter with the spiritual realm.[4]

---

1. Baker, "The Laying on of Hands," 2.
2. MacCulloch, "Hand," 492–99.
3. Gonzalez, *Laying-on of Hands*, 40.
4. Sazonova demonstrated well the crucial role the hands play in magical consciousness of paganism. Sazonova, 'Binarnyye Oppozitsii Kontsepta (Binary Oppositions)," 123–30.

The encounter between the sacred and the profane can, of course, take place without any material mediators. Baptists often emphasize the primacy of the spiritual over the corporeal, treating material signs of faith with disdain. But from a biblical perspective, matter matters, and there is no escape from materiality and corporeality. Christ took on material flesh and transformed it through his resurrection. Material mediators also have an important function in church life. The laying on of hands is no exception. It is a sign that not only indicates and manifests the divine presence but also serves as an instrument that God uses to bring about changes.

The principal tools Christ gave us to build his church are baptism and the Lord's Supper. Through baptism, God brings new converts into the church's fold, and through the Supper, he nourishes and strengthens them on their way to the heavenly kingdom. But through laying on of hands, God authorizes various workers who are to carry out the building of the house of God, supports those who are weakened, testifies to the unity of all members of the body of Christ, and blesses those in need.

Like water baptism and the Lord's Supper, laying on of hands fulfills all the characteristics of the church sacrament: the encounter between God and man. Chapter 1 outlined those attributes. In particular, the laying on of hands has a biblical basis, is characterized by its repeatability, and takes place in the locus of the community. It is mediative in that it mediates between the spiritual and material worlds while the prayer of laying on of hands is being said. It has a material component: the hands that focalize the participants' faith. Overall, laying on of hands is anthropological and performative because it is consciously performed by human beings and changes the ordained person through the power of God's Spirit. In the case of ordination for ministry, the status of the ordained changes; in the case of healing or blessing, their inner state is transformed.

Most Christian denominations practice the laying on of hands on five occasions: when church ministers are appointed, at post-initiation rites (like post-baptismal confirmation or blessing[5]), when those who committed grave sins get reconciled, at prayers for healing, and at blessings.

---

5. Tertullian, Hippolytus, Cyprian, Cyril of Jerusalem, and the Apostolic Constitutions tell us that in the early church, baptism was followed by anointing and the laying on of hands. The imposition of hands was associated with the descent of the Holy Spirit. Interestingly, in the pre-Nicene Syrian churches, as Munson has shown, both the laying on of hands and anointing with oil as a sign of the descent of the Holy Spirit took place *before* water baptism. See Manson, "Entry into Membership," 26.

There is no consensus in the Baptist tradition on how to understand and perform this ritual. Early Baptists insisted on the mandatory use of the laying on of hands at the ordination of ministers and the prayer following baptism. Over time, however, this issue became the subject of many controversies and schisms, and nowadays, many Baptist churches treat ordination loosely, considering it permissible but not mandatory. There is no record of Baptist churches practicing hand imposition as a means of welcoming back into the congregation those who have fallen away and repented of their apostasy, although it is occasionally practiced. Still, many Eastern European churches, as well as numerous charismatically oriented congregations, observe the use of laying on of hands during healings (with or without oil anointing). However, this is not a universally accepted practice.

The prayer with the laying on of hands is usually done at the request of the sick person by a group of elders, its biblical basis being James 5:14–15, Mark 6:13, and Mark 16:18. It is important to note that the laying on of hands is a face-to-face meeting with the sick person. It is not simply a prayer *for* the sick person from a distance but an act of sympathy and personal involvement. It is a prayer *with* the sick person, during which the ministers embrace their grief and helplessness. This kind of physically intimate prayer helps the sick person to realize that they are not alone but are included in the *koinonic* fellowship. It is clear that healing occurs through the faith of those involved, but Nikolai Kolesnikov, one of the leaders of the Soviet Baptists, remarks: "Oil in this ministry is as necessary as water at baptism [and] bread and wine at the commemoration of Jesus Christ's suffering."[6] In other words, the oil serves as a material sign that concentrates faith and, thus, is a kind of indicator of the divine presence.

Both early and modern Baptists have widely practiced the laying on of hands when praying for blessing (of children, married couples, each other, those present at prayer meetings, etc.). This gesture signals a special, enhanced, and intensified prayer. Despite the prominence and popularity of this practice, however, little attention has been paid to its theological justification and the theory behind it.[7] When Baptists did discuss the imposition of hands, the

---

6. Kolesnikov, *Khristianin, Zhayesh li ty?, (Christian, Do You Know?)*, 56.

7. This practice is most commonly discussed in the literature dealing with church ministry and priesthood. See, for example, Strauch, *Biblical Eldership*; Hammett, *Biblical Foundations for Baptist Churches*; Van Dam, *The Elder*.

Recently, the topic has also been addressed in academic periodicals. Of particular note is Fowler's original view on ministerial ordination in Fowler, "The Meaning of Ordination," 33–36.

debate tended to focus on the practical aspects of ministerial ordination and the act of laying hands on those who had been baptized.

The Laying on of Hands in the Baptist Tradition

Early Baptists did not question the practice of ordaining ministers. The *Short Confession* of 1610 states that "the investing into the said service is accomplished by the elders of the church through the laying on of hands."[8] All Baptist confessions of the seventeenth century approve of this practice. For example, the *Orthodox Creed* modeled after the *Westminster Confession* speaks of three categories of ministers: bishops, or messengers; elders, or pastors; deacons, or overseers of the poor. All of them should "be chosen thereunto by the common suffrage of the church, solemnly set apart by fasting and prayer, with imposition of hands, by the bishops."[9]

The necessity of laying hands on ministers as part of the ordination was not a matter of debate among early Baptists. Instead, the controversy centered on the question of what authority was conveyed to the minister through the act of hand imposition. As Ernest Payne notes, the eighteenth-century Baptists unanimously agreed that the laying on of hands did not convey grace, authority, or office in the church. Ordination was, rather, in an early Baptist author's words, "an orderly way of separating men to that work and office in the church, for which they were already qualified by the gifts and graces of the Holy Ghost, and to which they were duly qualified by the church."[10]

There are numerous historical accounts of Baptists ordaining their ministers for all kinds of church offices. For example, we know that Carey and many other missionaries had been ordained before they were sent into the ministry. Yet, there is also evidence that this practice came to be questioned in the Victorian era, as Baptists at that time grew extremely suspicious and critical of any sort of ritualism. The famous Spurgeon not only straightforwardly rejected ordination but even ironically remarked that ordination was but the imposition of "empty hands on empty heads."[11] This tendency led to heated debates and even schisms over ordination within the Baptist community, which went from the eighteenth century onward. At that time, American Baptists held firmly to the necessity of ordination, as reflected in the *Philadelphia Confes-*

---

8. McGlothlin, *Baptist Confessions of Faith*, 61.
9. McGlothlin, 146–47.
10. Payne, "Baptists and the Laying," 205.
11. Michael, *Spurgeon on Leadership*, 139.

sion of Faith,¹² drafted under the influence of Benjamin Keach and his son Elias. British Baptists criticized the practice, and it was not until the end of the nineteenth century that the laying on of hands made a comeback, as noted in *The Meaning and Practice of Ordination among the Baptists*. The document observes: "By 1880 references to ordination had become infrequent and it was not until after the First World War that they come into prominence. Since that time ordination has gradually become the regular practice with or without the laying on of hands."¹³

William McGlothlin summarizes the ebb and flow of attitudes toward ordination among Baptists thus:

> It may be said that the Baptists have almost uniformly ordained both pastors and deacons by prayer and the laying on of hands, and in the old days fasting preceded the ceremony as in the case of Barnabas and Saul, several of our old confessions of faith prescribing fasting as a part of the ordination exercises.¹⁴

In the Eastern European Baptist movement, the concept of the necessary ordination of congregationally elected ministers also caused considerable controversy. The Northern Revival, ignited by Redstock, who came to St. Petersburg in 1874, emphasized only conversion and a subsequent change of one's lifestyle. Its leaders rejected any ceremonies, and hence, the nineteenth-century evangelical Christians from the north of the Russian Empire did not deem it necessary to ordain their ministers. The issue became a serious point of disagreement with the Southern (Baptist) revival, influenced by the German Baptist tradition. The Baptist churches of Eastern Europe regarded laying on of hands as the only authorized manner of ordination: "By ordination, we mean the ordinance which the Holy Scriptures teach us, that the elders of this or other congregations set those whom the Church has chosen for the ministry apart by laying their hands upon them and praying for the office for which they have been called."¹⁵

In contrast, the eastern European evangelical Christians interpreted laying on of hands as merely a special kind of prayer. Their prominent leader, Prokhanov, wrote an article on laying on of hands in 1922 when discussions between

---

12. As already noted, the *Philadelphia Confession* of 1742 follows the *Second London Confession* verbatim but adds two more articles, affirming the necessity of communal singing and the laying of hands on both ministers and all those receiving water baptism.

13. Hayden, ed., *Baptist Union Documents*, 94.

14. McGlothlin, "The Laying On of Hands," 42.

15. Sannikov, ed., *Istoriya Baptizma (The History of Baptist Movement)*, 428.

Baptists and evangelical Christians were in full swing. There, he concluded that the ministerial ordination performed with the laying on of hands was not necessary but "useful as a special solemn prayer of the church for its minister [which] does not confer on the ordained person any special rights with regard to baptism, breaking of bread, etc."[16] Nevertheless, understanding the importance of laying on of hands in the cultural context dominated by the Eastern Orthodox Church and apparently wishing to relieve the tension between the Baptist and evangelical Christian unions, Prokhanov decided to receive ordination. On 1 April 1924, in Prague, the ministers of the Czech congregation, who considered themselves the heirs of Jan Hus, ordained him. This step, however, did not lead to the merger of the two unions.

The question of the laying on of hands after baptism remained a doctrinal cause of division in the Eastern European churches until the so-called Unification Congress, which was held at the behest of the Soviet government on 26–29 October 1944.

The *Regulations of the Union of Evangelical Christians and Baptists* the congress adopted read: "Clause 7: All congregations of Evangelical Christians and Baptists should, as far as possible, have ordained presbyters and deacons according to the Word of God: Tit. 1:5; Acts 6:1–6 and 1 Tim. 3:1."[17] From this time on, more and more churches accepted the principle that only ordained ministers could perform church ordinances. Ten years later, the practice became universal and was practically mandatory during the Soviet period.

One of the leaders of Evangelical Christians and Baptists Union, Peter Shatrov, explained in the *Bratskiy Vestnik* journal that "the laying on of hands is a visible sign of divine blessing during ordination when praying for the sick, and when receiving the Holy Spirit.... Only ministers to whom the Lord has entrusted this sacred act may perform it."[18] Another distinguished minister Kolesnikov wrote:

> If anyone dares to perform sacred acts without being ordained, he shows willfulness (Col. 2, 18), and does it on his own out of pride and arrogance (Jer. 23, 21–22 and 29, 32), creates disorder (2 Thess. 3, 7) and, of course, fulfills only a form [of a sacred act], which yields nothing.[19]

---

16. Prokhanov, *Izlozheniye Yevangel'skoy Very (An Exposition)*, 87.
17. "Polozheniye o Soyuze (The Regulations of the Union)," 33.
18. Shatrov, "Deyaniya Svyatukh Apostolov (The Acts of the Apostles)," 24.
19. Kolesnikov, *Khristianin, Zhayesh li ty, (Christian, Do You Know)*, 48.

However, since the 1990s, the evangelical Christians' churches, some of which do not attach any significance to the laying on of hands, have left former Evangelical Christians and Baptists Union to form their own church associations.

There has been a particularly heated debate in the history of both Western and Eastern European Baptists over the imposition of hands on just-baptized people. This practice is known to have first appeared in England around 1644.[20] It was grounded on Hebrews 6:1–2, where the laying on of hands is one of the "six first principles" of the Christian life. Adherents of this position insisted that the observance of all six principles was a necessary condition one needed to meet before they were allowed to join the local community and partake of the Lord's Supper. Thus, they soon became known as "Six-Principle Baptists."

Not all Baptist churches, though, approved of the idea of mandatory hand-laying on the baptized, and because of this, church splits ensued. However, in the early eighteenth century, the most influential Baptist association in America, the *Philadelphia Baptist Association*, made the practice standard and universal. The *Philadelphia Confession* of 1742 states, "We believe that laying on of hands (with prayer) upon baptized believers, as such, is an ordinance of Christ, and ought to be submitted unto by all such persons that are admitted to partake of the Lord's Supper."[21] McGlothlin specifies that in early Baptist communities, only the ordained minister would lay hands upon those who had been baptized. In other cases, the imposition of hands was considered invalid.[22]

By the nineteenth century, however, the practice had become less common in particular Baptist churches, but it had persisted longer among general Baptists. In 1783, the *Philadelphia Association* even amended its previous regulations and now admitted to the Lord's Table both those who had received the laying on of hands after baptism and those who had not.[23] In 1806, the clause concerning the hand-laying was dropped from the *Confession* altogether.[24]

Since then, schisms and controversies over the laying on of hands have virtually ceased. Researchers find it difficult to explain why an issue that long provoked fierce debate, mutual dissent, and excommunication had rapidly lost its appeal to Baptist ministers and theologians. Ernest Payne suggests that

---

20. Roger Williams, one of the founders of the American Baptist movement, published a paper in London in 1644 before his departure to the New World. There, he defended the practice of laying hands on the newly baptized, citing Hebrews 6:1–2. Payne, "Baptists and Christian Initiation," 151.

21. McGlothlin, *Baptist Confessions of Faith*, 297.

22. McGlothlin, "The Laying on of Hands," 49.

23. McGlothlin, 49.

24. Payne, "Baptists and Christian Initiation," 152.

this was due to the influence of the Great Awakening and the shift of attention from intra-church life to mission beyond church walls.[25]

In the Eastern European context, the issue of hand-laying after baptism also loomed large in the first half of the twentieth century. Churches and individual ministers regularly accused each other of deviating from biblical practice. However, a resolution was reached at the 1944 Unification Congress. It reads:

> Paragraph 9. Baptism and marriage, whether performed with or without the laying on of hands on those being baptized or on those being married, have the same validity. But in order to achieve full uniformity of practice among the churches, it is recommended that baptism and marriage be celebrated with the laying on of hands.[26]

As with the ministerial ordination, this practice quickly took hold in evangelical Christian churches and became ubiquitous.

Since the turn of the millennium, due to the active influence of American missionaries who came to this part of the world, the laying of hands on the baptized has come to be viewed negatively as an Eastern Orthodox influence. Now, many younger churches are treating it loosely or somewhat critically.

Today, however, there is a tendency to revisit the Baptist legacy. Perhaps, as John Parratt observes, early advocates of the laying on of hands after baptism, such as Keach,[27] "possessed an insight into its complement in New Testament initiation which has largely eluded their present day successors."[28] In other words, the laying on of hands is finding its way back to the list of established church practices of Baptist communities.

Biblical Instances of Hand-Laying

To grasp the deeper meaning of the imposition of hands, it is first necessary to look at all the biblical instances of hand-laying and reflect on its function in different situations. After that, we may either find what is common and essential in all these cases or be forced to admit that despite their outward similarity, they differ in meaning and significance.

---

25. Payne, "Baptists and the Laying on of Hands," 214.
26. "Polozheniye o Soyuze (The Regulations of the Union)," 34.
27. Keach, *Laying on of Hands*.
28. Parratt, "An Early Baptist," 327.

We will not undertake an exegetical analysis of the scriptural texts where the laying on of hands is mentioned. Eminent biblical scholars have already done this more than once, even though they have often come to opposite theological conclusions. Also, from a holistic perspective, it is not necessary to analyze the Old Testament and New Testament cases separately, as the vast majority of scholars do.

The variety of all biblical cases of hand-laying can be reduced to five classes:

- Blessing
- Sacrifice and testimony (legal context).
- Ordination and sending on a mission (ecclesiastical and missional context)
- Post-initiation ceremony
- Healing

Blessing

Scripture records various instances of blessing. At its core, an act of blessing involves invoking the name of God and asking him to pour out grace, power, or other favor on a particular person or group of people. It is always a prayer that connects the material and spiritual worlds. Yet, in especially significant cases, the verbal element is reinforced by a material sign. It may be the raising, touching, or laying on of hands, even though the gesture itself is not a channel for conveying the blessing. The hand-laying gesture is meant to shape or strengthen people's faith and to add solemnity to the occasion, turning it into the sacrament of man's encounter with God.

A typical example of a special blessing is the detailed account of Jacob's blessing of his grandsons, the sons of Joseph (Gen 48:14, 17–18). Joseph brought his two sons to his dying father so that they could receive a momentous, existential blessing from the patriarch. This was the kind of benediction Rebecca had been given by her mother and brother when she was about to leave home, but in that case, there was no imposition of hands because of the peculiar patriarchal culture. Jacob had received this kind of blessing from his father Isaac (Gen 27:27–30) and then gave it to all his sons before his passing (Gen 49:1–33), although there is no clear evidence of the laying on of hands in these stories.

This particular type of blessing was different from the ordinary benediction people often said when meeting each other or sealing an important deal. When Jacob met Pharaoh, he blessed him verbally (Gen 47:7, 10). Similarly,

Jesus encouraged his followers to bless people, whether they said good things or cursed them, regardless (Matt 5:44). An existential blessing, as distinguished from purely verbal benediction, is a prophetic act. It changes the life or situation of the one being blessed. This is why Jacob and his brother Esau struggled so hard for their father's blessing[29] that they were ready to kill each other (Gen 27:4–41).

Existential blessings were important not because of the power of the one blessing, but because of the divine presence. In such an act, God did not merely aver the future but preordained it, which was reflected in the prayer over the initiate. The blessing, therefore, became a sacrament whose key agent was God. He bestowed grace on the one being blessed through the one blessing. The laying on of hands that accompanied the prayer was the sacramental sign of this act.

The very gesture of laying on of hands signified a spiritual identification, the purpose of which was the transmission of divine blessing. The hands imposed marked a channel of spiritual communication between God and the one being blessed through the one blessing. The physical contact testified to the spiritual contact, helping to focus the faith of both participants. That is why the symbolism represented by material signs was so important in this case. Sometimes, the symbolism was emphasized by the superiority of the right hand, which in the Old Testament tradition represented strength, power, and victory.[30] As a result, the laying on of hands singled out the existential blessing, separating it from the ordinary, everyday benediction. Nevertheless, God was never bound by material signs or dependent on human gestures.[31] He also bestowed prophetic blessings through ordinary touch or, sometimes, with no intervention of human hands at all.

A striking example is Aaron's high priestly blessing (Lev 9:22). It was performed through the utterance of designated words and the raising of hands over the whole people of Israel. The gesture was similar to the imposition of hands. Given that it was practically impossible to lay hands on the entire assembly, the

---

29. It possible that when blessing his sons, Isaac also placed his hands on them, but the Bible does not mention it explicitly.

30. The Old Testament portrayals of Yahweh (e.g., Exod 15:6; Ps 16:11), as well as references to human beings and their power (e.g., Ps 137:5; Isa 41:13), highlight the prominent symbolic role of the right hand.

31. Therefore, when the biblical text speaks about the blessing of Joseph's sons and similar situations, the verbs *sim* and *shith* are used interchangeably and say nothing about the significance of the event.

Lord sanctioned a flexible form of blessing.[32] The Talmudic tradition requires that the text of the Aaronic blessing (Num 6:24–26) be recited exclusively in Hebrew with hands raised upward.[33] This is how it has been practiced in synagogues up to the present day.

The New Testament mentions the utterance of prayer-blessings many times. James even warns that they should not come from the same mouth that utters curses (Jas 3:9–10). But a special blessing with the laying on of hands appears in only a few instances. Simeon took the baby Jesus up in his arms in the Jerusalem temple (Luke 2:28), which was analogous to the imposition of hands, and pronounced a prophetic blessing (Luke 2:29–35). During Jesus's earthly ministry, Jewish parents, seeing his extraordinary divine power, would bring their children to him so that he could lay his hands on them and bless them. The Lord never refused to do it, despite the discontent of his disciples (Matt 19:13–15; Mark 10:13–16; Luke 18:15). Mark and Luke speak of the parents' desire at least to touch Jesus, while Matthew provides a more detailed account. He emphasizes the parents' wish for Christ to lay his hands on their children and tells us that this is exactly what he did (Matt 19:15). Interestingly, Mark uses the terms meaning "to touch" and "to lay hands" interchangeably, showing that in response to the parents' request to touch their children, Jesus placed his hands on them (Mark 10:16).

Luke narrates another important event involving hands. Just before his ascension, Jesus blessed the disciples by lifting his hands (Luke 24:50–51). Clearly, there was no need nor opportunity to touch each one in that instance. Instead, Christ acted like Aaron when blessing the people of God (Lev 9:22). When he bade his disciples farewell, he raised his hands and, in addition to his missional instructions, he pronounced words of blessing, handing them over to the care of the Holy Spirit, as he had promised earlier (Luke 24:49).

Thus, on all three New Testament occasions, as well as in all similar instances found in the Old Testament, the touching, laying on, or lifting up of one's hands emphasized the importance and solemnity of the event in contrast to the ordinary verbal benediction. It was a special encounter with the divine presence. The hands allowed for and helped to bring about the connection or

---

32. John Tipei draws attention to this feature when he says that the laying on of hands in the case of the Aaronic blessing was impossible. Hence, the raising of hands functioned as its equivalent. Tipei, "The Laying on of Hands in the New Testament," 16.

33. The mishnaic *Seder Nashim*, tractate *Sotah*, prescribes: "In the sanctuary one says the Name as it is written but in the provinces, with a euphemism. In the provinces the priests raise their hands as high as their shoulders, but in the sanctuary, they raise them over their heads." *Mishnah Sotah* 7:6.

identification between the blesser and the blessed. Still better, they created a kind of channel that made it possible to fulfill God's plan to impart the prophetic wisdom, power, health, or grace of God to those being blessed.

Sacrifice and Testimony

Another class of instances in early biblical history, when hands were laid on someone, were sacrifices and other legal acts.

The Lord established the system of sacrifices, carefully prescribing and specifying the occasions, forms, and procedures for their performance through Moses. In virtually all cases, there was a requirement to lay hands on the sacrificial animal before it was slain.[34] It was the case with burnt offerings (Lev 1:3–9), peace offerings (Lev 3:1–5), and sin offerings (Lev 4:2–12). Only the guilt offering (Lev 7:1–5) seems to be exempt from this requirement, but this conclusion does not follow given the close connection and similarity that existed between the sin offering and the guilt offering (Lev 7:7). The only difference between the two had to do with "full restitution" expected of those who committed a minor sin and now needed to make a guilt offering (Lev 6:1–7). This similarity allows us to suppose that even when the guilt offering was made, the sacrificer had to lay his hands on the head of the animal to be sacrificed.

Significantly, in all these cases, it was the sacrificer, not the priest, who put his hands on the sacrifice. If there was a collective guilt offering, then the community's representatives, the elders, were to act in the name of the community (Lev 4:13–21). The leaders of the people placed their hands on the sacrificial animals on behalf of the entire assembly. This is what King Hezekiah did when he introduced religious reforms (2 Chr 29:20–24).

The sacrifice was an important turning point in the sacrificer's life. Before the sacrifice, man was a sinner in the eyes of God, and usually, he knew it. After that, it was as if their sin had been erased. In the full sense of the word, animal sacrifices could not cleanse one's sin, but they pointed to sin and to the true sacrificial Lamb, Jesus, who would take away the sin of the whole world and set sinners free from punishment. The death of the sacrificial animal pointed to the substitutionary atoning death of Christ. The sacrifice itself was the event of the sacramental encounter between the sacrificer and God, in which the person, or the community, received the assurance of forgiveness. One could say

---

34. At the ordination of Aaron, Moses made the offering, but Aaron and his sons laid their hands on the sacrificial bull's head (Lev 8:13–15).

that it was an existential event that changed the person's status in the spiritual world: a sinner became a righteous person.

The very act of hand-laying indicated the embodiment of the offerer and his sacrifice in a legal sense. Many authors believe that this gesture symbolizes the transfer of sin from the sacrificer to the sacrifice.[35] However, according to a holistic approach that considers the totality of cases of hand-laying, it is more accurate to speak not of a transfer, but of identification. Before the spiritual world, the sacrifice after the hands were laid on it, represented the sacrificer himself, and its death represented the death of the sinner who offered it. It was not an abstract sin that was dying but a particular sinner who was identified with the sacrifice through the laying on of hands. Thanks to the substitution in death, the sinner received an undeserved right to life. In this way, the imposition of hands during the sacrifice became an ontological rather than merely symbolic act.

Analyzing sacrifices in different world religions, the famous anthropologist Edwin Oliver James comes to the conclusion that "expiatory offerings entailing the death of a victim involve the idea of substitution of its life for that of the sacrificer with whom it is identified at its consecration."[36] Hence, the identification resulting from the laying on of hands constituted an essential element of atonement.

This statement is illustrated particularly well by the imposition of hands as practiced on the Day of Atonement. The law says, "Then Aaron shall lay both his hands on the head of the live goat, and confess over it all the iniquities of the people of Israel, and all their transgressions, all their sins, putting them on the head of the goat" (Lev 16:21, NRSV). The expression "sins on the head" is a Semitic idiom that is similar to the saying "Your blood be on your head" (2 Sam 1:16; 1 Kgs 2:37). It is a reference to one's full culpability. To place sins on one's head means to declare someone absolutely sinful. Aaron, as the high priest representing the whole nation, identified with the sacrificial animal in regard to the sins, faults, and offenses of the whole nation through the laying on of hands. From that point on, the sacrificial animal represented the entire sinful nation. Their sins and offenses were sent as if to nowhere, with no possibility of return. This is what the sending away of the sacrificial goat to a remote wilderness, to "a barren region" (Lev 16:22, NRSV), symbolized. Thereby, the sin was removed, and the people were forgiven.

---

35. Daube, *The New Testament*, 226; Baker, "The Laying on of Hands," 1–12; Rowley, "The Meaning of Sacrifice," 83; Noordtzij, *Leviticus*, 22–33 and others.

36. James, *Sacrifice and Sacrament*, 34.

The identification in terms of guilt or innocence reflects the legal, judicial aspect of the laying on of hands. It manifested itself not only in the tradition of sacrifices, where it pointed to sin and forgiveness, but also in other legal procedures. For example, the law stipulated that when punishing a blasphemer, witnesses had to lay their hands on the offender (Lev 24:14). It was necessary to confirm his crime and remove the blame for his death from the witnesses because the Scripture says that he who speaks evil against God shall bear his own sin (Lev 24:15). The gesture of hand-laying indicated the identification of the witnesses with the offender in legal terms.[37] By doing so, they confirmed that they had indeed heard him say blasphemy, and in the case of perjury, the blood of the murdered man (that is, the guilt) fell on them.[38] Michael Sansom notes, "The charge is such a serious one that it demands this kind of attestation; 'may the Lord do the same to us and more also if we are not telling the truth,' we may imagine them saying."[39]

The same legal aspect is hinted at in Job's exclamation, "There is no umpire between us, who might lay his hand on us both" (Job 9:33, NRSV). This ancient custom showed the identification of each disputing party with an impartial arbiter in their joint quest for justice. Each party would swear an oath to the truth and nothing but the truth. An episode in the story of Susanna and the elders, as recorded in the deuterocanonical section of the book of Daniel, alludes to the same custom. To prove the truth of their testimony, the elders laid their hands on her head (Add Dan 13:34).

Thus, in legal procedures involving deliverance from sin, whether they took place before the altar or in the courtroom, the laying on of hands demonstrated a spiritual identification of the one laying his hands with the one – either human or animal – on whom the hands were laid. It allowed the power from above to operate in the one imposing his hands either to cleanse or to convict him.

---

37. It is interesting to note that the high priest, condemning Christ for blasphemy, only tore his garment. But neither he nor other Sanhedrin members laid their hands on Jesus. Perhaps by Jesus's times, this legal requirement had been forgotten due (at least in part) to the prohibition to put someone to death without the sanction of the Roman authorities, or perhaps these men did not want to take responsibility for Jesus's death publicly.

38. David Daube suggests that in this case, the witnesses were considered tainted by the crime committed and had to transfer to the criminal the guilt that he had put on them. "Or, maybe, the witnesses by anticipation threw back on the criminal the blood-guiltiness which would rest on them as a result of his execution." In either case, Daube agrees that the issue at stake has to do with legal procedures. Daube, *The New Testament*, 227.

39. Sansom, "Laying on of Hands," 326.

Ordination to Ministry

The judicial aspect mentioned above is echoed in ceremonies of ministerial commissioning and/or ordination, which legalize certain types of ministries. The ordination of Joshua, Timothy, the Levites, the seven deacons, and others immediately comes to mind as belonging to this category. The consecration to a certain ministry took place when the higher authority delegated some of its powers to the assistants or executors appointed to an important task.

The first mention of such consecration is found in the story of Moses appointing seventy elders to assist him. This group was chosen on the advice of Jethro, Moses's father-in-law (Exod 18:21–25). After another revolt of the people, the Lord, wanting to relieve the burden Moses carried, ordered these men to assemble outside the tabernacle, where he spoke to Moses. Then he took from the spirit that was upon him and gave them to the seventy (Num 11:24–25). Outwardly, it manifested itself in that all of them began to prophesy, including the two who remained in the camp and were not near the tabernacle (Num 11:26–27). It was a one-time act, attesting the authority of these newly elected ministers and the continuity between their ministry and the work and spirit of Moses himself.

It is unlikely that Moses laid his hands on them or raised his hands when speaking to them. It was clearly a divine act. Yet, its crucial element was the spiritual identification obtained between Moses and his helpers, who now had one purpose and one ministry: to govern the people of God. Moses was not merely a passive channel for the transmission of God's spirit. The elders were to act in the spirit of Moses, using his methods of governing the people, his principles, and his values.

Rodney Hutton rightly observes,

> That empowering spirit is at one and the same time precisely the spirit that is Moses' very own. Here Moses is conceived not simply as a mere accessory or funnel who plays at best a passive role. Rather Moses is himself the repository of "the spirit." The spirit that the seventy receive is not discontinuous with human experience or with the human spirit. This spirit does not stand over against the human spirit, but is at one with it.[40]

In these particular circumstances, when the Lord was just beginning to form the tradition and continuity of stewardship, he acted himself, but later on, he

---

40. Hutton, *Charisma and Authority*, 27.

preferred to perform similar actions through his ministers, often using the laying on of hands as a means.

As in all ordinations, the appointment of the seventy elders implied a certain level of identification. Of course, it was not complete identification, for it did not transfer Moses's identity to each of the ordainees. Moses remained a distinct person, just like each of the seventy, but there was now a spiritual synchronization between them. That is, in respect of office, each elder now represented Moses himself, and the people were to regard them as Moses himself. The official consecration was a sign of legal induction after the election, or in modern parlance, the public presentation of leaders and conferring on them a license for ministry.

A similar procedure took place when the Levites were consecrated to serve in the tabernacle, but in this case, the Scriptures clearly established the ritual to be observed (Num 8:5–20). The Lord announced that he was taking to himself the sons of Levi as a substitute for all the Israelite firstborns who belonged to him by right as a consequence of the tenth plague of Egypt. After the Levites had been ritually purified, Yahweh commanded Moses to gather the people and tell "the Israelites [to] lay their hands on the Levites" (Num 8:10, NRSV). The act of hand-laying was meant to establish the identification of the people with the Levites, who were henceforth to represent all the firstborn of Israel. In this way, the Levites obtained from the whole nation the right and duty to stand before Yahweh.

It is difficult to say exactly how this ordination happened in those ancient times. Obviously, it was impossible for every Israelite to participate in the ceremony, nor is it clear whether hands were laid on each single Levite. Most likely, elders, heads of families, and other official representatives of the people laid their hands on the Levites' heads, and Aaron said the prayer of consecration, according to the Lord's instruction: "Aaron shall present the Levites before the LORD as an elevation-offering from the Israelites, that they may perform the service of the LORD" (Num 8:11, NRSV). The physical touch was, of course, important, but, as previously noted, this requirement was not absolutely binding before the Lord. It helped to concentrate and focus the faith of the participants, while the result depended primarily on spiritual factors. Still, without the actual laying on of hands, whatever its form, the Lord's provision for the Levites would not have been fulfilled. The event described was in itself a solemn sacramental meeting between Yahweh and the Levites dedicated to him. They represented the whole people of God, and by accepting them, the Lord accepted his people.

The next, one might say, classic case of the ministerial appointment is recorded in Numbers 27:15–23. Before the Israelites crossed the Jordan, the Lord showed Moses the promised land from Mount Abarim and foretold his coming death. Then Moses, knowing by experience how difficult it was to govern the people of Israel for forty years, began to ask God for a successor "so that the congregation of the LORD may not be like sheep without a shepherd" (Num 27:17, NRSV).

The Lord revealed who should take up the leadership after Moses and what procedure should be followed: "So the LORD said to Moses, 'Take Joshua son of Nun, a man in whom is the spirit, and lay your hand upon him'" (Num 27:18, NRSV). It is important to note that the role was, essentially, that of a pastor and the basis for the appointment was the will of God. But the Spirit of God was already at work within the candidate for the ministry, which is why he was chosen. However, after his ordination, "Joshua son of Nun was full of the spirit of wisdom, because Moses had laid his hands on him" (Deut 34:9, NRSV).

This is how the Bible describes the sacramental event in which God, through Moses, gave Joshua the power, honor, and, most importantly, the authority and spirit of wisdom that his mentor had. The laying on of hands was the culminating manifestation of Moses's spiritual identification with his apprentice. It resulted in a new status and ontological position of the ordained person. There was no transfer of spirit or personality from Moses to Joshua, as Daube, Parratt, and some other scholars have suggested,[41] but an identification of the two in and for a specific mission: to lead the people of Israel. God used the spirit that was in Joshua to give him a new ability to lead and govern as a wise shepherd. On the surface, it looked as if the person was filled with the spirit in a manner similar to the New Testament accounts of the Holy Spirit descending upon and filling the apostles who had already had the Holy Spirit. Integral to this sacramental event was the verbal instruction that Moses gave both to Joshua, the son of Nun, and all the people before his ordination.

The New Testament mentions the imposition of hands as part of the ordination ceremony six times (Acts 6:6; 13:3; 14:23; 1 Tim 4:14; 5:22; and 2 Tim 1:6). The first reference is to the appointment of seven deacons in the Jerusalem church (Acts 6:1--6). This is the fullest biblical description of ordination to ministry, although not all early manuscripts[42] support the traditional reading, according to which the text implies the laying of the apostles' hands on the appointees. Some of the manuscripts suggest that the text speaks only of the

---

41. Daube, *The New Testament*, 226; Parratt, "The Laying on of Hands," 210–14.
42. See, Nestle-Aland *Novum Testamentum Graece*, , 229.

election of deacons. Still, the overall pattern is unambiguous. Luke maps the process of gradual institutionalization of primitive Christianity. The ecstatic mode of being of the Jerusalem congregation, governed directly by the apostles, had to give way to and be inevitably replaced by governance through organized structures. The tension caused by the lack of attention and support for the Hellenistic widows was the initial impetus for this process. The apostles made the wise decision to elect deputies who would "wait on tables."

Analyzing this choosing of the seven, Daube[43] draws a parallel with the Jewish tradition of appointing "seven from the city" who would represent the whole Jewish community, while Ferguson, accepting the Jewish roots of this apostolic decision, stresses how Luke's account evokes a custom of Greek and Roman civic elections.[44] R Alan Culpepper and some other scholars believe that the seven were not assigned a permanent life-long ministry[45] but merely a specific short-term commission, but this theory hardly fits the context. It is more plausible to suggest that they fulfilled this ministry as long as the Jerusalem congregation existed, although they certainly combined deaconry with other ministries. For instance, we know that Stephen and Philip were active evangelists.

The major exegetical and theological debate revolves around the question of whether it was the people or the apostles who laid hands on the seven. The grammatical structure of verse six allows us to assume that it was the people, not the apostles, who did it, but many manuscripts clearly speak of the apostles as the main agents. Theological and logical arguments also support this interpretation: first there are obvious parallels between the choosing of deacons and the election and ordination of Joshua by Moses;[46] second, it was practically impossible for all members of the Jerusalem church to lay hands on the electees. In any case, only a few people – not the whole audience – should have imposed their hands on the appointees. It is logical that (some of) the apostles, as the most authoritative representatives of the congregation, should have done so. Daube writes that after the seven deacons were elected, they were presented to the apostles who "'leaned their hands on them,' thus making them into their representatives, their extended selves, vis-a-vis the apostles."[47] The

---

43. Daube, *The New Testament and Rabbinic Judaism*, 237.
44. Daube, 237.
45. Culpepper, "The Biblical Basis for Ordination," 477–78.
46. The parallel has been discussed in detail above.
47. Daube, *The New Testament and Rabbinic Judaism*, 237.

laying on of hands, in this case, was a sign of identification and appointment to a particular work.[48]

As in the case of Joshua's ordination, the deacons in Jerusalem became full representatives of the apostles in the distribution of food and the management of material resources. Thus, the hand-laying was not merely a symbolic action but a real sacrament in which the apostles, the deacons, and the Lord acted together. Elected ministers were filled with the Holy Spirit even before ordination, as was Joshua. Being filled with the Holy Spirit implies a repeated and manifold process that makes manifest the work of the Spirit in a regenerate person who has already had "the firstfruits of the Spirit" (Rom. 8:23). The Spirit empowers people to witness (Acts 4:31), to work miracles (Acts 13:9–11), or for some other ministry. In this particular case, the Lord equipped deacons at the time of ordination with the ability and gift of stewardship (1 Cor 12:28). The apostolic prayer emphasized the sacramental character of ordination (Acts 6:6).

A vivid description of ordination as a sacramental act is found in Acts 13:1–3. The leaders of the Antioch church had received an explicit command from the Holy Spirit to set apart Barnabas and Saul for missions, and they did so through fasting, prayer, and the laying on of hands. The imposition of hands was, in a way, a point of reference, an outward sign of the meeting of the Lord in the Holy Spirit with Barnabas and Saul through the hands of the Antioch prophets and teachers. It was a sacrament signaling the beginning of their new ministry. Thus, the laying on of hands was both an indication that Barnabas and Saul had become official representatives of the Antioch church and a sign of the church's blessing and commitment. By performing this act, the congregation, as it were, set out with its missionaries on their evangelistic trip and promised to support them prayerfully, financially, and spiritually. In other words, it identified itself with them as its chosen representatives.

Many scholars tend to think that this commissioning of missionaries was a one-time assignment, a specific work to which the Holy Spirit called them.[49] However, given Barnabas's and Paul's many years of missionary service, the work the Spirit assigned them was a lifelong endeavor. Baker notes, "If Acts 13 is a parallel to Numbers 8, perhaps the setting apart of Paul and Barnabas was not of limited duration either."[50]

---

48. Culpepper writes: "The verb in the clause 'whom we may appoint to this duty' (6:3) appears elsewhere in Acts for official appointments (7:10, 27, 35; cf. 17:15) and in Titus 1:5 for the appointment of elders." Culpepper, "The Biblical Basis for Ordination," 477.

49. Tipei, "The Laying on of Hands," 235.

50. Baker, "The Laying on of Hands," 9.

The installation of leaders who were apparently to serve in the church for life is described as the ordination of elders in Asia Minor: Lystra, Iconium, and Antioch. Following their successful preaching and planting of new groups of Christ's followers, Barnabas and Paul "appointed elders for them in each church, with prayer and fasting they entrusted them to the Lord in whom they had come to believe" (Acts 14:23, NRSV). Speaking of the appointment of ministers, Luke uses the verb *cheirotoneo* (χειροτονέω). As John Tipei points out, the original meaning of the word was to elect by ballot (by raising one's hand), but by the first century, thanks to its adaptation by Philo of Alexandria and Josephus, it came to be used in the sense of appointing to or inducting into office.[51] In patristic Greek, the verb acquired the meaning "to appoint with the laying on of hands." It is in this sense that χειροτονέω occurs once in the *Didache* and three times in Ignatius of Antioch, referring to the selection of the churches' official envoys. It is not clear whether Luke uses the word in the older Hellenistic meaning "to elect" or in the later Christian meaning "to appoint," implying ordination. Ferguson views Acts 14:23 in conjunction with Titus 1:5, where the word καθίστημι is used, more akin to appointment than election. He writes: "The method Titus was to employ in installing elders was probably the same as in 1 Tim. 5:22, imposition of hands."[52]

The connection of χειροτονέω in Acts 14:23 with fasting and praying gives reason to think that this was not a simple election when people raised their hands supporting this or that candidate. Rather, the text speaks about a customary Christian appointment to the ministry, that is, the real sacrament of Christ's meeting with his ministers. It is more likely, as Tipei believes, that the leaders (elders, presbyters) in the newly formed home churches emerged naturally and that Barnabas and Paul, having verified the validity of the nomination, confirmed it through ordination. In this case, the gesture of hand imposition signified the apostles' confirmation of or identification with the newly elected ministers. Now, the apostles were leaving them in their stead and, by ordaining them, certified their ministerial credentials. From a procedural standpoint, it is most likely that Barnabas and Paul used the pattern of their own ordination in the Antioch church.

Another vivid description of ordination involves Timothy. In his first letter to Timothy, the apostle Paul advises his apprentice to develop the gift he had received "through prophecy with the laying on of hands by the council of elders" (1 Tim 4:14, NRSV). In his second letter, Paul reiterates the same

---

51. Tipei, "The Laying on of Hands," 242.
52. Ferguson, "Ordination in the Ancient Church IV," 141.

thought, instructing Timothy "to rekindle the gift of God that is within you through the laying on of my hands" (2 Tim 1:6, NRSV). Both accounts mention the charisma (the gift of grace) and link it with the ordination, the only significant difference being the reference to the supposed authorities (in plural) who laid hands on Timothy. The most natural interpretation, favored by the majority of commentators and endorsed by Daube, is the view that several elders laid hands on Timothy (1 Tim 4:14), including Paul (2 Tim 1:6). This is quite understandable in the framework of the rabbinic tradition in which Paul stood, and to which Timothy as his disciple also belonged. Then, the event Paul recalls reflects a sacramental encounter with Christ when the Lord endowed Timothy with a certain spiritual ability necessary for his ministry. The very act of ordination, undoubtedly accompanied by prayer, testified to the teacher's and his fellow ministers' identification with the disciple, who received from the Lord what his senior brothers possessed: spiritual gifts, ministerial authority, right to lead the church, administer the sacraments, train disciples, and so on.[53]

What Paul and other elders did, now Timothy could do. Therefore, Paul the mentor's warning to his young mentee makes perfect sense: "Do not be hasty in the laying on of hands, and do not share in the sins of others. Keep yourself pure" (1 Tim 5:22). This admonition has been a subject of much discussion. What is the procedure the text hints at? Is it the reinstatement of elders who have committed a grave sin or the appointment of new elders? It is hard to say. The principal evidence for interpreting this text in terms of the reinstatement in the office of those who have sinned usually comes from the context of verses 19–20 and is found in Tertullian's *De baptismo*, but this evidence dates from no earlier than the third century. Verse 21 seems to introduce a new theme in Paul's reasoning; therefore, most scholars are inclined to believe that the broad context of the pastoral epistles and Paul's list of requirements for and qualifications of a bishop (1 Tim 3:2–13, especially 3:6) suggest the appointment of new elders.[54]

---

53. Ferguson thinks that the charisma Timothy received was not necessarily associated with his church office. Perhaps it had a double purpose: to impart him with a spiritual gift and to appoint him to the ministries of the word and evangelism. Ferguson, "Ordination in the Ancient Church IV," 140.

54. See Tipei, "The Laying on of Hands," 260–64, for a detailed survey of interpretations. Brian Irwin proposes a new, original interpretation of the text, believing that the best understanding of the expression in 1 Timothy 5:22 is to associate it with the laying on of hands as a sign of accusation. He associates this passage neither with ordination nor with the readmission of those who have fallen away, reading it, instead, as a warning against the hasty accusation of presbyters (elders) of wrongdoing. Irwin, "The Laying on of Hands," 123–29.

The warning not to share in other people's sins has been sometimes interpreted as the possibility of being "contaminated by darkness,"[55] although this interpretation rests primarily on the practice of Christian counseling rather than on any biblical text. Fee reads this warning as follows: "Do not be yourself involved in those kinds of sins that have caused some elders to need to be judged."[56] This explanation loosens significantly the connection between the laying on of hands and involvement in the sins of others. Another interpretation stipulates that Paul is warning against ordaining unqualified pastors who do not meet biblical standards or have not passed probation.

Despite the ambiguities surrounding Timothy's ordination, it is undeniable that he *was* ordained and obtained the right to lay hands on others. This fact, together with Paul's admonitions, shows a clear connection between the physical laying on of hands and the spiritual world, which precludes considering ordination as a mere symbol of appointment or blessing. On the contrary, the Timothy case allows us to speak about ordination as a sacrament. Still, Tipei correctly writes that this church ordinance "has no magical functions. It does not guarantee the conferral of power (it is not an *ex opere operato* communication) nor does the gift so received become the possession of the receiver."[57] Sacrament occurs through the faith of those involved. Moreover, the gift received should be "rekindled" and can be lost.

Thus, all instances of ministerial ordination in both the Old and New Testaments point to and imply the identification of the one laying hands with the one on whom the hands are imposed. The latter is to become the successor of the former in their ministry. Through this sign, the Lord sacramentally renews the spirit of the person being ordained, giving them additional grace, authority, and, in some cases, charisma to carry on the ministry that the older minister has begun.

Post-Initiation

A small group of biblical cases of hand-laying relate to initiation procedures, that is, the admission of neophytes into the church. As stated earlier, initiation is a comprehensive process typically involving three stages: preparation (hearing and receiving the word), initiation per se (special prayers and water baptism), and post-initiation practices (joyful greetings, hand-imposition, etc.).

---

55. Zaibel', *Tserkov' Iisusa?, (Jesus's Church?)*, 151–4.
56. Fee, *1 and 2 Timothy, Titus*, 132.
57. Tipei, "The Laying on of Hands," 266.

Beasley-Murray points out that the most common initiation practice is presented in Acts 2:38. Here, repentance and the ensuing water baptism for the forgiveness of sins are accompanied by the gift of the Holy Spirit and occur in a relatively short period of time. Yet, other instances of conversion described in the Book of Acts and in subsequent church history show the diversity of God's workings with sinners. Therefore, Beasley-Murray continues by noting: "Variations from this norm (notably Acts 8:14ff.; 10:44f.; 19:1ff.) reflect the variety of circumstances and of experiences of the Spirit in a period of transition."[58] In the two cases of conversion Luke describes, the ministers used hand imposition as a sign of the Holy Spirit's descension, but in other cases, no laying on of hands is mentioned. From this, it is reasonable to conclude that this action was not practiced on a regular basis. Both cases exhibit exceptional circumstances requiring unconventional action.

In Acts 8:14–17, Luke tells us that the inhabitants of a Samaritan village had believed in Christ the Messiah through Philip's preaching. When the Jerusalem congregation learned that the Samaritans had accepted Jesus Christ and were baptized, they sent Peter and John there. The two apostles came and laid their hands on the new believers, after which these Samaritan Christians received the Holy Spirit. This brief account indicates that, in contrast to what happened at Pentecost, the Holy Spirit descended upon those who believed and were baptized only after the apostles imposed their hands on them. This event was to demonstrate the co-identification and unity of the two once antagonistic social groups. When Peter and John, the first leaders of the Christian community, laid their hands on the Samaritan believers, they identified themselves with them and testified that, henceforth, in Christ, there were neither Samaritans nor Jews. The hand-laying was much more than a symbolic act of reconciliation. It was a sacrament of encounter with Christ, the invisible mediator and reconciler. Only his divine presence ensured the impossible unity.

The second episode is recorded in Acts 19. Paul arrives in Ephesus and meets the disciples of John the Baptist, who were probably waiting for the Messiah but knew nothing about Jesus Christ or the Holy Spirit.[59] Having expounded the gospel message to them, Paul or one of his companions baptized them in the name of Jesus Christ, and, after the laying on of hands, the Holy Spirit descended upon them (Acts 19:1–7).

---

58. Beasley-Murray, "Baptiso," 146.

59. There are scholars who deny that these Ephesians were John the Baptist's followers, but Dunn and others argue for this view. Dunn, *Baptism in the Holy Spirit*, 83–89.

Many theologians argue that the case of the Ephesian disciples should be seen in parallel with the story of Samaritan believers. They assume that Luke deliberately emphasizes the similarity between the ministries of Peter and Paul, endowing them with the same apostolic authority.[60] Both narratives (Acts 9 and 19) arise from exceptional circumstances. As Gonzales writes, "In both events, apostles are seen as embracing a group of believers who are viewed as defective in some fashion and, therefore, in need of a reassuring ministry, thus, the use of laying-on of hands."[61]

Paul poses questions that disclose his bewilderment at the unusual situation. The wording of the first question implies that an obligatory part of Christian initiation is the reception of the Holy Spirit, and the second question highlights the necessity of water baptism (Acts 19:2–3). The laying on of hands after these disciples' baptism was a sign confirming that the spiritual process of conversion had gone well. As a result, the Holy Spirit came upon them.

Of course, baptism does not automatically and necessarily lead to the Holy Spirit's descent. The correlation between these phenomena occurs through the faith of the recipient, as Dunn correctly states. But even then, it is not possible to draw the unambiguous causal connection between the hand-laying and the descent of the Spirit, even though Tipei and some other scholars insist that this is the most plausible interpretation.[62] In fact, it is more natural to think that the laying on of hands was a sign of the sacramental encounter of the Ephesian disciples with Jesus, who received them into his body. The apostle's hands indicated the disciples' identification with all other members of the Christian community, and the outpouring of the Spirit was a consequence of this association, which signaled that all the gifts centered in the body of Christ now became available to these newly joined members. Thus, one may infer that both post-initiation cases were occasional sacramental encounters with Christ through identification with his ministers (in some respect).

Healings

Conventionally, the laying on of hands is often associated with healing, but the scriptural basis for this is scant. There are virtually no instances of healing through hand imposition in the Old Testament, although some healing stories mention tactile contact. Ancient Semitic peoples certainly knew the practice

---

60. Hull, *The Holy Spirit*, 115.
61. Gonzales, "Laying-on of Hands," 160.
62. See the detailed analysis in Tipei, "The Laying on of Hands," 202–4.

of placing hands upon the sick person or touching them with one's hand for the purpose of healing. The evidence for that is the expectations Naaman had of his potential healer. He thought a prophet would lay his hands upon him to cure him of his leprosy (2 Kgs. 5:11). However, this view has to do more with commonly held customs than with explicit biblical teaching.

The New Testament describes many healings that Christ performed. Apparently, he deliberately used a variety of methods: sometimes he healed by word alone (e.g. Mark 2:11); occasionally by touch, including laying his hands on people (e.g. Matt 8:3); sometimes he made mud out of dust and saliva (e.g. John 9:6). This diversity of healing methods was to show that healing was accomplished by the will of God through faith, not by magical rituals involving hands or certain objects. But people often needed tangible signs to strengthen their faith, and so many asked Jesus to lay his hands on the sick. For example, Jairus begged the Lord to lay his hands on his daughter to make her well (Matt 9:18), and the relatives of a deaf man with a slurred tongue asked for the same (Mark 7:32). Yet, in most cases, Christ himself chose the manner of healing. It seems that he made little use of the hand-laying and did not practice it as a ritual in the contemporary sense.[63] But his statement in Mark 16:18 suggests that one may resort to laying on of hands for healing purposes. Obviously, the healing touch was something the sick in Jesus's time expected and valued, and according to the gospel accounts, the Lord used it more than twenty times, sometimes touching the sick, sometimes taking their hand into his, and occasionally putting his hand on them.

The Book of Acts likewise contains a few healings, some of which were accompanied by the laying on of hands as a special ritual. The most illustrious of these stories are the healings of Saul (Acts 9:17) and of Publius's father (Acts 28:8).[64] Both instances link the gesture with prophecy or prayer. It is important to note that the cure of Saul's blindness was accomplished by divine command, whereas Ananias saw himself as only a conduit of divine power. The comment that immediately after he had laid his hands on Saul, "something like scales" fell from Saul's eyes indicates that this was not a merely symbolic action but a very real communication of divine favor.

---

63. A possible exception is Jesus's attitude to the people of Nazareth, his hometown. Mark summarizes it briefly: "he laid his hands on a few sick people and cured them" (Mark 6:5, NRSV).

64. There are other instances of healing through physical contact in Acts, such as the healing of the lame man at the Beautiful Gate (Acts 3:7), but the laying on of hands is explicitly mentioned only twice.

All of this suggests that the gesture of hand-laying in all biblical cases of healing signifies a sacramental encounter between the sick person and the healing power of God, transmitted by faith. James Dunn, commenting on these healings, explains, "No doubt a flow of energy from healer to healed was actually experienced in many cases through the physical contact (cf. Mark 5.28f. pars.)." Nonetheless, he is not sure "whether the energy was thereby simply released from the latent resources of one or other, or channeled through the man of faith to the sick person from sources outside of himself."[65]

From the standpoint of the biblical theology espoused by Eastern European Baptists, it is beyond dispute that instances of healing demonstrate the power of God and that the laying on of hands is a sign of identification of the healer and the healed with respect to health and physical strength. As Tipei notes, "In fact, one may even consider that for Luke a healer's hand functioned like a 'mediating substance', interposed between the real source (God) and the receiver; they are both carriers of numinous power."[66]

Of course, the communication of God's healing power is possible not only through direct physical contact but also via the mediation of material objects[67] or without any contact at all. Still, the actual imposition of hands, like other tangible acts, is often an indispensable means that enhances and concentrates the faith of the recipient who seeks healing. The minister's identification with the sick seems to tell the sick person: "Christ has taken your infirmities and diseases upon Himself, and henceforth, the health, strength, and grace that He bestows upon all the members of His body belong to you."

Thus, there is a variety of contexts in which the laying on of hands is practiced. These include sacrifices, healings, blessings, ordinations, post-initiation rites, and other occasions. All of them may be explained in terms of a sacramental encounter with divine power, which is channeled for various purposes through the medium created by the participant's faith. The outward sign of faith is the minister's or fellow believer's hands, which signify identification (association) in some respect between the one laying hands and the one on whom they are imposed.

---

65. Dunn, *Jesus and the Spirit*, 165.

66. Tipei, "The Laying on of Hands," 147.

67. Note, for example, the healing effect of Peter's shadow (Acts 5:15) and Paul's personal belongings (Acts 19:12).

The Laying on of Hands from a Theological Perspective

As has been shown, both the Old and New Testaments reveal a wide variety of sacred actions in which the hands play a crucial instrumental role. The imposition or laying upon of hands was practiced on occasions so diverse that, at first glance, they appear to have almost nothing in common. This ceremonial gesture came to the fore when people made sacrifices, were ordained as ministers (ordination) or appointed to certain offices (commissioning), sought a blessing or healing, went through post-initiation ceremonies (for example, confirmation), and so on. Some biblical scholars try hard to find a shared meaning and common significance of this phenomenon, while others believe that the laying on of hands has different meanings in different contexts. Still, others believe it to be a relic of ancient rituals that has no relevance today.

It is fascinating and valuable to explore the origins and prehistory of Christian hand-laying, seeking to determine with certainty whether the early church adopted it from pagan or rabbinic practices or, perhaps, directly modeled it on the biblical example of Moses and Joshua.[68] Even more important is to understand the essence and deeper meaning of hand imposition because this may help us to apply it appropriately in contemporary contexts.

Tipei, who has presented arguably the most detailed and thorough dissertation studying the laying on of hands, remarks: "It is surprising, then, that this topic has received little scholarly attention."[69] Michael Patrick Whitehouse's dissertation corroborates the same conclusion.[70] Both researchers identify only four seminal works on the subject in the last fifty years.[71] Johannes Behm's study, which both Tipei and Whitehouse highly acclaim, leads readers to the conclusion that, "for the first Christians, the gesture was more than a symbol; it was an effective symbol (*symbolum efficax*)."[72] Joseph Coppens' book emphasizes the sacramental nature of the laying on of hands. In his view, it signifies communion with the Spirit, which is accompanied by signs and

---

68. On this point, see the discussion between Arnold Ehrdardt, who denies the influence of rabbinic tradition on Christian practice, and Everett Ferguson, who sees a continuity between the two. Ehrhardt, "Jewish and Christian Ordination," 125–38; Ferguson, "Jewish and Christian Ordination," 13–19.

69. Tipei, "The Laying on of Hands," 2.

70. Whitehouse, Manus Impositio, 3.

71. It is interesting to note that there is virtually no treatment of the laying on of hands in popular systematic theology textbooks. Thus, Millard Erickson's *Christian Theology*, Wayne Grudem's *Systematic Theology*, and Michael Bird's *Evangelical Theology* do not analyze hand imposition when discussing the ordination of ministers.

72. Tipei, "The Laying on of Hands," 4, citing Behm, *Die Handauflegung*, 198.

wonders, empowering Christians to witness.[73] Karl Gross, as Tipei notes, sees no common pattern in the various instances of hand-laying in the Old and New Testaments and explains each case differently. He points out that for both Jews and Christians, this action conveys the right to instruct others, thereby ensuring the transmission of a tradition.[74]

An outstanding contribution to the biblical-theological understanding of the laying on of hands has been made by Daube. The section on "The Laying on of Hands" in *The New Testament and Rabbinic Judaism*[75] gave a new impetus to the discussion. Daube believes that we should carefully distinguish between the different types of hand-laying, given the difference in the Hebrew terms used to describe them. The vocabulary suggests two kinds of hand imposition.

The first is called *samakh* and means an intensive use of hands ("to lean/press"). It is a "heavy" hand imposition that represents a way of transferring something very significant from the agent to the recipient of the hand-laying. Daube writes:

> In all probability, by leaning your hands upon somebody or something, by pressing in this way upon a person or animal, you were pouring your personality into him or it (the simile of pouring also may be found in Rabbinic literature); or in other words, you were making him or it into your substitute.[76]

Alternatively, there is a pair of terms *sim* and *shith*, which mean "to place," and Daube explains their meaning differently: "The idea no doubt was that, by placing your hands on a person, some magic attaching to them took effect upon him. At a later stage, maybe your hands were conceived of as transmitting an influence from above, one might almost say, like conductors."[77] Meanwhile, he adds: "It indicates the transference of something other than, or less than, the personality; it means the employment of a special, supernatural faculty of one's hands."[78] This may be said to be a "light" touch in contrast to the "heavy" one, mentioned above. Hence, *sim* or *shith* is used to refer to blessing and, sometimes, healing. However, it is impossible to draw a clear-cut demarcation line between the "heavy" hand imposition (*samakh*), the utterance of solemn

---

73. Coppens, *L'Imposition des Mains*.
74. Gross, *Menschenhand und Gotteshand*.
75. Daube, *The New Testament and Rabbinic*.
76. Daube, 225.
77. Daube, 225
78. Daube, 229.

formulae, and use of one or two hands, on the one hand, and the "light" touch (*sim* or *shith*), accompanied by less significant words, on the other hand.

The hypothesis according to which the heavy hand imposition (*samakh*) and its use in the New Testament imply the transmission of personality is very intriguing, but the author fails to clarify what he means by *personality*. Obviously, he does not have in mind what twenty-first-century theology or psychology understands by this complex term. It is precisely this vagueness that has caused much criticism of his work. Notable biblical scholars such as Jeremias, Howard Marshall, and others have favorably evaluated his exegetical analysis.[79] At the same time, other, no less influential, scholars were quite skeptical of his ideas. For example, Ferguson rightly points out that the Septuagint, later Judaism, and the New Testament do not distinguish between different types of hand-laying.[80] John Meier makes a similar argument against Daube's hypothesis, particularly with regard to the pastoral epistles, which were written in Greek and could not account for differences in Hebrew terminology.[81]

Since the second half of the twentieth century, the main attention of researchers has been directed to the origin of the practice of laying on of hands and to the search for the meaning of this gesture both in terms of the process and the outcome. Put differently, the fundamental question is this: what happens during the laying on of hands in different contexts, and what effect does it bring about? With this starting point, the main discussion revolves around the question of whether something is conveyed in this act, or if it is just a symbol.

While analyzing Acts 6:6 and 13:3, Ferguson comments: "There is no indication that any sacramental power, or more particularly the Holy Spirit, was conferred by the laying on of hands in these passages."[82] In his publications,[83] this author insists that hand imposition is merely a sign of prayer and a symbol of blessing so that there is no transfer of power, authority, Spirit, or anything else.

John Tipei, in turn, writes:

> On the basis of our findings upon the examination of each use of the LH [the laying on of hands], it is our conclusion that in

---

79. Jeremias and Strobel, *Die Briefe an Timotheus und Titus*.; Marshall, *The Pastoral Epistles*.

80. Ferguson, "Laying on of Hands," 1.

81. Meier, "'Presbyteros' in the Pastoral Epistles," 339.

82. Ferguson, "Laying on of Hands," 252.

83. Ferguson, "Laying on of Hands," 1–12; Ferguson, "Jewish and Christian Ordination," 13–19.

the New Testament the gesture signifies always transfer of some positive *materia*: blessing, "life-force," the Spirit and *charismata*. The transference motif is also predominant in the Old Testament.[84]

He goes on to state: "Human hands are literally channels of power by which charisms for ministry are transferred from God, the divine source, to those so appointed. The established leaders of the church act as both petitioners of numinous power (in this case charisma for ministry) and mediators of such power."[85] In other words, Tipei comes to the conclusion that in the laying on of hands, there is a real transmission of something, although he identifies a few exceptions to this rule.

Brian Irwin considers the laying on of hands, at least in some contexts, to be a public identification or authentication of a testimony or declaration.[86] John Poirier, while supporting the idea of identification, believes that during hand-laying, the Spirit can be transferred as if "pouring from vessel to vessel," to use the language of the homiletic midrash *Bemidbar Rabba*.[87] Poirier builds on and develops Sansom's theory that stipulates that the imposition of hands has slightly different effects depending on whether one or two hands are involved.[88] Sansom believes that the number of hands determines the purpose of the rite. He divides the cases of hand-laying into two groups and applies the theory of transference to some and the theory of identification to others. He asserts that "two basic meanings emerge, then: transference on the one hand and acknowledgement or identification on the other. It is just conceivable that they may correspond to the use of two hands or of one."[89] However, the strict association of one or two hands with different cases of hand imposition is problematic because it is not supported by all the cases reported in the Bible.

According to Daube, in early rabbinic literature, hand-laying signified the transfer of office, authority, or power from one person to another. He says:

> We may also mention two similes which the Rabbis introduce again and again: though Moses "leaned his hands on Joshua," he did not lose his own faculties because he was "like one kindling

---

84. Tipei, "The Laying on of Hands," 275.
85. Tipei, 275.
86. Irwin, "The Laying on of Hands," 129.
87. Poirier, "Spirit-Gifted Callings," 88.
88. Sansom, "Laying on of Hands," 323–26.
89. Sansom, 326.

a light with a light"; and when he "put of his honour upon him," he was "like one pouring from vessel to vessel."[90]

At the same time, Lawrence Hofmann challenges Daube's conclusion and opines that "in rabbinic Judaism of the tannaitic period, *i.e.* the first two centuries, there is no evidence of a rite of ordination by laying on of hands."[91] Other scholars, though, cautiously support the idea of pre-Christian rabbinic ordination.[92]

Sullivan believes that the laying on of hands is polysemous: "Of the two meanings for this gesture in the Old Testament – as a symbol of prayer for a blessing from God and as a sign that the one imposing hands is sharing something with the other – it seems that when this gesture was used by Jesus, the latter symbolism was primary."[93] He concludes: "the laying on of hands can symbolize both the sacramental kind of prayer for which people are ordained, and the charismatic kind of prayer that is an exercise of the priesthood of all the faithful."[94]

It is clear from this brief overview that there is a wide range of theological interpretations of the meaning of laying on of hands. However, a holistic view embracing the unity of God's actions suggests that there is a common spiritual basis to all the instances of hand imposition that the Bible documents because, in addition to human parties, God himself is invisibly present there. Thus, we can look for an underlying unity that manifests itself in different ways in different contexts. We just have to broaden our horizons in order to discover it. It is necessary to analyze not only the actual gesture but also the very event that forms the background of hand-laying.

Researchers have mainly focused on the act (gesture) of laying on of hands and debated whether the effect depends on the laying on of one or two hands, whether it is a touch or a firm pressure, and whether it is possible to speak about any effect at all. But if we consider the event during which the prayer, hand imposition, and other accompanying movements take place, it is obvious that we are dealing with a sacrament, during which a person meets God, and hands become the visible sign of this meeting. The hands not only point to the sacramental encounter but function as a visible sign of divine presence. Just as during baptism or the Lord's Supper, there is an encounter between the

---

90. Daube, *The New Testament and Rabbinic*, 232.
91. Hoffman, "Jewish Ordination on the Eve," 11–41.
92. Lohse, *Die Ordination im Spätjudentum*; Baker, "The Laying on of Hands," 4–5.
93. Sullivan, "The Laying on of Hands," 44.
94. Sullivan, 54.

participants and the Lord through the medium of material signs and physical operations; the same holds true for the rite of laying on of hands. The one laying his hands serves as a minister or steward who coordinates the encounter. Both the pastor administering baptism, the minister breaking the bread, and the bishop imposing his hands are executors of God's will, not owners of divine grace, spirit, health, or gifts.

The very act of laying on of hands presupposes a spiritual personification, an identification of the minister imposing his hands with the one being imposed for a specific purpose. It is the purpose or intention that determines the outcome of each case. For sacrifices, the purpose is identification with substitutionary sacrifices; for blessings, it is the transfer of benefits and favor; for healing, it is personification in terms of health; for post-initiation, it is identification in terms of acceptance into the community with the reassurance of rights and duties; and for ordination, it is identification in and for a specific ministry (whether for life or for a certain time).

Thus, the hand-laying ritual is multifarious in its purposes and effects but one in its core meaning – it is a sacrament wherein an encounter with God happens via the spiritual equating of human agents. The diversity is manifested in the unique purpose of each occasion, which is determined by prayer, and the unity lies in the fact that all instances involve the identification of the one who lays his hands and the one on whom they are laid. As the renowned historian of liturgy, Cyrille Vogel has accurately noted, "The imposition of hands, a ritual gesture that of itself is polyvalent, acquires its specific meaning from the prayer that accompanies it and the context of worship in which it is practised."[95] All the contexts have something in common that unites the different biblical cases under one umbrella. It is the notion of a spiritual identification.

Perhaps Daube was referring to the *equating* of persons when he wrote about the transfer of personality during the *samakh*. Identification is equating rights, abilities, access to something, power, health, and so on. It does not mean that the one laying his hands conveys to the one being ordained something uniquely his own, something that is his possession. In spiritual identification, it is the Lord who works.

Outwardly, it seems that something is transferred from the greater to the lesser, but in reality, there is no transfer. There is only an equating in properties, position, role, or something else. This is the aim of the ritual, and it is usually expressed in the accompanying prayer. What once belonged to the ordainer now becomes the property of the one on whom the hands are laid. In the spir-

---

95. Quoted in Sullivan, "The Laying on of Hands," 53.

itual world, mutual identification has taken place. It is not a physical merger of personalities but an identification in status: I am who you are in a particular respect, my status is your status, my rights are your rights, and so forth. Such identification leads to a change in the mode of being of the ordained; that is, it produces an ontological effect.

Such an identification is impossible without the presence of a higher spiritual power. To change one's status means more than just delegating new functional authority or confirming a new leadership position. All these are purely external manifestations of ordination. At the same time, God transforms the existential or ontological state of the ordained. A new modality of being emerges, not just a new mode of activity. Just as God changes the inner spiritual identity of the person offering the sacrifice from that of a sinner to that of a righteous person, so he changes one's identity at ordination from that of a sheep in God's flock to that of an empowered pastor. In John Colwell's words, "To be ordained implies a change of being and not merely a change of function. Those ordained are not just separated to perform certain sacramental functions, they are separated themselves to be sacramental mediations of God's presence and action."[96]

Only the Lord can make the encounter happen. He meets the ordained person in prayer and physical gestures. His is the power that accomplishes the needed identification and brings about the subsequent change. He is the third party involved in ordination. It is from him that any analysis of ordination must begin. Fiddes explains: "Ordination is a moment of special encounter with the triune God in which, like Baptism, there is grace to help shape heart, mind and character."[97] In this, the hands become outward signs of the spiritual processes that God is accomplishing. They not only point to spiritual identification but also confirm it; the laying on of hands becomes equivalent to a legal document, a testimony before the material and spiritual world about the event that has taken place in reality.

Practical Aspects of the Laying on of Hands

The efficacy of the act of ordination depends, as in the case of water baptism and the Lord's Supper, on the work of the Holy Spirit and the faith of the participants. Whether it is a blessing, healing, or ministerial ordination, the Holy Spirit must move and lead the participants. Fulfilling the necessary formalities

---

96. Colwell, *Promise and Presence*, 220.
97. Fiddes, *Tracks and Traces*, 101.

is not enough for ordination to become a sacramental encounter, a meeting place between the one being ordained and God; there must be an explicit will of God.

Biblical practice affirms that the efficacy of all types of hand imposition was defined by God's will: they all took place because God directly commanded it or gave his consent. The ordination of Joshua was done by the direct command of God (Num 27:18). The same was true of the separation and consecration of the Levites (Num 8:6–19). Sacrifices were to be made according to the law God gave through Moses (Leviticus 1–7). The healings that Christ performed were surely in harmony with God's will, while Christ's disciples healed others following their master's instructions (Mark 16:18). By God's command, Barnabas and Saul went on a mission; by God's consent, ministers were appointed in the churches they had planted.

Therefore, ordination is not valid when the individual or even the church wants it, but only when God wills it. The laying on of hands as ordination always follows the election by the local congregation and the examination of the minister's qualities against biblical standards (1 Tim 3:2–12). This is how it was practiced in apostolic times (Acts 6:3) and in the pre-Nicene period.[98] This is also what I. Ya. Miller, a well-known minister of the Ukrainian Baptist movement at the beginning of the twentieth century, says about the ordination of ministers: "By ordaining, the church proves that it has understood God and His work. She prayed to God, discussed the issues pertinent to His cause, understood the voice of God and the state of the work, and saw God's hand bringing forward a particular brother."[99]

In addition to divine will, there is something that depends on humans, for the spiritual powers do not produce ministerial identification unless the human free will consents to it. There must be mutual trust between the three parties. It creates a bridge in the spiritual world between the one(s) laying hands and the one(s) on whom they are laid, linking the two with an invisible spiritual power. The theologians of the World Council of Churches put it this way: "Ordination is a sign performed in faith that the spiritual relationship signified is present in, with and through the words spoken, the gestures made and the forms employed."[100]

---

98. Afanasiev and Myshtsyn, Eastern Orthodox historians of liturgy, confirm it. See Afanasiev, *The Church of the Holy Spirit*, 61–64; Myshtsyn, *Ustroystvo Khristianskoy Tserkvi (Internal structures of the Christian Church)*, 15–16.

99. Miller, "O rukopolozhenii (On the Laying on of Hands)," 21.

100. World Council of Churches, *Baptism, Eucharist and Ministry*, 28.

The ordination to ministry (*cheirotonia*[101]), as practiced in Eastern European evangelical churches, usually consists of three stages: the election of ministers by the local congregation under the direction of the current ministers, a probation period during which the candidates are to perform the functions assigned to them, and the ordination itself.

At present, there is no accreditation procedure, such as that adopted by the British Baptist Union, which helps to assess the minister's competence and provides an opportunity to involve the wider church structures in the ordination process. However, introducing accreditation would help not only to raise the level of ministerial training but also to strengthen inter-church ties and enable a local minister to be seen as representing both the local congregation and the wider church. This process would ensure a more accurate interpretation of the gospel, which is entrusted to the whole church of Christ rather than to a single congregation. Somewhat equivalent to accreditation is the interview that a representative of a Baptist union or local association normally conducts with a candidate before ordination. The involvement of such a representative testifies to the unity and shared fellowship between this particular community and other churches.

The laying on of hands as ordination is reserved in this part of the world for those who are to directly lead the church and teach it on a regular basis – for presbyters (pastors) and deacons. The rite is taken to confer upon them an office, duties, and rights. The *Beliefs of Evangelical Christians-Baptists* of 1906 reads: "The church elects from among its members the elders (presbyters), teachers, and ministers, who through consecration are endowed with the office of ministry."[102] Preachers, Sunday school teachers, and other lay ministers who have no permanent functions in the church do not require ordination. They may be elected by the congregation or appointed on the basis of the general priesthood of all believers. When they are appointed to the ministry, a prayer with the raising or laying on of hands is often practiced, but it means blessing, not ordination. According to the Eastern Orthodox tradition, this type of hand-laying (blessing) is called *cheirothesia* and changes the ordained one functionally but not ontologically.

---

101. In the Eastern Orthodox Churches, the ministerial ordination is usually called *cheirotonia* (from the Greek χειροτονία). Originally, the term referred to any hand-laying but in ecclesiastical circles, it came to refer to the laying on of hands that accompanies the ordination to the priesthood.

102. *Veroucheniye Russkikh* (*The Beliefs of the Russian*), 9.

The analogous prayers of blessing, involving the laying on or raising of hands but without ordination, are performed when an ordained minister is assigned a new ministerial task or when the church sends out a missionary or appoints a chaplain. Outwardly, the laying on of hands for blessing is similar to the laying on of hands during ordination, but the purpose is different, even though the encounter between God and the ordained occurs in both cases. This distinction between the ordination to ministry (*cheirotonia*) and the blessing for ministry (*cheirothesia*) – both of which involve some hand gestures – does not suppress but rather fosters the development of various ministries within the people of God.

Hand imposition as ordination or consecration to a church office confers upon the ordained person additional rights and duties. The 1906 *Beliefs* state explicitly that elders (presbyters) govern the congregation and provide soul care, while teachers are responsible for preaching.[103] However, these offices may be combined, as has often happened in practice. Only these properly ordained ministers are allowed to carry out all of the church ordinances: water baptism, the Lord's Supper, and ordination (or laying on of hands).[104] Deacons, in turn, are ordained to do the practical housekeeping work in the congregation.

It is impossible to ordain elders and deacons independently from the local congregation.[105] Symbolically, the act of ordination (*cheirotonia*) amounts to a divinely accomplished union or conjunction of the minister and the church. In contrast, the consecration of a missionary or chaplain (*cheirothesia*) is a blessing that the church gives for a particular ministry, assuming the obligation to support the one sent. Such hand-laying (as a blessing) does not change the status of the ordained, but, as an intensified prayer, it calls for and signifies the special blessing by and support of the church. The same applies to laying hands on the sick, children, etc. These practices certainly indicate an encounter in the broad sense of the word, which takes place at the moment of spiritual identification. The outcome is similar in all these instances: the functions, office, or state of the ordained person may change, but his essence and status before God remain the same.

---

103. *Veroucheniye Russkikh* (*The Beliefs of the Russian*), 10.

104. As I stated earlier, the Northern (St. Petersburg) Revival followed this rule rather loosely.

105. This view was prevalent even in the early patristic period. Thus, Rule 6 of the 4th Ecumenical Council (of Chalcedon) expressly forbids ordaining ministers without designation to a particular local church. If such an ordination occurred, it was to be considered invalid.

As Stephen Holmes has shown, the ordination of ministers should be considered from a trinitarian perspective, reflected in the life of the church.[106] Both hierarchy and concurrent equality are essential properties of the inner life of the Trinity. It preserves a certain hierarchy and the order of precedence, which Christ repeatedly emphasized in the Gospels (John 14:28), and at the same time, there is the absolute unity of persons (John 10:30). The doctrine of *perichoresis* (mutual penetration in love) is counterbalanced by the doctrine of correspondence (appropriation), according to which each divine hypostasis fulfills a certain role. The church, as the body of Christ, reflects this truth. The laying on of hands as ordination and the direct involvement of God confer additional authority and dignity on certain church members, in addition to assigning them to certain functions. Their ontological status changes, and they become, as they were, angels of the church, acquiring the right and responsibility to shepherd the flock of God. As Miller noted in his 1928 paper on ordination, "[I]t would be ridiculous if the flock led the shepherd . . . at ordination, we receive a [particular] brother as a gift from God, as our chief, educator, and messenger of God."[107]

There arises a kind of duality. On the one hand, ordained ministers are subject to church discipline, and the congregation has authority over them because it elects them and delegates some of its powers to them. On the other hand, ministers obtain a prophetic voice and receive authority from above. This is the authority to serve and not to govern the church. Paul Fiddes remarks that an ordained pastor is called to love and follow Jesus like any other believer, but he is also called to shepherd his sheep, which becomes his permanent, inevitable responsibility.[108]

Ministers receive additional authority because ordination is a sacrament that has both a horizontal dimension – the election by the church – and a vertical dimension – God's work in establishing his minister. It is this understanding that provides the theological rationale for the indelibility of ordination (from Latin *indelebilis*, "impossible to erase/delete"). An ordained minister retains his *charisma*, even when the minister's function or position in the church changes, and he no longer holds the office of *episcope*. Some scholars deny

---

106. Holmes, "Towards a Baptist Theology," 258–62.
107. Miller, "O Rukopolozhenii (On the Laying on of Hands)," 22.
108. Fiddes, *Participating in God*, 296.

the indelibility of ordination.[109] But if we take into account the indelible and performative nature of biblical hand-laying that produces ontological changes in the one on whom hands are laid during healing, blessing, sacrifices, etc., then it becomes clear that ordination also produces something substantial and inalienable in the one being ordained. This is why Paul states that the calling of God is irrevocable (Rom 11:29).

Thus, ordination is an encounter between God and a human being at the moment of spiritual identification and consecration for a specific purpose. Like any encounter with God, it is mysterious and, therefore, sacramental. In some cases, it changes the ordained person's status; in others, it brings them closer to God; whatever the specifics, it is always performative to the extent of their faith.

Other Church Ordinances

When considering church life in a sacramental context, one can say that any act performed in and through the church contains a sacramental element to it, as long as the Holy Spirit is at work in the community. Not only baptism, the Lord's Supper, and ordination are sacramental, but any other element of worship is meaningless if the lord is not manifested in and through it. Only the divine presence makes church singing and doxology meaningful; it alone confers power on the preaching of the word of God; only through the mysterious work of the Holy Spirit do people come to repentance and accept Christ; the Spirit alone can lift the supplications of those present up to the throne of grace; and so on.

Yet, it is beyond the scope of this study to consider the sacramental character of all the elements of worship. I would limit myself to emphasizing the pivotal role of repentance, which is the medium through which the repentant sinner meets the forgiving God. It is, therefore, an encounter between the prodigal son and the loving father. Similarly, it is vital to acknowledge the role of worship, which, without the mediating work of God, easily degenerates into a concert. On the contrary, when God joins the earthly choir with the heavenly

---

109. See Paul Beasley-Murray's claim that ordination has to do with the function of leadership rather than the ministry of word and sacrament. Beasley-Murray, *Anyone for Ordination?*, 161, 166. Paul Fiddes, in turn, takes an intermediate position, saying that ordination only gives grace for a new way of life, and although this grace is irrevocable, like that of baptism, and provides a new way of being, it can take on a new form of life and being. It seems to follow that both the ministerial position and ordination itself are potentially revocable or effaceable, albeit Fiddes does not explicitly say it. Fiddes, *Tracks and Traces*, 101–3.

one, then the glory of God is indeed multiplied. Now, however, we must turn our attention to the sacramental function of biblical preaching, which occupies a pride of place in the Eastern European Baptist tradition.

The Sacramentality of Biblical Preaching

As chapter 1 has suggested, the Bible itself can be viewed as a divine sacrament because of its dual God-human nature. The mystery of the incarnation points to this, for "the Word became flesh" (John 1:14). The Bible, by definition, contains and reveals, albeit in part, the mystery of divine presence. However, the sacramentality of Scripture is rarely addressed. More often than not, the Bible is treated as an ordinary book that one can understand by applying standard historical and grammatical tools. But it is not true. In fact, the biblical text contains a certain prophetic mystery that eludes and defies conventional textual analysis.

In a way, any text can be said to have a mystery. Following poststructuralists, we may even say that to understand a text is to decode it, and this process depends on the interpreter's culture, thought paradigms, and other factors. No one can guarantee that the recipient reconstructs the exact meaning of what they read because they bring their own experience and connotations into the text. Therefore, the search for the authentic meaning of the text simply does not make sense. It is no accident, then, that poststructuralism loudly proclaims *the death of the author*. The written text is deprived of its "author-father."[110] The reader is left alone with a text whose meaning they grasp to the best of their abilities. Such equivocality and mysteriousness of any text can be called the mystery of incomprehension. Hence, there is a multiplicity of meanings (or interpretations) and a lack of an objective criterion against which to determine the exact meaning of the text.

The picture changes completely if we take the biblical text as a sacrament, as the mystery of God acting in reality – not only when the text was being written, but also when it is interpreted here and now. The prophetic mysteriousness is brought to light by the work of the Holy Spirit, who elucidates the text. This is why Christ, and the New Testament writers interpreted the Old Testament texts, taking as their point of departure not their cultural context

---

110. Socrates, in Plato's dialogues, showed this perfectly well, saying that when a written text is "faced with rudeness and unfair abuse it always needs its father to come to its assistance, since it is incapable of defending or helping itself." Plato, *Phaedrus* 275e, 70.

but the revelation of the Spirit, who was promised to Christ's followers as their guide (John 16:13; 1 John 2:20).

When the Holy Spirit interprets a biblical text, even though the human author-father who wrote it down is uncertain, the text remains under the protection and care of the divine father who instilled meaning into it. This father is actually present in the reading and is never "dead." Translating this statement into biblical terms, we can say that the Spirit opens the reader's eyes (Ps 119:18) and speaks to them through the text, revealing to them the meaning, sense, and substance of what is written. Therefore, for Christians, reading Scripture is fundamentally different from reading any other text because of the divine author's omnipresence.

The illuminating work of the Spirit ensures that the God-intended meaning of the biblical text is there at all times and in all cultural habitats because it puts the divine ideas of the text into meaningful concepts that are most readily accessible to individual readers. This insight allows Vanhoozer to state,

> I reject any plurality that assumes the meaning of a text changes at the behest of the reader, at the influence of an interpretive community, or as a result of the Spirit's leading. On the other hand, I affirm a "Pentecostal plurality," which maintains that the one true interpretation is best approximated by a diversity of particular methods and contexts of reading. The Word remains the interpretive norm, but no one culture or interpretive scheme is sufficient to exhaust its meaning, much less its significance.[111]

Thus, understanding Scripture as a mediating sacrament that connects the divine author and the human reader offers a hermeneutical key to finding the meaning and significance of the text that is needed in the here and now.

There is another dimension to the sacramentality of Scripture. It can be seen not only as sacramental in its meaning but also as a sacrament that *transforms* the recipient of that meaning. The Bible is more than a book that conveys information about distant historical events, divine principles, and commandments. It produces a change in the reader. Colwell observes that when one takes up the Bible, "[s]omething is expected to be understood, but nothing is expected to 'happen'. There is expectation to be informed, but little expectation to be transformed."[112] Assuming Austin's speech act theory, we should accept that words do not just convey information; they produce something. Put dif-

---

111. Vanhoozer, *Is There a Meaning*, 419.
112. Colwell, *Promise and Presence*, 88–89.

ferently; speech has both locutionary and perlocutionary (performative) functions. At times, the audience can participate in the process of communication without undergoing any change. But sometimes, the text as a locutionary act produces a *perlocutionary* effect. It influences the audience, making something in them or through them. This is the mystery of the encounter of God and man, that is, the sacramental work Christ performs through his word on the spiritual nature of the one hearing it. In fact, the Bible appears to be a double sacrament: when the word of God is read, the Spirit expounds what is heard and, at the same time, transforms the hearer from the inside.

This twofold effect is especially evident when the Bible is preached in a church setting. The word spoken in the community of believers creates a fertile ground for the Holy Spirit's work because where two or three are gathered in Jesus's name, Christ moves and acts among them (Matt 18:20). Of course, he reveals the meaning of what is written even to those who read the Bible on their own, but a more accurate understanding is reached when reading and expounding the text in the community (Acts 8:31). This activity mirrors the wider tradition of Bible reading in miniature. One grasps the meaning of each word and phrase and comes to a fuller comprehension of the biblical text through the historical legacy of the Christian church. A person is able to understand anything at all only when they live in and proceed from a certain cultural and historical context. In the church, the expository and transforming work of the Holy Spirit through the word is grounded in the community's tradition, its convictions, and the broader church legacy.

Thus, the Bible is seen as an interlocutor through conversation with whom man discovers God. It leads one to faith if they respond to what God is saying and doing. It is the instrument of God's grace. When the sacramental, performative quality of the Bible as the word of God is ignored, it becomes a trivial collection of instructions and doctrines. When we, on the other hand, understand the Bible as a sacrament, it becomes the locus for the encounter of God with man.

5

Practical Aspects of Church Ordinances

Baptist Liturgy

The ecclesiastical rituals embedded in worship inevitably compel one to consider the entire Baptist liturgy to understand their purpose and meaning correctly. A few explanations are in order.

Typically, evangelicals avoid applying the word *liturgy* to their worship services other than ironically. Liturgy is believed to be a set of clearly defined and strictly fixed utterances, particular rituals, well-ordered actions, appropriate clothing, etc. But this is a very narrow view. The word "liturgy" (λειτουργία) is made up of two Greek words: *laos* and *ergon*, meaning "people" and "action" or "work," respectively. In the New Testament, this word denotes the various ways the people of God may serve God together. For example, in Philippians 2:17, instructing the church at Philippi, the apostle Paul speaks of the "service coming from your faith" (λειτουργίᾳ τῆς πίστεως). In Luke 1:23, this word (λειτουργία) describes the divine office Zechariah performed in the Jerusalem temple. Similarly, the practical ministry of the Corinthians, who donated to the needs of the believers in Judea, is referred to as "the ministry of this service" (ἡ διακονία τῆς λειτουργίας ταύτης, 2 Cor 9:12, ESV). But as time passed, the word acquired a more specific and narrow meaning.

In the Christian East, liturgy came to designate the eucharistic celebration, while the West tends to understand it as the church's written and rigorously structured service. In other words, for the Christian West, liturgy is a broader concept that encompasses both the celebration of the Lord's Supper and everything that takes place during the worship service within the church walls.

For Baptists, as representatives of free churches, the notion of liturgy as a fixed set of rites is unacceptable. Historically, Baptist congregations in Britain,

America, and Eastern Europe have valued spontaneous worship centered on a sermon delivered by an emotional preacher who could quote the word of God by heart and expound it without a preconceived outline, applying scriptural texts to the particular situation of his audience. He required neither pulpit nor extensive theological knowledge, but his ardent sermon was able to present the most important Christian doctrines. The main idea of this type of service was to attract new church members by converting the unbelievers to Christ.

The call to repentance, that is, an invitation to make a commitment to Christ, was the pivotal moment of these worship services. Later, they also came to include the elements of teaching and instructing the hearers in the basics of Christian life. Over time, christened folk music, typically simple and sentimental, was introduced for didactic purposes, while self-composed poems embellished the congregation's meetings. Spontaneous prayers played a significant role in these loosely organized gatherings, but eventually, they evolved into a fairly standardized repetition of lofty phrases. In the Eastern European evangelical movement, the form of worship has been free and mostly spontaneous even to the present day, although some of its elements easily become fixed over time. Thus, while verbally rejecting the idea of liturgy, Baptists actually practice it. This is why Philip Thompson, in a *Review & Expositor* editorial, boldly declared, "Baptists have liturgy because Baptists worship and serve God in community."[1]

Although liturgy is often understood as an activity centered around worship, Ruth Gouldbourne expands on this concept. She argues that Baptist liturgy, unlike that of Catholic or Eastern Orthodox Churches, consists of three parts:

> (1) The liturgy proper, conducted during the local congregation's general assembly. Such gatherings are often called worship services in the Western tradition and divine services among Eastern European Baptists;
>
> (2) quasi-liturgy that includes casual gatherings for Bible study, Sunday school, discipleship groups, prayer groups, etc.
>
> (3) auxiliary meetings such as communal meals and fellowship, post-service coffee breaks, informal house-to-house gatherings, family worship services, recreational programs, retreats, Summer camps, etc.[2]

---

1. Thompson, "Baptists and Liturgy – ," 318.
2. Gouldbourne, "Liturgical Identity Carriers," 382.

From the Baptist perspective, Gouldbourne is certainly right. One cannot reduce free church liturgy as the joint action of the children of God exclusively to what happens during Sunday services. After all, community and communal life are the bedrock of evangelical tradition. Of equal importance to the Baptist community are the quasi-liturgical and auxiliary meetings. Each of them implies that members of Baptist congregations come together to serve God and one another. Therefore, these events can safely be called liturgical, even though they may be very loose, informal, and not called worship.

Baptist liturgy is difficult to grasp because of its elusive and flexible nature. In historical churches, liturgy exists in the form of clearly defined texts that one may analyze, tracing their historical formation and sources. But in Baptist communities, one finds a wide variety of liturgical experiments.[3] In fact, it is impossible to single out and describe *the* Baptist liturgy because Baptists, especially in Eastern Europe, do not have a strictly regulated and fixed set of liturgical practices that are supposed to take place during each worship service. Some Easter European Baptist churches recite the Lord's Prayer aloud, and others do not; there are congregations that celebrate the Lord's Supper weekly and those that do it monthly; the order and form of the eucharistic service may vary widely; and so on. Furthermore, the form and style of worship can vary from one congregation to another and may even change in any congregation over time.

Evangelicals share many liturgical practices with other Christian traditions, although they are carried out in distinctive ways. These include prayer, preaching, communal singing, water baptism, the Lord's Supper, etc. There are also practices unique to free churches, such as for example, "table fellowship," which combines communal meals and fellowship (sometimes happening immediately after the service); congregational discussion of Scripture texts (Bible study or "the scrutiny of the word,"); communal social ministries; group evangelism; recreational programs for the whole congregation; and so on. All of these practices are rather fluid and often unique to a certain community, but there is much in Baptist worship and all quasi-liturgical activities that is shared. Therefore, when a member of one Baptist congregation visits another that they know nothing about, they quickly adapt to the new environment and start feeling at home.

---

3. The most extravagant experiment in Baptist liturgics so far is the transformations that have taken place in the Baptist Union of Georgia under the leadership of its president, Malkhaz Songulashvili. See Songulashvili, *Evangelical Christian Baptists of Georgia*, as well as an analysis of these experiments in Eastwood, "Georgian Baptists: Church Reform."

The liturgical assembly of a Baptist congregation is sometimes called the "worship service." Its recognizable features are democracy, spontaneity, distrust for fixed motions and verbal formulas, involvement of a large number of church members, sometimes communal discussion of the Bible readings, and critical approach to the sermon and all liturgical elements. As Christopher Ellis observes, the Puritans, from whom the early Baptists emerged, adhered to Martin Luther's position concerning worship practices, in which whatever was not forbidden was permitted. Nevertheless, the Baptists followed Jean Calvin's ideas about the organization of church services even more radically than Calvin himself. They believed – and many Eastern European Baptist communities still subscribe to the view – that for a liturgical practice to be permitted, it should be rooted in and justified by the Scripture. Whatever is not permitted in the Bible is forbidden. Thus, Baptists have tended to adhere to rigorous biblicism, which creates many difficulties for them.[4]

Overall, the Baptist mentality is hardwired in such a way as to regard every element of church service as the Lord's ordinance. Hence, in addition to the Lord's Supper and baptism, the ordinances include other liturgical elements. But in order to justify a particular worship practice, the Baptists often have to develop a complex and volatile exegesis of the biblical texts. This is especially true with regard to the manner of worship, the attire of the participants, worship songs, and music styles.[5]

This approach inevitably results in heated debates about what Scripture actually prescribes because any biblical text is bound to be read through the cultural lenses of its readers and can be interpreted differently. The demand to ground everything in Scripture leads to a lapidary style of worship. It is characterized by stark simplicity, the absence of any imagery out of fear of idolatry, and a strict timetable for the worship service. It should contain nothing superfluous or distracting, while the central place is reserved for the word of God. These are the distinctive features of the Baptist liturgy.

Despite the lack of uniformity and standard "order" of liturgy, it is possible to identify the following common elements in Baptist worship. Here, I present them listed in order of their importance to the Baptist tradition:

---

4. Ellis, "Duty and Delight," 335.

5. Ellis quotes John Fawcett's stern injunction: "No acts of worship can properly be called holy, but such as the Almighty has enjoined. No man, nor any body of men have any authority to invent rites and ceremonies of worship . . ." John Fawcett, *The Holiness Which Becometh the House of the Lord* (Halifax: Holden and Dawson, 1808), 25. Quoted in Ellis, "Duty and Delight," 337.

1. The Word

Central to the service is a maximally intelligible sermon in the congregation's language, with elements of didactic instruction. Sometimes, it takes the form of a homily, when the Bible reading is followed by running commentary on and exposition of the Scripture, with possible discussion of the readings by the whole community.

Communicating faith verbally is the keystone of the Baptist tradition, which is why religious scholars sometimes call this movement *rational sectarianism*. The narrow focus on the Bible certainly looks attractive and commands respect, but, unfortunately, the dominant role of preaching has almost supplanted all other forms of worship.

Today's Baptist liturgy in Eastern Europe cries for a restoration of its integrity. The verbal forms of worship should be accompanied by visual and tactile – broadly speaking, aesthetic – expressions. Of course, the sermon should continue occupying the pride of place in the Baptist liturgy but not at the expense of other forms of worship. At present, we can observe a wide variety of liturgical experiments in Eastern Europe, whose aim is to balance verbal, visual, and tactile means of communicating divine truth.[6] The increasing contacts of Baptist ministers with representatives of other Christian traditions and, especially, the influence of the charismatic movement have played a major role in this.

2. Music

Christian music and singing, whether communal or individual, are part and parcel of Baptist worship. One may hear the whole congregation sing as well as enjoy listening to the choir or solo singers. In any case, music and poetry serve the double purpose of praising God and/or edifying people.

This ministry has traditionally been viewed either as an emotional release and spiritual encouragement between sermons or as another form of proclaiming the word. David Peterson says that psalms, hymns, and spiritual songs should be seen as "the means of teaching and admonishing one another."[7] In other words, they actually fulfill the same function as preaching, albeit serving

---

6. A leader of Georgian Baptists Malkhaz Songulashvili, describing the reforms their Baptist union underwent to bring the church closer to the Eastern Orthodox Church, writes: "Human beings have five senses and all of them may participate in worshiping God: sight (Christian arts), hearing (Word of God), touching (anointing with oil), taste (Eucharist), smell (incense)." Songulashvili, *Evangelical Christian Baptists of Georgia*, 414.

7. Peterson, *Engaging with God*, 221.

as an additional, idiosyncratic expression of faith, praise, and thanksgiving to God. On the one hand, the music ministry contextualizes and shapes theology in many ways, and on the other hand, it serves as an instrument that directly glorifies God. The *dogma* and the *doxa*, teaching and praise, go hand in hand in the music ministry.

Congregational singing occupies a very special place in Eastern European Baptist worship. It is a phenomenon of mass rather than elitist culture. This singing is a form of folk music indigenous to the region and usually has a simple, memorable tune. Such music is always local and, therefore, by default, acceptable. The lyrics for congregational singing are usually written by ordinary church members who have no theological training but, instead, possess a keen grasp of the central tenets of their faith. This feature renders these songs poetic and accessible to the bulk of the people in the church. Had these texts been written by academic theologians, they would hardly have had a chance to win people's hearts and become truly congregational songs.

Nowadays, the music ministry is gaining prominence as a distinct form of worship. The content of spiritual hymns is becoming less didactic and more focused on glorifying God. It certainly reduces their semantic content but fills in the emotional, sensual, and spiritual components of the worship service.

3. Prayer

By prayer, I, by and large, mean doxology or the public prayers of both ministers and laypeople, be they loud or silent.

Public prayers have always been a free and spontaneous outpouring of the spiritual emotions and thoughts of those participating in the Baptist worship service. Usually, a few people in each church display an active prayer life and do not hesitate to express their feelings and needs in public. However, over time, these people's public prayers become more formal and monotonous, and a heightened awareness of their responsibility for their words makes their prayers excessively cautious and full of clichés. Therefore, realizing the necessity for and importance of sincere prayers of as many community members as possible, some Baptist ministers began to encourage short public prayers of thanksgiving and promote praying in small groups (of two or three people) during worship services. At times, they introduce other forms of communal prayer life.

4. Repentance

For Baptists, repentance is a call to confess one's sins and commit oneself to Christ and an invitation to renew one's spiritual life publicly, showing other people how God works in and changes their lives.

Revivalism was a major hallmark of the Baptist movement in the nineteenth and twentieth centuries. Baptists frequently organized special evangelistic services like old-time frontier camp meetings. This worship focused primarily on the conversion of sinners and invited the audience to repent, not so much on the public worship of God by the already converted. At the beginning of the twenty-first century, when well-known American evangelists, such as Billy Graham, Louis Palau, and others, arrived in Eastern Europe, the call to repentance came to be replaced by an invitation to give one's heart to Jesus, commit oneself to Christ, and so on.

Nowadays, many ministers believe that the effectiveness of these seeker-oriented events is declining. Bill Leonard admits: "Times are tough for Baptist evangelists. A once thriving vocation now seems in serious transition if not decline."[8] In the last decade, not only has the popularity of evangelistic "calling" meetings declined, but also the testimony about one's conversion to Christ, a crucial element of early Baptist liturgy, has become increasingly rare. These testimonies supplied examples to emulate, and functioned as an authentication process for those who wanted to join the congregation. They helped to synchronize the individual and communal faith, giving the local church a tool to "verify" the authenticity of one's conversion and welcome the convert into its fold. Today, some worship services no longer include a call to come forward, confess one's sins publicly, and repent. Nevertheless, this liturgical element is still of great importance for Baptists.

5. Rituals

These include the public administration of water baptism, the Lord's Supper, ordination, consecration, and other ceremonies.

Traditionally, the Baptist movement has shunned ritualism. So much so that the very terms "ritual" (or "rite") and "ceremony" have been consistently avoided because, for Baptists, these words refer to a written and uniformly replicated sequence of religious acts. However, in practice, within each community, the unwritten tradition of performing certain actions develops, gradually becoming a set of habitual, recurring words and gestures with sacred

---

8. Leonard, "Salvation and Sawdust," 6.

meaning. Still, it is not the correctness of gestures, words, or movements that matters most but the sincere, free-form prayer and the reading of the relevant Scriptural text. These two elements validate the rite.

All rituals, being part of the liturgical life of the congregation, contribute enormously to the formation and spiritual integration of church members because they are, in a sense, performances, dramatic actions that engage people in a qualitatively different mode of being a Christian. Rituals exhibit the visibility and tactility that other elements of Protestant worship lack.

6. Koinonia

Basically, *koinonia* is the unity and solidarity among church members that is realized through announcements, intercessory prayers about people's needs, issues, and joys, informing everyone about congregational events, and demonstrating the interconnectedness of different communities through the exchange of greetings and messages (written and oral).

Many contemporary ministers do not fully appreciate the significance of this liturgical component. They often downplay or ignore it altogether, relegating all the communication about the congregation's life exclusively to an online format. Yet, the announcements of church activities, prayer needs, events in other congregations, etc., provide an opportunity for church members to share in each other's lives, provide help, and offer prayerful and financial support to those in need.

As John Carleton has convincingly shown, "The New Testament church is a worshipping fellowship, a koinonia, a group, an organism. This is not a coming together of privately saved souls; it is the collective creation of Christ."[9] At present, this communal dimension in the liturgy is obscured, but the information about the active life of the community continues to be its vivid witness.

7. Contemplation

It is a quiet and silent spiritual reflection on God, an experience of the reality of divine mystery and majesty, and reverent silence before the almighty and loving Father.

Contemplative worship is the least developed part of the Baptist liturgy. This state of mind should not be confused with hysterical religious ecstasy or a sensual outburst of intense emotions. Kolomiytsev calls this practice "the

---

9. Carlton, "The New Emphasis," 312.

worship of standing before God," which consists of putting aside all mental and spiritual clutter and entering the reality of God's presence.[10] Unfortunately, contemporary liturgies have very little room for silent reflections.

Viktor Lyakhu explains: "According to the biblical understanding, contemplation is an important and valid experience. It is by no means trance or ecstasy nor a sudden vision of a transcendent flash of light. . . . It is a religious perception of God."[11] In contrast to contemporary meditation practices promoted by the New Age movement and various Eastern cults, biblical contemplation focuses on the living God, not on a mantra. Spiritual contemplativity as an element of liturgical practice distinguishes theater-like worship from worship that makes room for an encounter with the living and acting Jesus.

Baptist liturgy is more often man-centered than God-centered. This is a common problem that free churches face all the time. John Carleton writes:

> In its essence worship is the adoration of God, the ascription of supreme worth to him, and the manifestation of reverence in his presence. John Calvin insisted that worship is not designed primarily to bring the consolations of grace to the sin laden soul but that it was a solemn offering of confession, homage, and thanksgiving on the part of the whole congregation of the elect. Calvin maintained that man's efforts to derive religion from mere human aspirations and needs issued in religiosity rather than pure religion.[12]

For Baptist devotional practices, man-centeredness is a great temptation. All things were created for man, but man was made for Christ (Col 1:16); this is the Creator's will. Therefore, when making Baptist worship services seeker-centered, church ministers should keep in mind that worship might become so man-centered that the direct worship of God will fade to almost an afterthought. The attendees should be taught to give sincere thanks without asking for anything, to praise God selflessly while expecting no immediate benefit, and to worship Christ zealously while contemplating the magnificence of his deed on the cross.

These are the basic structural elements of Baptist liturgy. Some of them may be occasionally omitted. For example, some congregations do not use musical instruments or avoid singing; others do not make public calls to repentance;

---

10. Kolomiytsev, *Pridite, Poklonimsya! (Come, Let Us Worship!)*, 223–48.
11. Lyakhu, "Bogosluzheniye Kak Sozertsaniye (Worship as Contemplation)," 65.
12. Carlton, "The New Emphasis on Worship," 312.

sometimes there is no room for personal contemplation during the service; the individual liturgical components may be ordered differently; etc. Still, for the most part, Baptist worship services tend to consist of these structural elements.

The primary purpose of Baptist worship is to ensure that the participant meets Christ in his word through the Holy Spirit. Therefore, the liturgy is designed in such a way as to facilitate communal worship and celebration of Christ, embodying the values of his kingdom, participating in the *Missio Dei*, and attracting new worshippers to his church. Thus, worship becomes a place where, focusing on Christ, people discover true life in him, get transformed through him, and grow spiritually with him.

The Reality of Evangelical Ordinances

The grace, beauty, and power of church ordinances in evangelical communities inevitably make one pose the question: how and under what conditions may a person benefit fully from the riches of divine grace contained in water baptism, the Lord's Supper, the laying on of hands, and other ordinances? What is the relationship between an ordinance and the realities of the Christian life? Is this connection purely mental, or does participating in the ordinances accomplish something for and in those involved? If something happens there, under what conditions does it happen, and when does it fail to happen?

Validity and Efficacy

The reality of each particular ritual is determined by its validity, which is the opposite of being illusory and invalid, and its efficacy, which is the opposite of ineffectiveness. This means that baptism, the Eucharist, and ordination must (1) occur in reality and (2) produce a certain effect.

Validity and *efficacy* are key concepts in sacramental theology. Something is called valid when it exists in reality and is contrasted with the imaginary, illusory, possible, or potentially existing. As early as Aristotle and, later, the scholastics realized that matter itself was passive, a formless possibility and that only an idea and force from the outside could turn matter into something actually existing. Actuality, the actual world, is something larger than the empirical reality per se. Material objects or physical phenomena do not exhaust the notion of actuality. An actual being is a being that embodies an idea, a conception, or a vision. It embraces both the physical reality and its spiritual principles, which logically and ontologically precede actual beings.

Vladimir Solovyov wrote:

> Between the concepts of "actuality" and "reality" there exists a logically clear, though empirically always relative, distinction. Something possessing an internal actuality cannot be realized, and as a consequence cannot possess reality. The creative idea of an artist possesses actuality but is deprived of reality until it is realized in external material.[13]

In other words, reality becomes actuality in the full sense of the word when a potency is fully realized. This applies to both human creativity and divine creativity.

Let us take the notion of actuality as an embodied, realized idea as our starting point. From it, we may infer that the actuality and, hence, the validity of any sacrament is its fulfillment in such a way that its effect is revealed, its function performed, and the power inherent in the sacramental event manifest.

A passport is invalid if it cannot fulfill its purpose, for instance, when it has expired or was obtained illegally, even though it may look like new. A church ordinance may also look right and be carried out in full accordance with established procedures, but if it does not fulfill its function, failing to usher in an encounter with Christ, it is neither valid nor effective.

The concepts of *validity* and *efficacy* have been explored in legal studies for centuries, which may have influenced how this pair of concepts was used in sacramental theology. This tendency to think of sacraments in legal terms has been particularly common in Catholic theology, which frequently frames the discussion under the headings of legal validity and invalidity, technically called *liceity* and *illiceity*, respectively. Something can be valid but illicit (*valida sed illicita* in Latin). That is, an act can occur in reality and produce a real result but still be unlawful from the legal point of view.

Catholic lawyer Robert Rodes notes that modern theology has developed a contemptuous attitude towards the legal dimension of sacramental theology.[14] It came to insist that the encounter with the living Christ occurs even in Christian communities that reject the idea that only the sacraments administered by ministers who stand in apostolic succession are licit. Rodes argues for the need to retain legalism in sacramentalism. He says that sacraments, like any other legal transactions, are effectuated by means of "performative utterances," which are performed properly and have effect only upon the condition that

---

13. Solovyov, *The Philosophical Principles*, 166.
14. Rodes Jr., "On Validity and Invalidity," 580–600.

they are performed in a particular legally appropriate context. In his view, one cannot simply dismiss the topic of the sacrament's validity because the sacrament's effect is properly valid and licit only if it is recognized as such by the entire church community.

Liceity does help to remove ambiguity or contestability of an act, but liceity itself depends on established rules and procedures. Consequently, the sacramental validity, as the Catholic Church defines it, may be at odds with what is recognized as licit in an Eastern Orthodox or Baptist context. Therefore, any discussion about the legal validity of the sacraments will hinge directly on the social context that sets the norms for liceity and illiceity of certain ecclesial practices. It means that interdenominational debates about the supposed (il)liceity of sacraments in other traditions are doomed because each tradition establishes its own rules, norms, and legal (canonical) procedures.

For this discussion to bear fruit, a radical shift of focus is needed. One should stop asking whether this given sacrament is valid and start thinking about whether it has ushered in an encounter with Christ. This is the question biblical sacramentalism deems worth asking. After all, one can imagine, verbally describe, and theologically justify an encounter with Christ. It may even be formally licit (valid). But still, it may not have actually happened for all of its participants. At least two factors must come together for it to occur. There should be, first, the presence of Christ, who administers the sacrament, and second, the faith of the participant.

Christ's objective presence is the primary, decisive factor determining the validity of the sacrament. The Lord is willing to meet everyone who comes to him; he is really present at each baptism and each communion, but every single participant, as well as the entire local church, needs to recognize his presence. When the Lord is surely present, is the sacrament's validity determined by the legitimacy of its procedure or by the effect it produces in participants?

Medieval Christian theology tended to embrace the view that the sacramental action derived its efficacy from the lawfulness and propriety of its procedure. The sacrament was to be administered by a priest who had been properly ordained by the bishop standing in apostolic succession and who correctly performed the sacramental acts. In such a case, the effect was expected to occur "from the work performed by the Church" (*ex opere operato ecclesiae*). In other words, if a rightly appointed priest celebrated the Lord's Supper or water baptism and the procedure was carried out in accordance with the order of liturgy, God would necessarily bestow grace on the participant in virtue of his promise, and such a sacrament would be valid. The sacrament's effect – its efficacy – would still depend on the recipient's willingness and disposition, but its validity would remain intact.

This is the approach based on the proper administration of the sacrament. It has at least three weaknesses. The first one has to do with the legal system, which determines the parameters of the sacrament's validity. Every Christian denomination has its own tradition. Both Eastern Orthodox and Roman Catholic Churches hold that the continuity of episcopal ordinations going back to the apostles constitutes the canonical grounds upon which the notion of sacramental validity rests. But what justifies and makes this norm valid? Neither Christ nor the apostles are known to have established this system. This norm is based on sound logic and tradition that developed later when pre-Nicene Christianity sought to justify the legitimacy of its orthodox doctrines and ecclesiastical structures in the struggle against the Gnostic ones. Is it the only possible approach that correctly reflects the laws of the kingdom of God?

Given what Jesus said and did, according to the New Testament, the validity and efficacy of Christian practices is determined neither by the verified "standing" in the apostolic succession nor by being born into a Christian culture, nor by formal signs of belonging to the people of God through water baptism, nor even by the extraordinary ability to perform miracles and prophesy. The only thing that matters is the fruit Christians bear to the Lord (John 13:35; Matt 7:22–23).

If a sacrament, in Beasley-Murray's words, is the sinner's *trysting place* with God,[15] is there any point in talking about its validity? Let us expand on the image Beasley-Murray proposes. Imagine young people agreeing to have a date in the park and then having a great time together, chatting, laughing, holding each other's hands, and admiring the fallen leaves around them. It is hardly possible to describe this meeting in terms of validity or efficacy. One needs to use a different set of terms to grasp the meaning and value of this meeting. We should switch to the language of encounter that is better suited to discussing the communication between two persons: God as a person and a human being as a person.

Second, the *ex opere operato* principle completely excludes the human will from the equation and only fits the theology of radical determinists. But biblical texts consistently speak of the conjunction of divine initiative and human responsibility, which both play their part in the kingdom of God (Matt 16:24;

---

15. Beasley-Murray writes that baptism is a "trysting place of the sinner with his Saviour; he who has met Him there will not despise it. But in the last resort it is only a place: the Lord Himself is its glory, as He is its grace." Beasley-Murray, *Baptism in the New Testament*, 305.

Acts 8:37; Rom 8:13, etc.). It is beyond dispute that God does a lot of things by his sovereign will alone, with absolutely no regard for human desire or volition. But in matters of spiritual growth and personal transformation into the image of Christ, human endeavor plays a rather significant role, according to Scripture. If this observation is correct, it would be odd, to say the least, to ignore or underestimate the individual Christian's contribution to such important practices as water baptism and the Eucharist, both of which are instrumental in building up the church and spiritually nourishing its members.

Third, the emphasis on the process of *doing* sacraments, regardless of those performing and participating in them, smacks too much of magical thinking, whereby a magician makes a spiritual force fulfill what he asks for by uttering the correct words and making the right gestures. Undoubtedly, the actions performed, and words spoken during baptism and the Lord's Supper address the living God rather than an unknown spiritual force, which partially removes the accusation of magical thinking. Still, the procedure, the manner, and, most importantly, the very idea of *ex opere operato* are, by and large, analogous to what we expect of magical techniques. In such an approach, an unbiased observer will immediately detect an attempt to oblige God to act in a certain way in response to the rite being correctly performed. But obviously, one cannot compel Jesus to do something merely because the recipient believes he has promised to do it. He acts out of his own will and not according to a mold, however correct and reasonable. Jesus promised to wait for and welcome the one who comes to him, but the validity of the encounter depends largely on the participants, whether they recognize Jesus and rush to him or pass him off as a stranger on his way to Emmaus. This is why, from the New Testament perspective, it is most natural to define the validity of the sacrament in terms of an encounter (the reality of the meeting) rather than the legal categories of liceity and legitimacy.

Fourth, an encounter presupposes a change in those who meet. If the baptism or the Lord's Supper is truly valid and a real encounter with Christ has occurred, then there will be some kind of spiritual change in the participant. The validity of the sacraments, in other words, necessarily manifests itself in their efficacy.

It may happen that a person receives baptism or participates in the Holy Communion thoughtlessly by simply doing the ritual and expecting no real encounter with Christ. In this case, they do not experience any spiritual transformation and leave the church just as they have entered it. It means that the authentic encounter failed to occur because of the participant's lack of faith or outright disbelief. Faith is the driving force that opens the communicant's eyes and lets them see the Lord awaiting them and pointing to his wounds. Responsive faith brings about the encounter so that the encounter turns out to be a work of faith. Faith shapes and actualizes the event whose validity depends on faith and whose efficacy, in turn, strengthens faith. It is well-known that "without faith it is impossible to please God" (Heb 11:6). We may extend this principle by applying it to sacramentology and saying that without faith, any sacrament remains an empty shell, an external form lacking spiritual content.

To summarize, the validity of sacraments is determined not by formal legal norms but by the fact of the participants' encounter with Christ in the local church setting. A valid encounter is necessarily efficacious. For this to happen, the participants must perceive baptism as a decisive step in entering into a covenant with the Lord and the beginning of a genuine Christian journey. They also should approach the Lord's Supper not as a mere memorial, an encounter with the historical Christ of the past, but as a desirable and authentic encounter with the living and actually present Jesus.

The Sacred and the Profane

One of the most debated issues is the status of the signs pointing to the sacramental encounter with Christ: How sacred are they? If the water of baptism, the bread and wine of the Eucharist, and the hands performing the ordination are all signs of a sacrament, at what point do they become valid signs, and how should they be treated afterward? Especially poignant is the controversy over eucharistic signs.

Christ's words are clear. Pointing to the eucharistic bread and wine, He said, "This is my body and my blood," and commanded his disciples to eat and drink them regularly. But these words raise many questions. How should we treat the eucharistic substance? Do the bread and wine always represent the body and blood of Christ or only from a certain moment on? Why does the old Baptist tradition consider them holy signs after the prayer of consecration, while contemporary Baptist churches seem to abandon this notion altogether? Where is the boundary between the sacred and the profane?

Most Christian traditions believe that from a certain point in the liturgy, the Eucharist becomes sacred. Until that point, the bread is just bread, and the wine is nothing but ordinary wine. After that point, their status changes. This belief is firmly established in the historical churches, but many Baptists and other Evangelicals, especially in the East, also subscribe to this view.

Chapter 3 showed that many early Baptist confessions defined bread and wine as holy signs separated from common use[16] and that Eastern European Baptist churches clearly display a reverent and pious attitude toward the eucharistic substance, considering it holy and even *most holy* (compare with Exod 30:29).[17] Thus, Andrei Blinkov, describing the sacraments from an evangelical perspective, opines that

> it is completely unacceptable to treat the consecrated elements, the bread and wine, carelessly. Carelessness may include scattering bread crumbs or spilling the wine. . . . Any remaining pieces of consecrated bread should be consumed by the communicants or given to other believers participating in the sacrament. The same applies to the consecrated wine (juice). It should be drunk completely.[18]

This opinion corresponds to what the authoritative Ukrainian Baptist Union's ministers recommend doing.[19] It is safe to conclude that many Baptist ministers and laypeople treat the consecrated bread and wine as something sacred, understanding Christ's words of institution as performative and not simply descriptive. They produce what they announce, creating a new reality.

In the historical churches, the high point of the eucharistic prayer (anaphora) after which the bread and wine are separated from profane use is called the epiclesis (ἐπίκλησις, invocation). It is essentially the invocation of the Holy Spirit, who is able to enact the ontological change (conversion or transubstantiation) of the ordinary bread and wine into the body and blood of Christ. Both the form and the exact timing of this moment have been subject to much debate between Catholic and Eastern Orthodox theologians.[20] The Western Catholic tradition holds to an ascending epiclesis, implicitly containing an invocation to God the Father or the Trinity to accept the eucharistic sacrifice,

---

16. For example, the *Orthodox Creed* of 1678, Article XXXIII reads: "And the outward elements of bread and wine, after they are set apart by the hand of the minister, from common use, and blessed, or consecrated, by the word of God and prayer, the bread being broken, and wine poured forth, signify to the faithful, the body and blood of Christ." Lumpkin, *Baptist Confessions of Faith*, 321.

17. See Matviyiv, *Svyashchennodiyi Pastora (The Pastor's Sacred Acts)*, 56; Prokhorov, *Russian Baptists and Orthodoxy*, 160–61.

18. Blinkov, *Sem' Tainstv Tserkvi (The Seven Sacraments of the Church)*, 37.

19. Matviyiv explains: "What should be done with the bread leftovers? Once the service is over, the brethren (ministers and preachers) stay and eat them." *Svyashchennodiyi Pastora (The Pastor's Sacred Acts)*, 72.

20. Kern, *Yevkharistiya (The Eucharist)*, 231–47.

while the Eastern tradition opts for a descending epiclesis wherein the Holy Spirit is explicitly requested to come down and effect the conversion of the eucharistic substance.

The evangelical eucharistic theology does not specify or analyze the particular moment when the entire community encounters Christ in the Eucharist, after which the bread and the cup truly manifest the body and blood of Christ. It only implies that this happens after the prayer over these signs. In fact, this holds true for all sacraments. For example, before water baptism, the pastor says a prayer over the water in which the baptism will be performed. However, since there are no biblical instructions regarding the water of baptism, the question of its sacredness is not raised at all, and it is, therefore, believed to play a purely instrumental role.

With regard to bread and wine, most Christians, including many Eastern European Baptists, agree that after the epiclesis, the eucharistic elements become holy. It is, therefore, important to clarify what this means and how the bread and wine should be treated after the prayer of consecration. As shown in chapter 3, it is biblically ungrounded and philosophically incoherent to speak of transubstantiation whereby the substance of the bread miraculously changes while its accidents miraculously remain the same, even though no external evidence suggests that a miracle has actually occurred. Therefore, the evangelical tradition claims that the substance of the Eucharist does not change ontologically. But then, why is it called *most holy* and treated with great reverence? Why is no crumb allowed to fall to the ground or be disposed of as refuse? What is a holy thing, and how does the holy differ from the profane?

The concept of holiness has its origins in the idea of God. It is believed that holiness is an essential divine attribute. The *Holy One* is one of his most common names (Isa 43:15; Isa 57:15; Job 6:10). The Old Testament term for holiness is *kadosh* (קדוש), meaning "cut off," "alien," or "radically different." It corresponds to the New Testament term ἅγιος, which means "set apart" or "dedicated to God."

In classical Protestant theology, as Richard Muller[21] has shown in his seminal work, the holiness of God was mainly understood in two senses. First, it was identified with God's infinite supremacy over all inferior and created things. This feature is sometimes called the *majesty-holiness* (1 Sam 2:2). It is grounded on the unbridgeable gap between God and creation because he is, by nature, totally different from everything else in the world. Second, holiness emphasizes the moral goodness and perfection of God, who in principle cannot sin and

---

21. Muller, *Post-Reformation Reformed Dogmatics*.

has no part in evil (Heb 7:26). He is holy in himself, irrespective of creation and being in its totality; he is holy inherently, unconditionally, essentially, and not just in contrast to creatures. His nature manifests itself in certain moral and ethical principles he established for himself and revealed to humankind in Holy Scripture. Put simply, holiness is both divine transcendence and his moral purity. However, in recent decades, evangelical scholarship has begun to revisit and clarify this notion.

Drawing on the work of the French evangelical theologian Claude Costecalde, Peter Gentry has made the following conclusion: "The basic meaning of the word (holiness) is 'consecrated' or 'devoted.' In Scripture, it operates within the context of covenant relationships and expresses commitment."[22] Gentry analyzes Exodus 3, which refers to the *holy ground* that God set apart for himself when he met Moses; Exod 19, which speaks of the *holy nation* of Israel with whom God made a covenant dedicating them to himself; Isaiah 6, which demonstrates God's holiness to the prophet as a commitment to social justice; and other texts. His research shows that the overall meaning of holiness is commitment and dedication. God requires total commitment to himself (people, land, temple, and so forth) from his people, and at the same time, he himself is committed to the principles he has declared in the covenant with his people.

God is the only source of holiness, its condition, cause, and fullness. Nothing can, in principle, become holy on its own. Yet, it can be consecrated to and set apart for God, thereby becoming separated from the ordinary reality and, hence, holy. Outside of God, holiness may be only imputed and imparted by God. As such, it implies separation from other things and dedication to him.

Imputed holiness has two most essential and inextricably linked characteristics: first, it implies otherness and separation from the ordinary, everyday, and profane; and second, it is dedication, consecration, givenness, and commitment to God. Other characteristics of holiness, such as integrity, beauty, purity, spiritual perfection, the highest moral standards, and so on, are all derived from these two. It follows that holiness is not a substantial property, for it does not change the essence of a thing, phenomenon, or person. That which is separated from ordinary use and dedicated to God remains ontologically intact. Its substance and accidents remain the same as before the consecration, but their purpose has changed. In other words, a teleological change takes place.

The teleological approach seeks, first of all, to discover the purpose and ultimate meaning of the processes and phenomena. It seeks to understand why

---

22. Gentry, "The Meaning of 'holy,'" 417.

something happens, to what end, and for what purpose, and only then to determine the specific causes that produced the phenomenon in question. It makes perfect sense to interpret the concept of holiness from a teleological perspective, thinking about a change in purpose rather than an ontological alteration.

Some examples from the Old Testament vividly illustrate the teleological meaning of holiness. God made the seventh day of the week holy (Gen 2:3) and required that Israel keep it dedicated to God (Exod 20:8), avoiding any ordinary work on that day. The essence of the day did not change after the consecration. This day was still no different from any other day, but its purpose changed after God had set it apart for himself. Mount Sinai, upon which the Lord descended, was called holy (Exod 19:23), but ontologically and purely physically, it did not change during or subsequent to the divine presence. The cauldrons, basin, lampstand, altar (Exod 40:10–11, etc.), and other objects used in worship remained the same after their dedication to Yahweh as they had been before, but their purpose changed, and it had serious consequences for all those who approached them.

Before the dedication, one could freely ascend Mount Sinai, but when it became holy, set apart for the Lord, even touching it could be fatal (Exod 19:12–13). The ark of the covenant became a deadly hazard after it was set apart for the Lord. When Uzzah touched it, his life tragically and abruptly ended (2 Sam 6:6–7), even though it could have been touched without any consequences prior to the consecration. Another good illustration would be the story of the temple utensils that the conquerors took to Babylon. When King Belshazzar used the sacred vessels from the Jerusalem temple during his banquet, reassigning them to his gods (Dan 5:2–30), he was severely punished by the Almighty. The holiness of the Jerusalem goblets did not inhere in their essence after their dedication but came from their purpose. Thus, we can conclude that *the sacred differs from the profane not substantively but teleologically*.

With regard to the sacraments, their sacredness is to be explained in the same way. For example, during baptism, the physical immersion into water spiritually joins the baptized person with Christ. But when people from the Christian East call the act of baptism holy, it is not because the water changes substantially and becomes holy but because it changes its purpose and, instead of purifying the body, serves as a sign of the washing away of sin. This belief corresponds well with what Ananias said to Saul: "And now what are you waiting for? Get up, be baptized and wash your sins away, calling on his name" (Acts 22:16).

Likewise, the bread and wine do not change their essence after the prayer of consecration. Both their physical composition and their metaphysical substance remain the same, but they undergo a teleological change. There is a change in purpose, the transformation of the eucharistic elements' *raison d'être* that removes them from ordinary use and makes them serve not for the sustenance of the flesh but for the renewal of the spirit. By partaking in the bread and wine physically, the Christian becomes a partaker of the body and blood of Christ spiritually. These two processes are interconnected following the divine commandment, the commandment of Christ.

The bread and wine brought to the Lord's Table are entirely consecrated to the Lord, but not all of it is consumed during the celebration of the Lord's Supper. Are the leftovers of the consecrated eucharistic substance still holy?

On the one hand, they certainly remain holy in the sense of being detached from common usage. For this reason, they are to be treated with reverence as something that has already been given to God and used to glorify him and usher in the encounter with him. Consequently, it is unacceptable to treat the remnants of the eucharistic bread and wine with negligence not because they have magically become flesh and blood of Christ but because they have been dedicated to God, having acquired a new purpose. Just as it was unacceptable to use temple vessels for domestic needs, the eucharistic substance requires a careful and pious approach after the prayer of consecration.

At the same time, there is no place for superstitions that paganism bestows on artifacts, places, or material objects. If, by chance, someone spills the wine or drops the crumbs of the consecrated bread on the floor, they should not be accused of sacrilege or desecration because what happened was not conscious, that is, a purposeful, teleological violation of the sacred object. Christ repeatedly underscored this thought by citing the example of David, who had eaten the temple bread that he had not been allowed to eat (Matt 12:4) and whom the Lord did not punish. What is consecrated to the Lord is meant to serve man, not enslave him.

Dedication to the Lord involves pastoral prayer, during which the Holy Spirit works, combined with the proclamation of Christ's words, "This is my body; this is my blood." Do these words produce any effect or merely convey information? Many people believe that they are purely informative, but McClendon applied Austin's theory of performative acts to the baptism and Lord's Supper and came to a conclusion that many Baptists found surprising. McClendon showed that Christ's words of institution should be understood as *performative* speech-acts.[23]

---

23. McClendon Jr., *Doctrine: Systematic Theology*, 388–89.

The New Testament sacramental language frequently features performative utterances, linking the spiritual and material worlds. This is particularly evident in various ritual words. Their most important characteristic is that they convey very little or sometimes no meaningful information at all. Since the language of liturgical religious rites is based on a fixed text that is well known to all participants, the actual (locutionary) utterance does not tell the hearers anything new. The presbyter's speech act has no communicative-informative function but is undoubtedly performative, referring to the past but operative in the present. The phrase, "This is my body," that Jesus said long ago at the Last Supper and the same phrase uttered during the eucharistic celebration nowadays are performative rather than descriptive. They do not describe reality but create it. From this moment on, the bread in Christ's hands changes its purpose and begins to function as an operative sign/acting sign without ontologically changing into Christ's physical body.

When and why is this new reality created? Austin argues that the context or circumstances of the utterance determine the meaning of performative speech acts.[24] For these words to take effect, they need an appropriate setting. Yet, as Jacques Derrida demonstrated, what is important for successful and effective performativity is not just the context, which is fluid and elusive, but the rules and conventions that have been established in this context, that is, a particular social environment.[25] In this case, the performative utterance is merely a reception of these norms and conventions.

In sacramental speech acts, the performative utterance is customary, repeatable, and effective not because of an implicit social contract, established conventions, or other peculiarities of the context. McClendon notes that words spoken, and actions performed during sacramental celebrations, particularly during the Lord's Supper, have *double agency*. He claims that "the authentic prophet speaks God's word not just her or his own; in the Lord's supper, the deacons feed the flock, and *eo ipso* Christ feeds the flock."[26] This *double agency* guarantees the performativity of the words spoken during the breaking of bread. Broadly speaking, though, in sacraments, the agency is actually *triple*: there are God's, the candidate or communicant's, and the church's actions. A new alternative reality emerges from the interplay of the word, the Spirit, and one's faith in the context of the communal liturgical act, under appropriate conditions, and in response to certain expectations. It constructs a new com-

---

24. Austin, *How to Do Things*, 15–138.
25. Derrida, "Signature – Event – Context," 307–30.
26. McClendon Jr., *Doctrine: Systematic Theology*, 389.

munal identity that unifies people as well as renews each participant's status as they continue to grow in faith.

The Contingent Nature of the Encounter

A sacrament is a personal encounter between Christ and each sacramental participant. For a genuine encounter to take place, the faith of the receiver and the work of the Holy Spirit need to coalesce. Human faith and God's grace create a continuum that is rooted in and sustained by the Spirit on both sides of this interaction. The Spirit focalizes the faith of the one receiving the sacrament, and, on the other hand, he also communicates to them grace as an ineffable gift from God. Metaphorically speaking, the Holy Spirit is like the arch of a bridge over the abyss, whose one footing is Christ and the other the participant's soul.

However, here comes the practical question: how, when, and under what conditions does this faith arise, and what should be its level or quality that would allow the encounter to happen? How do divine and human agency relate in the encounter?

Most Eastern European evangelicals' belief that God's encounter with a given sacramental participant is not a pattern one takes for granted but a probability that depends on various factors. However, different groups of believers define the degree of probability differently. Some believe that the sacramental encounter occurs necessarily, with 100 percent probability, because God has promised to make it happen. Others assume that there are conditions under which an encounter with Christ can happen, or is guaranteed to happen, or never happens at all.

This approach allows one to analyze the encounter using the language of modal logic and, specifically, the concept of contingency, according to which every encounter constitutes coming into *con-tact*.[27] In other words, it is an event or a moment when two parties touch each other. The notion of *con-tact* demands that there must be two parties present. In the case of a sacramental encounter, they are both persons who have consciousness and free will; hence, their actions and reactions are not completely predictable and should be described as contingent.

---

27. The English word "contact" derives from Latin noun *contactus*, "touched," "grasped," or "bordered on," and the verb *contingo*, "touch (on all sides)," and "take hold of" which etymologically connects the root "touch" (*tangere*) and prefix "together with" (*con-*).

Contingency is what lies between regularity and pure chance. It is something that occurs with probability but is not subject to the law of random numbers. It is neither a completely random, accidental event nor an inevitable consequence of certain efficient causes. In terms of modal logic, contingency is a non-necessary consequent of a set of antecedents. Human behavior is contingent in this sense: it is non-preprogrammed and unpredictable, depending solely on the individual's free decision. It is neither random nor predetermined. Sometimes, contingency is defined as *non-necessary* or *non-impossible*, but placing it on the axis of necessity-chance would be a mistake. It has to do with the person's inner decision, provided one believes, as many East European Baptists do, that the individual is capable of making such decisions on their own. When two persons meet, the so-called *double contingency* emerges, as the major sociologist Talcott Parsons puts it.[28] *My* contingency (or "ego" in Parsons' terms) meets the contingency of the *other*. To analyze their interaction, one must understand both sides' attitudes, goals, and capabilities.

Suppose God constantly uses his omnipotent sovereign power. In that case, every interaction he has with humans will always turn into an encounter, becoming a recurrent pattern rather than a probability. Under this approach, if God wills to have an encounter with the person in the Eucharist, he will necessarily have it at the moment he chooses. And vice versa, if God does not want to meet the communicant, the encounter will not happen no matter how much effort the human being makes. In fact, the human being cannot make any effort at all because absolutely all of his endeavors are under God's full control. Many people find grounds for this understanding in the Bible, citing relevant texts and providing theological arguments in its support.[29]

The indeterminists, to whom most evangelicals in Eastern Europe belong, believe that God has given the human will the ability to make decisions consciously and responsibly, sometimes suppressing for some reason the strongest impulse in favor of a weaker one. Nobody can tell us what processes are at work in the soul at that moment. Only the person's own spirit within them knows what is going on inside (1 Cor 2:11). Still, even they cannot describe, analyze, and predict their future voluntary decisions because they are subject to many factors. Therefore, one's inner spiritual life is marked by unpredictability and ambivalence of feelings, desires, and spiritual stimuli leading to or influencing

---

28. Parsons, *The Structure of Social Action*, 353.

29. See, for example, Sammons's book, endorsed by John MacArthur, which repeatedly insists that God is the only agent involved in man's salvation and determining all of his actions. Sammons, *Reprobation and God's Sovereignty*.

the will's decisions and, ultimately, one's deeds. Of course, there is a certain, quite predictable, range of actions that a person performs influenced by different circumstances, but they do not follow a strict pattern.

Therefore, faith, which is necessary for actualizing the encounter with Christ, is often presented in this part of the world as an emergent contingent phenomenon. It comes suddenly and is usually irreducible to – sometimes even contradictory to – the person's earlier experience. Its emergence lies in the fact that faith cannot be deduced from previous states of mind, although they may prepare for its arrival. Its contingency consists in its unpredictability. Faith is the synergistic interplay between the impact of the word of God and its free acceptance by the human soul. As the Bible has it, "faith comes from hearing, and hearing through the word of Christ" (Rom 10:17, ESV). Faith is undoubtedly a gift of grace (Eph 2:8), but this gift can be either accepted or rejected by the intended recipient. Both one's embracing of faith and one's growing in faith result from the synergy between God's power that initiates the process (1 Cor 2:5) and the human recipient's acceptance of that power.

When encountering Christ, a person is called upon to exercise their freedom through faith. However, the level of faith, as a temporally variable value, may be insufficient. Perhaps the person has the "firstfruits" of faith, but many factors prevent them from focusing on Christ fully and seeing him through the eyes of faith. In order to help the newcomers form the proper faith, the ministers of traditional Baptist communities try to focus their attention on Christ and his word. In this respect, the combination of properly structured sermons, songs, and prayers of their friends and the whole church gradually shapes the inner world of the communicants, centering their spiritual gaze on the encounter with Jesus. The whole church setting should help the person to encounter Christ in baptism or the Lord's Supper. It means that the contingent factors that have a bearing on this experience include not only one's personal faith but also the faith of their parents, friends, and the entire church community.

Let us summarize this discussion of the reality of evangelical sacraments. It is more fruitful to consider it through the lens of the communicative language as a probable and temporally circumscribed personal encounter with Jesus Christ. Proper administration of a ritual cannot necessarily and inevitably produce the encounter because its "validity" and reality rests on the conditional, rather than unconditional, promises of God. On the divine side Jesus's presence is guaranteed by the aim and meaning of the gathering – it occurs in the name of Christ. On the human side, the key element is the participant's faith, which can change over time and depends on the inner state of the person as well as on some external factors. Faith is shaped by the synergy between God's actions and man's response. Therefore, faith is a conditional gift the human person may accept or reject. External factors that shape and strengthen faith are the word of God and intercessory prayers. The combination of these elements creates the contingency of each particular event of water baptism and the Lord's Supper so that it is impossible for an outside observer to determine whether an encounter has taken place in a given sacrament.

Practical Remarks on the Administration of Sacraments

The meaning and function of church ordinances are manifold and require adequate pastoral implementation. Ministers are responsible for creating the conditions for the communicants' encounter with Christ. But for this to happen, the whole congregation should have the right spiritual disposition. Specifically, the individual church members should be prepared through Christian counseling and mentoring, and the liturgy needs to be well-structured, balanced, and properly conducted.

The care for the church is first and foremost manifested in the formation of communality. All sacraments, and in particular water baptism and the Lord's Supper, have the potency to foster unity, reinforce fellowship, and knit together the wounded body of Christ. This potency should be the focal point of pastoral attention. Pastors teach their congregation to value one another and live together without losing diversity but maintaining unity. The image of the body to which the neophyte is joined at baptism, as well as the sign of the broken body of Christ at the Lord's Supper, both point to mutual responsibility for one another, especially for those who, for various reasons, cannot attend the service. Therefore, Eastern European Christians tend to celebrate water baptism with the whole congregation present, even though, in exceptional cases, the congregation may be represented only by a few members.

After each Eucharist, the ministers take the consecrated bread and wine and, whenever possible, financial aid to the sick and disabled church members who could not make it to the church. Symbolically, it signifies the belonging of the absent members of the local church to the common Lord's Table. This is why they are not served a separate Lord's Supper but are invited to share in the communal meal, receiving the same bread and wine the local church has prayed over.

Communal compassion finds expression in the prayerful intercession during each sacrament for those who are crippled by sin and sickness. In this, the reference to the suffering of Christ and communal love in action are combined *koinonically*. The vertical and horizontal dimensions of *koinonia* thus coincide. The same idea is emphasized by the insight that the Eucharist points both to the broken body of Christ on the cross and the suffering church as the living body of Christ in the world of evil and sin. In practice, it means that the celebration of each sacrament includes a time when the church prays for Christians enduring tribulations and persecutions around the globe and collects special offerings intended for missions and relief for believers in other regions.

Many people have noted Baptist activism. This is certainly a positive trait that distinguishes the movement from other denominations. However, in the liturgy, activism often takes the form of an endless series of sermons, songs, poems, and other activities so that the attendees become mere listeners and have no time for personal reflection, introspection, or the opportunity to hear the quiet whispering of the Holy Spirit. The pastor and ministerial team make sure that those present never have an idle minute. Keeping the church members as busy as possible during the worship service is considered a good idea.

Currently, many Eastern European churches have begun to critically revisit the Baptist liturgy, especially the assemblies in which the church ordinances are celebrated, with the goal of providing a time of silence and personal introspection. The communities also rethink and adopt more "moderate" forms of worship from other traditions. Until twenty to thirty years ago, worship had a pretty modest place in the Baptist liturgy. It was confined mainly to hymns of praise the church choir sang and doxology as part of spontaneous or "fixed" prayers, which tended to avoid excessive emotionality. Today, there is a tendency to allocate more time during the service for worship music, praise, and emotional expression. After all, worship service is the worship of God; therefore, people should address God directly. Music gives them a venue to do that.

A good, developed sermon is what distinguishes all strands of Protestantism. The Reformers used to capture Luther's position by saying, "The sacraments cannot be without the word, but the word can be without the sacraments."[30] In this sense, Baptists have continued the Lutheran rather than Calvinist trajectory, viewing the Lord's Supper primarily as a parable pointing to Christ's death. It somewhat devalues the Eucharist, on the one hand, but, on the other hand, assigns pride of place to the Christ-centered sermon, which is meant to show the depth of Christ's sacramental presence and his power to transform people's hearts here and now.

In addition to caring for the whole congregation and the proper ordering of worship, there is another function a pastor needs to perform. The pasto-

---

30. Quoted in Vischer, "The Eucharist-Ritual and Reality," 204.

ral perspective on sacramentology requires that a system of pre-sacramental preparation be established for each church ordinance.

Preparation for baptism in the Eastern European Baptist movement has always been particularly thorough. In many ways, this practice resembles the austere approach of the post-apostolic church in the second and third centuries when lengthy catechization and the testing of the neophytes' faith preceded one's admittance to water baptism. This pre-baptismal training usually consists of a series of talks, held regularly for about half a year, in which those preparing for baptism learn a wide range of doctrines and familiarize themselves with essential biblical truths. Of course, it is difficult to find the unambiguous biblical basis for such catechetical practice or supply it with examples dating back to the apostolic period. Therefore, it should be treated mainly from an economic point of view as a helpful tool the church of a particular historical period uses. Viewed from this perspective, the approach has proven its effectiveness.

Catechization concludes with an interview when the candidate for baptism is interrogated by the ministers or, in smaller congregations, all members of the church. The purpose of these interviews is not only to get to know the new members of the congregation but also to obtain testimony of the neophytes' conversion, commitment to Christ, and assent to the congregation's disciplinary practices.

Special prayer meetings leading up to water baptism and eucharistic celebration are essential in preparing church members for these sacraments. Many Eastern European congregations still retain the old Baptist tradition[31] of fasting and praying the Friday before baptism or the Lord's Supper. Sometimes, an all-night prayer vigil for groups of twenty to thirty people is scheduled on Saturday night.

The purpose of these gatherings is to enhance the spiritual life and, for some people, to restore it. They usually consist of short biblical readings and longer periods for prayer, with everyone participating. Among the important themes that come up in these meetings are the call to reconciliation with God and one another, deliverance from sin, and prayer for the sick, weakened, and absent church members, as well as for brothers and sisters in distress. Ministers work to create conditions that would make the call to reconciliation culminate

---

31. In the English-speaking world, the examination practice before the Lord's Supper was widespread in the nineteenth and early twentieth centuries. James Cheesman writes that many American churches at that time held Saturday night meetings at which the pastor preached a sermon on self-preparation, and people often confessed their sins and repented. He cites several occasions when prominent nineteenth-century pastors publicly refused to participate in the Lord's Supper, deeming themselves unworthy to do so. Cheesman, "The Lord's Supper," 67.

in prayer and then lead to practical steps toward forgiveness, reconciliation, and mutual understanding.[32]

Sacraments in an Era of Existential Crises

Over the last decade, the world in which Christianity lives has changed dramatically, which has entailed irreversible and unprecedented changes in the lives of many churches. These processes have especially affected Eastern Europe. According to Giorgio Agamben, fear and panic have become the main features of the 2020s.[33] The numerous waves of terrorism that became a daily reality after the 9/11 attacks in 2001 propelled them into the foreground. On a much larger scale, fear gripped the world during the COVID-19 pandemic and in the wake of Russia's full-scale war on Ukraine. Fear has become an ever-present reality, especially in Eastern Europe. We see a new pandemic taking root, a pandemic of fear. People are afraid of terroristic attacks, new variants of coronavirus and other infections, as well as the real threat of World War III. It paralyzes them and creates ideal conditions for mass consciousness manipulation and the imposition of so-called emergency measures.

In this environment, apocalypticism, populism, and dystopias grow in popularity; conspiracy theories multiply, the number of end-of-the-world scenarios grows, and various internet fables, simulacra, and personal "revelations" spread. These circumstances force both individuals and entire church structures into an existential crisis, which is becoming permanent. Another new condition of life that significantly affects ecclesiology and eucharistic theology is the unprecedented influence of mass media and the internet.

Pandemics and wars have thrown the door wide open into online space. They compelled people to use the internet on a much bigger scale and moved whole sectors of economic, political, and social life into a remote mode. It has particularly affected education, church, and community life. In many ways, the internet has made life easier for humanity but has also exposed many new social-psychological and spiritual issues. Serious ecclesiological challenges have emerged, influencing many Christian communities, most notably evangelical free churches. The proliferation of online congregations and Zoom services has forced us to rethink our understanding of the church, its essence, and its functioning. A serious theological problem has come to light: what is the backbone of the local church? Is it preaching, common prayer, or church dis-

---

32. Romanyuk, *Tserkovne Slyzhinnya (Church Ministry)*, 40.
33. Agamben, "The Invention of an Epidemic."

cipline? Active supporters and promoters of online churches and their equally active critics raise their voices in support of quite divergent views.[34] Antonio Spadaro has inaugurated serious research on cyber-theology and the peculiarities of church functioning on the World Wide Web. It was he who posed the important question: how to remain a Christian in a new, strange world?[35]

Christian congregations are facing even more challenges due to the pressure that modern media tools are putting on them. The phrase "soft prison" has emerged, referring to the estrangement between people, rampant individualism, and growing self-isolation in the confined comfort of one's home, where the only communication available is through media. TV, streaming platforms, and the internet, rather than the church and communities of friends, are now the primary sources of values and worldviews – even of decisions and practices. That is to say, the private residence has become a center of media consumption, an observation capsule, and a place of voluntary confinement.

This is true not only for members of online communities who live permanently online but also for an overwhelmingly large number of ordinary church members who combine attending traditional worship services with watching sermons on YouTube, participating in Zoom conferences, and doing other "church stuff" on the internet. Ksenia Luchenko notes that "media institutions take away from religion its functions (i.e. they become moral and spiritual guides, give a sense of community, and so on) and equate religion with various forms of entertainment."[36]

In other words, the permanent crisis constantly fuels alarmist sentiments and pushes Christians onto the internet, which creates an illusion of vibrant church life. At the same time, Russia's war in Ukraine has demonstrated the power that mass media have on Christians. As Maksim Nesterenko has shown,[37] Christians in Russia trust the information from the mass media more than they trust the testimonies of their brothers and sisters who are eyewitnesses to real events. Thus, the manipulation of consciousness has reached an unprecedented level, and there is a real prospect of reformatting and reshaping the worldview of a large group of people in any way imaginable. It is now possible to indoctrinate the human community with certain values and convince them of the

---

34. Stefanovich, "Dobro Pozhalovat' v Onlayn-Tserkov'" ("Welcome to the Online Church"), 151–67.
35. Spadaro, *Cybertheology: Thinking Christianity*.
36. Luchenko, "The Digitalization of Worship Practices," 40.
37. Nesterenko, "Rossiyskiye Khristiane (Russian Christians)," 216–43.

expediency of certain practices using contemporary means of psychological influence rather than through the church.

In the early days of mandatory lockdown (spring 2020), virtually all evangelical churches moved their worship services online, and many began using videoconferencing tools to enable the interaction with and involvement of their members. Some communities used amateur forms of broadcasting on YouTube or Facebook, while others purchased semi-professional equipment and made broadcasting their worship services a regular practice. The full-scale war in Ukraine that broke out in 2022 resulted in the dissolution of many congregations due to the destruction of houses of worship and forced migration. Other churches lost significant numbers of their memberships. It further intensified the trend of moving worship services online.

This transition has compensated to some extent for the lack of spiritual nourishment and fellowship. But, as many forced "online Christians" – especially those in exile – admit, it has brought to light people's deep longing for a live, tangible community. In an effort to at least partially meet this need, some congregations have begun to actively cultivate a culture of liturgical co-participation, engaging remote church members in worship at their home church via Zoom, Google Meet, or other interactive technologies. It allows Christians who are away or forced to stay at home to engage in congregational Scripture reading, communal and solo singing, recitation of poems, prayers, etc. It turns out that engagement as a form of universal priesthood, difficult to achieve in classical worship service, is much easier to accomplish in an online or small group format. Thus, the media environment has made it possible for many people to be actively present in the liturgical action, experiencing emotional and even spiritual engagement (immersion) through digital means.

This kind of interactivity and immersiveness, which researchers have extensively explored in contemporary theatrical performances,[38] leaves participants free to choose their own manner of interaction and level of immersion in the worship service. They can engage in dialog or refrain from it. This flexibility remains regardless of the form of the worship service, be it online, offline, or hybrid. The organizers offer the choice of activity and method of communication, but it is up to each participant to decide what and how they want to do according to their individuality or current moods. This is undoubtedly a positive outcome of the crises we have lived through.

---

38. Kaydanovskaya, "Sovremennyi teatr (Contemporary Theatre)," 212–226; Repenko, "Interaktivnost' i Immersivnost' v Media (Interactivity and Immersiveness in Media)," 459–64; etc.

The Lord's Supper and the Pandemic

As the doors of many houses of worship closed due to lockdown and, later, warfare, baptisms became less frequent and usually with limited participation. The Lord's Supper, in turn, was either not celebrated at all or celebrated in whole or in part online.

For the historical churches, the discussion about the possibility of online communion hinges on a key question: is the conversion of the eucharistic substance possible when the priest administers it from a distance? Can the bread and wine be transformed into the body and blood of Christ in a private residence rather than the church, and would Christ's presence be real in this case?[39] For evangelical Christians who understand the reality of Christ in terms of the pervasive work of the Spirit and not through the notion of a substantial change, this kind of question is not an issue at all. The bread and wine before and after the prayer of consecration remain substantially the same, but the prayer changes their purpose, and thus, they become holy. Consequently, the restrictions of place and distance are not applicable to the eucharistic substance. For Baptists, the main point of contention has to do with a different cluster of questions: Is full communion among the partakers of the Lord's Supper possible? How can communality be maintained without slipping into extreme individualism? Is the disciplinary role of the community preserved intact? Is the degree of collective involvement and co-presence sufficient to enable the collective faith of all those present to confirm the validity of a particular form of the Eucharist?

This challenge prompted six professors from Odesa Theological Seminary to examine various ways of administering the Lord's Supper in a time of crisis. As a result of these discussions, a document with a number of recommendations was drafted. It was published on 2 April 2020 in Russian and Ukrainian[40] and was widely distributed in the evangelical community. According to numerous responses, it had a serious impact on determining the way in which the Lord's Supper was celebrated in Eastern European Baptist churches during the COVID-19 lockdown.

The text analyzes four approaches to celebrating the Eucharist and concludes that the choice of a particular way depends mainly on the hermeneutic

---

39. Additionally, Eastern Orthodox theologians have often discussed the question: is it possible to get infected by eating the real body of Christ? The official answer is no, it is impossible. But in practice, a stipulation has been introduced: it is possible to catch the virus not from the eucharistic substance but from a chalice or spoon with which Holy Communion is administered.

40. Bandura et. al., "Provedeniye Vecheri Gospodney (Celebrating the Lord's Supper)," 8–13.

the community employs. In particular, how broadly and comprehensively do the congregation and its ministers understand the essence of the Lord's Supper, and which dimensions of the event do they accentuate? In the ideal liturgy, all aspects of the Eucharist – remembrance, proclamation, thanksgiving, fellowship, self-examination, communion, and anticipation of what is to come – should be harmoniously interwoven. The very event of the Lord's Supper should usher in an encounter between the communicants and Jesus Christ. In other words, liturgical practice should create favorable conditions within which the encounter with Jesus can take place. In practice, however, this is not always the case.

If, for some ministers, the Lord's Supper serves only as a remembrance-commemoration and an opportunity for self-examination, then it can be celebrated independently of the community meetings and formal worship services. If others understand it to be holy communion with brothers, sisters, and Christ, providing reciprocal disciplinary support and encouragement, then the fullness of such an event is difficult to achieve by digital means without gathering physically in one place. Thus, different theological emphases shape the choice of particular eucharistic practices.

In times of crisis, the question arises: is it necessary for the community to gather together, joining each other in one topographical locus, or can it still be a community with no physical presence? What brings a congregation together? One premise? One Spirit? One word? It seems obvious that not everyone gathered in one room is part of a community, nor are all who hear the word a church. One Spirit certainly unites the congregation, but it is difficult to verify and specify the external markers that unambiguously show who has or does not have the Spirit. A visible congregation should have visible markers. The invisible body of Christ does not need such signs. God knows his own. But even in the visible world, there is always a boundary separating the body from what is not that body. If the Eucharist is celebrated by means of visible signs in a visible space within the visible congregation and only among the church members, then the clearest sign of the congregation as a community of saints is discipline and order. It is precisely discipline and order that, as Baptist congregations in Eastern Europe believe, establish the boundaries of the local church. Since it is difficult to monitor and oversee church discipline in the online format, many ministers are critical of the Lord's Supper celebrated online.

In this case, ministers receive no feedback and do not know who participates in the Supper and who does not. This approach to the sacrament is largely inconsistent with the eucharistic theology of Eastern European Baptists, who have a strict policy regarding participation in the Lord's Supper: only church members who have undergone the necessary preparation are admitted to the table.

Online communion gives the impression that a virtual community is being formed, whereas, in fact, it just imitates the church assembly as much as possible. As a result, the Lord's Supper turns into a purely individual affair between man and God. The imitation happens merely in the imagination because everyone sees only the minister on their screen, not fellow believers, and imagines their brothers and sisters praying, eating the bread, and drinking from the cup at this very moment. Of course, even when the Lord's Supper is celebrated face-to-face, it is not the case that each participant has fellowship with every other member of the congregation. Still, even incomplete face-to-face fellowship creates a sense of unity and wholeness.

The Lord's Supper and the War

Russia's full-scale war against Ukraine, which began on 24 February 2022, has caused the suffering of hundreds of thousands, and displaced up to ten million Ukrainian nationals. The pain and suffering the war has brought has taken on a personal, existential quality. Millions of families in Ukraine, Russia, and elsewhere have been affected by the war in one way or another. Aggression, pain, cowardly silence and passivity, solidarity, belonging, and similar feelings became embedded in the Christian experience. These experiences also had a bearing on the Lord's Supper. If the pandemic raised a number of theological questions, the war added ethical, social, and psychological ones. Anxiety, stress, pain, and apocalyptic forebodings have provided fertile ground for interpersonal and international conflicts, causing divisions in and radicalization of society.

A German pastor and theologian, Hermann Hartfeld, believes that political events in Ukraine, which began in 2014 with the annexation of Crimea and a military coup in the Donbas, have seriously radicalized evangelical Christianity. Both Russian and Ukrainian Baptists now often perceive each other as enemies; political events and virulent propaganda have undermined mutual trust between the two groups. In his paper given at the Nuremberg Radikalisierung im Namen der Religion Symposium, Hartfeld talks about the "Radicalization of Christianity" in the wake of this war.[41] He cites evidence that shows how

---

41. Hartfeld, "Radikalisierung des Christentums," 219–239.

Russian Christians and even church ministers[42] actively participate in the war against Ukraine and urge others to support it. On the other hand, Ukrainian Baptists are not only helping the Ukrainian army but are also directly involved in combat operations against the Russians.

The Eastern European Baptist community has never witnessed this level of internal spiritual division in its history. Even the extremely painful conflict within the Soviet Baptist brotherhood in the 1960s did not lead to such tragic consequences. Hartfeld visited Donbas in 2014 at the height of hostilities. Amazed at the intensity, sacrifice, and devotion with which young people were killing their fellow Slavs in south-eastern Ukraine, he wrote: "The killings are symptoms of a gradual brutalization that is being promoted by both sides, the Ukrainian and the Russian side."[43] This radicalization clearly stems from informational and spiritual aggression, which generates excessive anger, hostility, and, as a consequence, physical violence. In the end, it divides all people into "us" versus "them," provoking conflicts in Baptist churches between pacifists and militarists.

As is well known, the Eastern European Baptists have long held the principle that the use of arms, military service, and similar issues are matters of the believer's personal conscience and individual choice.[44] In other words, neither church congresses nor any other supra-church structures make or can make binding decisions with regard to the use of violence or nonviolence. In fact, most Eastern European evangelicals, influenced by the Mennonite theology up to the early 1990s, used to hold a pacifist position. But since 2014, and especially since winter 2022, the situation has changed dramatically, and the idea of limited violence, or the just war theory, has become dominant.[45] This shift in theological emphasis has been a source of additional tensions in the Baptist churches. The presence of a relatively large number of victims of physical, psychological, sexual, and spiritual violence contributed to the spiritual tensions, as well.

Such a thickening of negative conditions can be resolved in various ways, but one of the tools is the Lord's Supper. Because of its sacramental nature, as a venue for an encounter with Christ, the Eucharist becomes a powerful way of lifting and alleviating the negativity of war. It does not work directly, as men-

---

42. For example, Prokhorov, *Kipyashchiy Kotiol Iyeremiyi (Jeremiah's Boiling Cauldron)*, 34.

43. Hartfeld, "Radikalisierung des Christentums," 234.

44. Grigoriev, "Voyennyi Vopros v Istorii (The Military [Service] Issue in the History)," 91–104.

45. Tkachenko, "*Bellum Justum or War*," 105–154.

toring sessions do, but operates in a subtle and gentle manner. Encounter with Jesus helps to eliminate aggression and hatred because it restores true biblical *shalom*, renews the communicant's inner world, and makes them reconsider their condition in the light of gospel values. The Eucharist becomes a therapy for people suffering from the war and its consequences. It moves their inner self into safety, into the territory where they join and become emotionally involved in Christ's suffering for each and every one of us.

The estrangement that is removed by sharing a common meal the Lord himself hosts has become a defining feature of the 2020s. The pandemic brought with it a lockdown that divided people and fostered individualism and even solipsism. Now, as the war rages, emigration and political strife deepen the gulf even further. The dividing lines now often cross through the family. Moreover, whereas during the COVID-19 pandemic, it was the elderly or physically weak who were most vulnerable, the war largely kills the young and strong. The Lord's Supper, again, may be an appropriate Christian response to this state of affairs. In times of war, its indelible spiritual impact and healing effect are much more important than its form or manner of celebration. It exposes and cures the wounds of war because it is the medicine of life. The Eucharist always works this way, but its effect is more palpable in times of war because the wounds are deeper and more visible.

Pastor Aleksandr Nagirnyak of the Central Baptist Church in Mariupol recounts the Lord's Supper he served in the besieged city. It was, by far, the most unusual eucharistic celebration, he says.

> The believers had already been in the Central Baptist Church's basement for several weeks. They hardly ever went outside because of the bombing, for the bombs were falling on residential neighborhoods, on people's houses. One could not hide from them. No cellar could save anyone from a direct hit. On the contrary, when it happened, the shelters became mass graves.
>
> Our house of prayer is located near the Azovstal plant. Therefore, the bombing here was the most intense. But – amazing grace of God! – everything around the church building was destroyed; not a single building was left whole, but our church kept standing, protected by God's hand! We, while in God's house, were still alive in spite of the fact that the specter of death was walking around the city.
>
> On Sunday, 13 March 2022, we celebrated the Lord's Supper. We had some wine but no bread. Nevertheless, the sisters made

flatbread, which the brothers baked on the fire in the churchyard. We listened to the Word reading about the sufferings of our Lord, sang quietly and emotionally, and prayed earnestly. We participated in the Lord's Supper, knowing that for many of us, it could be our last [communion]. But still, despite all the dangers, we decided to try to leave the city. Staying any longer meant facing certain death. At 6 a.m. on 16 March 2022, a convoy of 25 vehicles and 110 people set out, and the Lord extended His mercy for us. By an incredible miracle, we managed to break through to Ukrainian territory.[46]

These kinds of testimonies demonstrate the Lord's Supper's unique role in forming Christians' stable spiritual condition.

War has complex spiritual as well as severe economic consequences. The global economic crisis and the depletion of energy and food supplies have the greatest impact on the poor and socially unprotected segments of the population. Therefore, it is appropriate to return to the practice of *agape*, the Suppers of Love or love feasts,[47] which the early church practiced by combining communal meals with the Eucharist. Each participant would bring some food to share, according to their ability. Therefore, small congregations could easily hold these meals on a weekly basis even today. They would not only serve the poor but also foster fellowship, create a culture of solidarity, and involve all members of the church in a collective endeavor.

In sum, the Lord's Supper celebrated today in a rapidly changing world poses many pastoral challenges as well as theological, spiritual-psychological, and organizational questions. The variegated but always scripturally rooted eucharistic practices of evangelical communities are currently searching for and formulating the answers to them. This quest will certainly produce many discussions, errors, and exciting findings, which is why we should actively encourage all kinds of theological reflection and open discussions.

---

46. Nagirnyak, "Khronika Dney Bedstviya (A Chronicle of the Times of Trouble)."

47. For instance, Fr. Cyril (Hovorun) recommends that Eastern Orthodox communities should resume the practice of agapes in extreme conditions. Horevoy i Derkach, *Fenomen onlayn-Prichastiya. Refleksii. Polemika. Perspektivy (The Phenomenon of Online Communion. Reflections. Polemics. Perspectives)*, 98.

Conclusion

One purpose of this study was to familiarize the English-speaking academic community with the traditions and principles of church rituals of Eastern European Evangelical Baptist churches. However, I deemed it even more important to explore the sacramentalism inherent in early Baptist thought that still persists in many contemporary Baptist churches and engage it theologically. To do this, I examined the Baptist sacramental tradition through historical and biblical lenses, followed by a theological analysis, synthesis, and practical reflections. This modest exploration has yielded several conclusions.

First, Baptists are not so rationalistic as to reject sacraments per se. Their perennial concern is their aversion to rituals that supposedly operate *ex opera operato*, that is, automatically, without the recipient's active involvement. For Baptists, however, baptism, the Eucharist, and other ordinances undoubtedly presuppose God's presence and people's sacramental encounter with him. This encounter depends on the Lord and the faith of those participating and may fail to occur if such faith is absent.

Without faith, the encounter with Christ remains an unapproachable mystery: baptism turns into a bodily washing, the Lord's Supper becomes an ordinary meal, and ordination degenerates into placing "empty hands on empty heads," as Charles Spurgeon put it. But if baptism, the breaking of bread, the laying on of hands, the proclamation of the gospel, worship, and other church activities are approached with faith and expectation of a meeting with the Lord, then Christ, in keeping with his faithful promise, is really, though not materially, present in all of them. He is *up there*, next to his Father in the kingdom of heaven, and at the same time, he is *down here* among the people of God. He meets the believer in the water of baptism and the bread and wine of the Lord's Supper and creates spiritual identification through the laying on of hands between the parties involved.

Second, many phenomena can be signs of the divine presence, beginning with creation and ending with the inner voice of the Holy Spirit. But there are special signs reserved for the church alone. They not only testify to God's presence but also produce certain effects by the power of God. They are performative signs that play a part in and contribute to the mysterious building of Christ's church (Eph 3:9). Through water baptism, new members join the church; through the Lord's Supper, the church nourishes and strengthens the communicants who gaze upon the crucified one and encounter him by receiving the bread and the cup; through ordination, ministers are appointed to supervise the construction of the house of God. Each such encounter with Christ produces an essential change in his followers.

Third, I want to emphasize that church sacraments are mysterious and incomprehensible. We may say we know them because we regularly perform them in the church, just as we may grasp their meaning insofar as it is revealed to us in Scripture, but each time we approach them, we are confronted with the profound mystery of divine presence.

Fourth, the study shows the importance of material signs through which the encounter with Christ takes place. This may seem strange to Baptists because they typically disregard the role of material mediums or "mediators." Nonetheless, the water of baptism, the eucharistic bread and wine, and the hands used in ordination become vehicles of the divine presence. They become holy not ontologically but teleologically. In other words, these material signs do not change their essence – water remains water, bread remains bread – but their purpose changes. After prayer, they become a medium through which God's presence manifests, and the Holy Spirit begins to work. This makes material signs holy because they are intended for the Lord and given away (consecrated) for him to use.

Fifth, the holistic approach to sacramentology allows us to see the unity of God's operations in water baptism, the Lord's Supper, the various instances of the laying on of hands, the sacramental dimension of preaching the word of God, and other cases. This demonstrates the advantages and validity of holistic methodology when applied to theological studies.

Baptist sacramentology is a young and developing field, and some scholars and pastors will certainly disagree with my conclusions. But I hope this book invites a fruitful dialog and reflection both within the Baptist tradition and in a broader ecumenical context.

Bibliography

Afanasiev, Nicholas. "Tainstva i Taynodeystviya (Sacramenta et Sacramentalia)." *Pravoslavnaya mysl* no. 8 (1951): 17–34.

———. *The Church of the Holy Spirit*. Translated by Vitaly Permiakov. Notre Dame: University of Notre Dame Press, 2007.

Agamben, Giorgio. "The Invention of an Epidemic." *European Journal of Psychoanalysis*, 26 February 2020. https://www.journal-psychoanalysis.eu/articles/coronavirus-and-philosophers/#block-1.

Aland, K. *Did the Early Church Baptize Infants?* London: SCM Press, 1963.

Andreev, A. V. *"The Quest for the Historical Jesus": from Reimarus to the Present Day*, Studia Religiosa. Moscow: New Literary Review, 2022.

Argyle, A. W. "Baptism in the Early Christian Centuries." In *Christian Baptism: A Fresh Attempt to Understand the Rite in Terms of Scripture, History, and Theology* edited by Alec Gilmore, 187–222. London: Lutterworth Press, 1959.

Atkinson, William P. *Baptism in the Spirit: Luke-Acts and the Dunn Debate*. London, Lutterworth, 2011.

Augustine. *Teaching Christianity (De Doctrina Christiana)*. Translated by Edmund Hill. Edited by John E. Rotelle. Vol. 1 of *The Works of Saint Augustine: A Translation for the 21st Century*. Hyde Park: New City Press, 2023.

Austin, J. L. *How to Do Things with Words*. London: Barakaldo Books London, 2020.

Austin Study Group. *Report on the Table of the Lord*. North American Conference of Faith and Order, September 3–10, 1957. Box 111, the Carlyle Marney Papers, David M. Rubenstein Rare Book & Manuscript Library, Duke University, North Carolina.

Baker, Donald. "The Laying on of Hands." *The Dunwoodie Review* 18 (1995): 1–12.

Bandura, Igor, et al. "'Provedeniye Vecheri Gospodney v Usloviyakh Karantina' (Celebrating the Lord's Supper during Lockdown).'" *Bogomysliye*, no. 26 (2020): 8–13.

Barth, Karl. *Church Dogmatics: Volume 1/1*. Translated by G. W. Bromiley. Edinburgh: T & T, 1975.

———. *The Teaching of the Church Regarding Baptism*. Eugene: Wipf and Stock Publishers, 2006.

Beale, Gregory K. *We Become What We Worship: A Biblical Theology of Idolatry*. Downers Grove: InterVarsity Press, 2009.

Beasley-Murray, George Raymond. *Baptism in the New Testament*. Grand Rapids: Eerdmans, 1973.

———. "baptiso," in *The New International Dictionary of New Testament Theology*, edited by Colin Brown. Grand Rapids: Zondervan, 1986.

Beasley-Murray, Paul. *Anyone for Ordination?: A Contribution to the Debate on Ordination*. Tunbridge Wells: Marc, 1993.

Behm, Johannes. *Die Handauflegung im Urchristentum nach Verwendung, Herkunft und Bedeutung in religionsgeschichtlichen Zusammenhang untersucht*. Naumburg a.S., Lippert, 1911.

Bender, Thorwald W. "A Theological and Functional Understanding of the Ordinances." A paper presented to the American Baptist Convention meeting in Detroit, 1963.

Bird, Michael F. "Re-Thinking a Sacramental View of Baptism and the Lord's Supper for the Post-Christendom Baptist Church." In *Baptist Sacramentalism 2*, 61–76. Eugene: Wipf and Stock Publishers, 2008

Blinkov, Andrei. *Sem' Tainstv Tserkvi: Yevangel'skiy Vzglyad (The Seven Sacraments of the Church: An Evangelical Perspective)*. LitRes: Samizdat, 2009.

Blount, Douglas K., and Joseph D. Wooddell. *The Baptist Faith and Message 2000: Critical Issues in America's Largest Protestant Denomination*. Lanham: Rowman & Littlefield Publishers, 2007.

Bornkamm, Günther. "Lord's Supper and Church in Paul." In *Early Christian Experience*, translated by Paul L. Hammer, 123–60. New York: Harper & Row, 1969.

Brachlow, Stephen, Philip E. Thompson, and Anthony R. Cross. *Recycling the Past Or Researching History?: Studies in Baptist Historiography and Myths*. Vol. 11. Eugene: Wipf and Stock Publishers, 2007.

Bradshaw, Paul F. *Reconstructing Early Christian Worship*. Liturgical Press, 2010.

Brewer, Brian C. "'Signs of the Covenant': The Development of Sacramental Thought in Baptist Circles." *Perspectives in Religious Studies* 36, no. 4 (2009): 407–20.

Bridge, Donald, and David Phypers. *The Water That Divides: The Baptism Debate*. Downers Grove: InterVarsity Press, 1977.

Broadway, Mikael. "Is It Not the Communion of the Body of Christ?" *Review & Expositor* 100, no. 3 (2003): 403–47.

Broadway, Mikael, Curtis Freeman, Barry Harvey, James McClendon Jr., Elizabeth Newman, and Philip Thompson. "Re-Envisioning Baptist Identity: A Manifesto for Baptist Communities in North America." *Perspectives in Religious Studies* 24, no. 3 (1997): 303–10.

Brunner, Emil. *The Divine-Human Encounter*. Philadelphia: Westminster Press, 1943.

Bulgakov, Sergius. *Yevkharistia (The Eucharistic Sacrifice)*. Moscow:Russkiy put'/YMCA Press; Paris: Russkiy put'/YMCA Press, 2005.

———. *The Eucharistic Sacrifice*. Translated by Mark Roosien. Notre Dame: University of Notre Dame Press, 2021.

Bullard, Scott W. "James William McClendon Jr., the New Baptist Sacramentalists, and the Unitive Function of the Eucharist." *Perspectives in Religious Studies* 38, no. 3 (2011): 267–88.

Bunyan, John. *Differences in Judgment about Water-Baptism, No Bar to Communion; Or, To Communicate with Saints, as Saints, Proved Lawful*. Private Circulation, 1673.

Bychkov, Alexey, and Arthur Mitskevich. *Dogmatika (Dogmatics)*. Moscow: ZBK VSEKhB, 1970.

Bychkov, V. V. *Malaya Istoriya Vizantiyskoy Estetiki (A Brief History of Byzantine Aesthetics)*. Kyiv: Put' k istine, 1991.

Calvin, John. *Institutes of the Christian Religion*. Translated by F. L. Battles. Louisville: The Westminster Press, 1960.

Carlton, John W. "The New Emphasis on Worship and Liturgy." *Review and Expositor* 64, no. 3 (1967): 309–21.

Carr, Warren. *Baptism: Conscience and Clue for the Church*. New York: Hold, Rinehart and Winston, 1964.

Carson, Donald A. *The Gospel According to John*. Grand Rapids: Wm. B. Eerdmans Publishing, 1991.

Carter, James E. "The Lord's Supper: A Baptist Perspective." *Southwestern Journal of Theology* 31, no. 2 (1989): 34–41.

Cason III, Harland James. "The Gathered Community as a Locus of Christ's Presence: A Historical and Theological Analysis of Baptist Sacramentalism in the Lord's Supper." *ProQuest Dissertations and Theses*. PhD diss., Southwestern Baptist Theological Seminary, 2011.

Catechism of the Catholic Church n.d. The Holy See, 25 March 2024. https://www.vatican.va/archive/ENG0015/__P4D.HTM.

Chauvet, Louis-Marie. *The Sacraments: The Word of God at the Mercy of the Body*. Collegeville: Liturgical Press, 2001.

Cheesman, James P. "The Lord's Supper among the Early Philadelphia and Charleston Association Baptists." *Artistic Theologian* 3 (2015): 55–67.

Child, R. L., ed. *The Lord's Supper: A Baptist Statement*. London: Carey Kingsgate Press, 1951.

Childs, Brevard S. *Memory and Tradition in Israel*. Vol. 37. Studies in Biblical Theology. London: SCM, 1962.

Chrysostom, Saint John. *Homiles on the Gospel of St. Matthew*. New York: The Christian Literature Company, 1888.

Chwolson, Daniel. "Poslednyaya Pashalnaya Vecherya Iisusa Hrista i Den Ego Smerti (The Last Passover Supper of Jesus Christ and the Day of His Death)." *Khristianskoye Chteniye*, no. 9–10 (1875): 430–88.

———. "Poslednyaya Pashalnaya Vecherya Iisusa Hrista i Den Ego Smerti (The Last Passover Supper of Jesus Christ and the Day of His Death)." *Khristianskoye Chteniye*, no. 11–12 (1877): 557–610.

———."Poslednyaya Pashalnaya Vecherya Iisusa Hrista i Den Ego Smerti (The Last Passover Supper of Jesus Christ and the Day of His Death)." *Khristianskoye Chteniye*, no. 5-6 (1877): 821-76.

———. "Poslednyaya Pashalnaya Vecherya Iisusa Hrista i Den Ego Smerti (The Last Passover Supper of Jesus Christ and the Day of His Death)." *Khristianskoye Chteniye*, no. 3-4 (1878): 352-419.

———. *Das Letzte Passamahl Christi Und Der Tag Seines Todes. Nach Den. Berichten Der Synoptiker Und Des Evangelium Johannis/Anhang Über Das Verhältnis Der Juden, Pharisäer Und Sadducäer Zu Christus*. Leipzig: Nachdr. d. verm. Aufl, 1908.

Clark, Neville. *An Approach to the Theology of the Sacraments*. London: SCM Press, 1956.

Clarke, Anthony. "A Feast for All? Reflecting on Open Communion for the Contemporary Church." In *Baptist Sacramentalism 2*, 25:92-116. Eugene: Wipf and Stock Publishers, 2009.

Collins, Adela Yarbro. "The Origin of Christian Baptism." *Studia Liturgica* 19, no. 1 (1989): 28-46.

Collins, William. *The Baptist Catechism of 1693*. https://credocovenant.com/2013/11/11/the-baptist-catechism/.

Colwell, John. *Promise and Presence: An Exploration in Sacramental Theology*. Eugene: Wipf and Stock Publishers, 2011.

Commission on Doctrine and Christian Unity BWA. "The Word of God in the Life of the Church. A Report of International Conversation between the Catholic Church and the Baptist World Alliance 2006-2010." Baptist World Alliance, 2013. http://bwanet.org/images/pdf/baptist-catholic-dialogue.pdf.

Coppens, Joseph. *L'Imposition des mains et les rites connexes dans le Nouveau Testament et dans l'église ancienne: étude de théologie positive*. Paris: J. Gabalda, 1925.

Cottrell, Jack. *Baptism: A Biblical Study*. Joplin: College Press, 1989.

Cross, Anthony R. "'One Baptism' (Ephesians 4:5): A Challenge to the Church." In *Baptism, the New Testament and the Church*, 173-209. Journal for the Study of the New Testament Supplement Series 171. Sheffield: Sheffield Academic, 1999.

———. *Baptism and the Baptists: Theology and Practice in Twentieth-Century Britain*. Milton Keynes: Paternoster, 2000.

———. "Spirit- and Water-Baptism in 1 Corinthians 12.13." In *Dimensions of Baptism: Biblical and Theological Studies*, edited by Stanley E. Porter and Anthony R. Cross, 120-48. Sheffield: Sheffield Academic, 2002.

———. "The Evangelical Sacrament: Baptisma Semper Reformandum." *Evangelical Quarterly* 80, no. 3 (2008): 195-217.

———. "Baptism among Baptists." In *Baptism: Historical, Theological, and Pastoral Perspectives*, Vol. 4, edited by Gordon L. Heath and James D. Dvorak, 136-55. Eugene: Pickwick Publications, 2011.

———. *Recovering the Evangelical Sacrament: Baptisma Semper Reformandum*. Eugene: Wipf and Stock Publishers, 2012.
Cross, Anthony R., and Philip E. Thompson, eds. *Baptist Sacramentalism*. Studies in Baptist History and Thought 5. Eugene: Wipf and Stock Publishers, 2006.
———, eds. *Baptist Sacramentalism 2*. Studies in Baptist History and Thought 25. Eugene: Wipf and Stock Publishers, 2009.
———, eds. *Baptist Sacramentalism 3*. Eugene: Wipf and Stock Publishers, 2020.
———. "Introduction: Baptist Sacramentalism." In *Baptist Sacramentalism*.
Cullmann, Oscar. *Christ and Time: The Primitive Christian Conception of Time and History*. London: SCM Press, 1962.
Culpepper, R. Alan. "The Biblical Basis for Ordination." *Review & Expositor* 78, no. 4 (1981): 471–84.
Daube, David. *The New Testament and Rabbinic Judaism*. Eugene: Wipf and Stock Publishers, 2011.
Derrida, Jacques. "Signature – Event – Context." In *Margins of Philosophy*, translated by Alan Bass, 307–30. Chicago: University of Chicago Press, 2009.
Dorodnitsyn, Alexei. *Materialy Dlya Istorii Religiozno-Ratsionalisticheskogo Dvizheniya Na Yuge Rossii vo Vtoroy Polovine 19 Stoletiya (Materials for the History of Religious-Rationalist Movement in the South of Russia in the Second Half of the 19th Century)*. Kazan': Tsentr. typ., 1908.
Dowley, T. "Baptists and Discipline in the 17th Century." *Baptist Quarterly* 24, no. 4 (1971): 157–66. https://doi.org/10.1080/0005576X.1971.11751344.
Dudnik, Alexandr. *Nachatki Ucheniya Khrista (The Beginnings of Christ's Teachings)*. Vol. 2 of *Svet Voskreseniya*. Makeyevka: Svet Voskreseniya, 1997.
Dunn, James. *Baptism in the Holy Spirit: A Re-Examination of the New Testament Teaching on the Gift of the Spirit in Relation to Pentecostalism Today*. Philadelphia: Westminster John Knox, 1970.
———. *Jesus and the Spirit: A Study of the Religious and Charismatic Experience of Jesus and the First Christians as Reflected in the New Testament*. Grand Rapids: Eerdmans, 1997.
Dyatlik, Taras. "Bogoslovsko-Ekzegeticheskiy Analiz Temy Suda v Vechere Gospodney (A Theological-Exegetical Analysis of the Judgment Motif in the Lord's Supper)." *Praktychna Filosofiya* 2, no. 68 (2018): 103–10.
Dyck, Johannes. "Fresh Skins for New Wine: On the Structure of the First Russian Baptist Congregations in South Russia." *Theological Reflections: Eastern European Journal of Theology*, no. 6 (May 2006): 114–28.
———. *U Kolybeli Bratstva: Iogann Vieler (1839–1889) i Obshchiny Pervych Evangel'skich Verujushchich v Rossii (At the Brotherhood's Cradle: Johannes Wieler (1839–1889) and Evangelical Christian Communities in Russia)*. Steinhagen: Samenkorn, 2017.
Eastwood, William. "Georgian Baptists: Church Reform, Orthodox Christianity, and National Belonging." Bloomington: Indiana University, 2010.

Ehrhardt, Arnold. "Jewish and Christian Ordination." *The Journal of Ecclesiastical History* 5, no. 2 (1954): 125–38.

Ellis, Christopher J. "Duty and Delight: Baptist Worship and Identity." *Review & Expositor* 100, no. 3 (2003): 329–49.

———. "Embodied Grace: Exploring the Sacraments and Sacramentality." In *Baptist Sacramentalism*. Vol. 2, edited by Anthony R. Cross and Philip Thompson, 1–16. Eugene: Wipf and Stock Publishers, 2008.

Erickson, John H. "Leavened and Unleavened: Some Theological Implications of the Schism of 1054." *St. Vladimir's Theological Quarterly* 14, no. 3 (1970): 155–76.

Fadyukhin, Sergei P. "O Tserkvi (On the Church)." *Bratskiy Vestnik (Brotherly Herald)*, no. 1 (1959): 57–69.

Fee, Gordon D. *1 and 2 Timothy, Titus*. New International Biblical Commentary. Peabody: Hendrickson Publishers, 1988.

Fee, Gordon D. *The First Epistle to the Corinthians*. New International Commentary on the New Testament. Revised Edition. Grand Rapids: Eerdmans, 2014.

Ferguson, Everett. "Laying on of Hands in Acts 6:6 and 13:3." *Restoration Quarterly* 4, no. 4 (1960): 250–52.

———. "Ordination in the Ancient Church IV." *Restoration Quarterly* 5, no. 3 (1961): 130–46.

———. "Jewish and Christian Ordination: Some Observations." *Harvard Theological Review* 56, no. 1 (1963): 13–19.

———. "Laying on of Hands: Its Significance in Ordination." *The Journal of Theological Studies* 26, no. 1 (1975): 1–12.

———. *Baptism in the Early Church: History, Theology, and Liturgy in the First Five Centuries*. Grand Rapids: Eerdmans, 2009.

Fiddes, Paul S. *Reflections on the Water: Understanding God and the World through the Baptism of Believers*. Macon: Smyth & Helwys, 1996.

———. *Participating in God: A Pastoral Doctrine of the Trinity*. London: Darton, Longman and Todd, 2000.

———. "Baptism and the Process of Christian Initiation." *The Ecumenical Review* 54, no. 1 (2002): 48–65.

———. *Tracks and Traces: Baptist Identity in Church and Theology*. Studies in Baptist History and Thought. Eugene: Wipf and Stock Publishers, 2007.

Fowler, Stanley K. "The Meaning of Ordination: A Modest Proposal." *Baptist Review of Theology* 2, no. 1 (1992): 33–36.

———. *More Than a Symbol: The British Baptist Recovery of Baptismal Sacramentalism*. Vol. 2. Eugene: Wipf and Stock Publishers, 2007.

———. *Rethinking Baptism: Some Baptist Reflections*. Eugene: Wipf and Stock Publishers, 2015.

France, Richard Thomas. "Chronological Aspects of 'Gospel Harmony.'" *Vox Evangelica* 16 (1986): 33–59.

Frank, Semen Li͡udvigovich. *Reality and Man: An Essay in the Metaphysics of Human Nature*. Translated by N. Duddington. New York: Taplinger Publishing, 1965.
Freeman, C. W. *Contesting Catholicity: Theology for Other Baptists*. Waco: Baylor University Press, 2014.
Garland, David E. *First Corinthians (Baker Exegetical Commentary on the New Testament)*. Vol. 1. Grand Rapids: Baker Academic, 2003.
Gay, David H. J. *Baptist Sacramentalism: A Warning to Baptists*. UK: Brachus, 2011.
Gentry, Peter. "The Lord's Supper." In *An Exposition from the Faculty of The Southern Baptist Theological Seminary on The Baptist Faith and Message 2000*, edited by Lawrence Smith and Bryan Cribb, 25–28. Louisville: Southern Baptist Theological Seminary, 2001.
Gentry, Peter J. "The Meaning of 'Holy' in the Old Testament." *Bibliotheca Sacra* 170, no. 680 (2013): 400–417.
Gilmore, Alec. *Christian Baptism: A Fresh Attempt to Understand the Rite in Terms of Scripture, History, and Theology*. Cambridge: Lutterworth Press, 1959.
Gnilka, Joachim. *Jesus of Nazareth: Message and History*. Peabody: Hendrickson Publishers, 1997.
Gonzalez, Rudolph Davila. *Laying-on of Hands in Luke and Acts: Theology, Ritual, and Interpretation*. Waco: Baylor University, 1999.
Gouldbourne, Ruth. "Liturgical Identity Carriers for Ecclesial Transformation." *American Baptist Quarterly* 31, no. 4 (2012): 379–91.
Grace, W. Madison II. "Early English Baptists' View of the Lord's Supper." *Southwestern Journal of Theology* 57, no. 2 (2015): 159–79.
Gray, Donald P. "Real Absence: A Note on the Eucharist." *Worship* 44, no. 1 (1970): 20–26.
Grigoriev, Igor'. "Voyennyi Vopros v Istorii Yevangel'Skikh Khristian-Baptistov (The Military [Service] Issue in the History of Evangelical Christians-Baptists)." *Bogomyslie*, no. 15 (2014): 91–104.
Gross, Karl. *Menschenhand und Gotteshand in Antike und Christentum*, edited by Wolfgang Speyer. Stuttgart: Anton Hiersemann, 1985.
Gura, Vitaly. "Pryroda Dukhovnogo Vplyvu Vecheri Gospodnyoyi Na Khrystyyanyna (The Nature of the Spiritual Influence of the Lord's Supper on the Christian)." L'viv: L'viv Theological Seminary, 2007.
Halbwachs, Maurice. *On Collective Memory*. Chicago: University of Chicago Press, 1992.
Hamilton, Andrew. "Eucharist in Retreat." *The Way. Supplement* 99 (2000): 109–19.
Hammett, John S. *Biblical Foundations for Baptist Churches: A Contemporary Ecclesiology*, 2nd ed. Grand Rapids: Kregel Academic, 2019.
Harmon, Steven R. *Towards Baptist Catholicity: Essays on Tradition and the Baptist Vision*. Vol. 27. Eugene: Wipf and Stock Publishers, 2006.

Harsch, Lloyd. "Were the First Baptists Sacramentalists?" *Journal for Baptist Theology and Ministry* 6, no. 1 (2009): 25–44.
Hartfeld, Hermann. "Radikalisierung des Christentums Am Beispiel Osteuropas." In *Zeitschrift Für Theologie Und Gemeinde*. Vol. 22. Нюрнберг: Gesellschaft für Freikirchliche Theologie und Publizistik e.V. (GFTP), 2016.
Hartman, Lars. *Into the Name of the Lord Jesus: Baptism in the Early Church*. London: A&C Black, 1997.
Hayden, Roger, ed. *Baptist Union Documents 1948-1977*. London: Baptist Historical Society, 1980.
Haymes, Brian, Ruth Gouldbourne, and Anthony R. Cross. *On Being the Church: Revisioning Baptist Identity*. Vol. 21. Eugene: Wipf and Stock Publishers, 2009.
Hein, Kenneth. *Eucharist and Excommunication: A Study in Early Christian Doctrine and Discipline*. European University Studies: Theology. Vol. 19. Bern: Herbert Lang, 1975.
Henry, Matthew. *An Exposition of All the Books of the Old and New Testaments*. Vol. 6 of 6 vols. Philadelphia: Ed. Barrington, 1806.
Hicks, John Mark. "Ordinance or Sacrament: Both/And Rather Than Either/Or." *Leaven* 22, no. 4 (2014): 204–8.
Hobbs, Herschel H. *The Baptist Faith and Message*. Convention Press, 1971.
Hoffman, Lawrence A. "Jewish Ordination on the Eve of Christianity." *Studia Liturgica Rotterdam* 13, no. 2 – 4 (1979): 11–41.
Holmes, Stephen R. "Towards a Baptist Theology of Ordained Ministry." In *Baptist Sacramentalism*, edited by Anthony R. Cross and Philip E. Thompson, 247–62. Eugene: Wipf and Stock Publishers, 2006
Hudson, H. "Omnipresence." In *The Oxford Handbook of Philosophical Theology*, edited by T. P. Flint and M. Rea. Oxford: Oxford University Press, 2011.
Horevoy, D., and T. Derkach, eds. *Fenomen Onlayn-Prichastiya. Refleksii. Polemika. Perspektivy (The Phenomenon of Online Communion. Reflections. Polemics. Perspectives)*. Kyiv: Fond pamiati Blazhennishoho mytropolyta Volodymyra, 2021.
Hughes, Philip Edgcumbe. "Grace." In *Evangelical Dictionary of Theology*, edited by Walter Elwell. Grand Rapids: Baker Academic, 2001.
Hull, John Howarth Eric. *The Holy Spirit in the Acts of the Apostles*. Cleveland: The World Pub, 1967.
Humphreys, Colin J. *The Mystery of the Last Supper: Reconstructing the Final Days of Jesus*. Cambridge: Cambridge University Press, 2011.
Humphreys, Colin, and Graeme Waddington. "Dating the Crucifixion." *Nature* 306, no. 5945 (1983): 743–46.
———. "Astronomy and the Date of the Crucifixion." In *Chronos, Kairos, Christos: Nativity and Chronological Studies Presented to Jack Finegan*, edited by Jerry Vardaman and Edwin M. Yamauchi, 165–81. University Park: Eisenbrauns, 1989.

Hustad, Donald P. "The Lord's Supper for Baptists: A Spiritual Meal, a Snack, or a Placebo?" *Review & Expositor* 106, no. 2 (2009): 171–87.
Hutton, Rodney R. *Charisma and Authority in Israelite Society*. Minneapolis: Fortress Press, 1994.
Irwin, Brian P. "The Laying on of Hands in 1 Timothy 5:22: A New Proposal." *Bulletin for Biblical Research* 18, no. 1 (2008): 123–29.
Ivanov, Mikhail. *Osnovy Sistematicheskogo Bogosloviya (Basics of Systematic Theology)*. Moscow: Protestant, 2002.
———, ed. *Posobiye Dlya Podgotovki k Vodnomu Kreshcheniyu (Preparation Manual for Water Baptism)*. Moscow: Otdel bogosloviya i katekhizatsyi RS YeKhB, 2005.
———. *Veruyem: Katekhizis Dlya Tserkvey Yevangel'skikh Khristian-Baptistov (We Believe: A Catechism for the Churches of Evangelical Christians-Baptists)*. Moscow: Russian Union of Evangelical Christians-Baptists, Department of theology and catechization, 2010.
Ivanov-Klyshnikov, Vasily Vasilievich. "O Pokayanii (On Repentance)." *Baptist*, no. 45 (1911): 6–7.
———. *Izbrannye Stat'i i Propovedi (Selected Essays and Sermons)*.
James, A. B. *Analogous Uses of Language, Eucharistic Identity, and the "Baptist" Vision*. Studies in Baptist History and Thought. Milton Keynes: Paternoster Press, 2014. https://books.google.com/books?id=2VelBAAAQBAJ.
James, Edwin O. *Sacrifice and Sacrament*. New York: Barnes & Noble, 1962.
Jaubert, Annie. *The Date of the Last Supper*. Staten Island: Alba House, 1965.
Jeremias, Joachim. *Infant Baptism in the First Four Centuries*. London: SCM Press, 1960.
———. *The Eucharistic Words of Jesus*. Translated by Norman Perrin. London: SCM Press, 1966.
———. *The Origins of Infant Baptism: A Further Study in Reply to Kurt Aland*. Eugene: Wipf and Stock Publishers, 2004.
Jeremias Joachim and August Strobel, *Die Briefe an Timotheus und Titus. Der Brief an die Hebräer*. NTD. Göttingen: Vandenhoeck & Ruprecht, 1975.
Jones, Brandon C. *Waters of Promise: Finding Meaning in Believer Baptism*. Eugene: Wipf and Stock Publishers, 2012.
Jones, Ray Carlton, Jr.. "The Lord's Supper and the Concept of Anamnesis." *Word & World* 6, no. 4 (1986): 434–45.
Kargel', Ivan. *Kratkoye Izlozheniye Veroucheniya Evangel'skikh Khristian (A Brief Exposition of the Evangelical Christians' Beliefs)*. St. Petersburg: the Second St. Petersburg Community of Evangelical Christians, 1913.
Karyev, A. V. "Vecherya Gospodnya: Yeyo Ustanovleniye i Znacheniye (The Lord's Supper: Its Institution and Significance)." *Bratskiy Vestnik*, no. 2 (1962): 13–20.
Kavanagh, Aidan. *The Shape of Baptism: The Rite of Christian Initiation*. Vol. 1. Collegeville: Liturgical Press, 1978.

Kaydanovskaya, Anna. "Sovremennyi Teatr: Immersivnyie Postanovki (Perfomans, Promenad, Interaktivnost) i Ikh Vliyaniye Na Preobrazovaniya Teatral'nogo Prostranstva (Contemporary Theatre: Immersive Productions, Performance and Its Influence on Spatial Transformations of Theatrical Structures)." *Architecture and Modern Information Technologies* 42, no. 1 (2018): 212–26.

Keach, Benjamin. *Laying on of Hands upon Baptized Believers, as Such, Proved an Ordinance of Christ*. London, 1698.

———. *The Baptist Catechism*. Philadelphia: P. Brynberg, 1809.

Kelly, Gerard. "Baptism in the Roman Catholic Church." In *Baptism: Historical, Theological, and Pastoral Perspectives* edited by Gordon L. Heath and James D. Dovorak, 26–52. Eugene: Wipf and Stock, 2011.

Kern, Cyprian. *Yevkharistiya (The Eucharist)*. Moscow: Khram Kosmi i Domiana, 2006.

Khrapov, Nikolai. "Dom Bozhyy i Sluzheniye v Nyom (The House of God and Ministry Therein." *Soyuz Tserkvey Yevangel'skikh Khristian-Baptistov* (blog), 1975). http://www.blagovestnik.org/books/00280.htm#5.

Klausner, Joseph. *Jesus of Nazareth: His Life, Times, and Teachings*. London: Macmillan, 1925.

Klawans, Jonathan. "Was Jesus' Last Supper a Seder?" *Bible Review Washington* 17, no. 5 (2001): 24–33.

Klippenstein, Lawrence. "Johann Wieler (1839–1889) Among Russian Evangelicals: A New Source of Mennonites and Evangelicalism in Imperial Russia." *Journal of Mennonite Studies* 5 (1987): 44–60.

Kloha, Jeffrey J. "Koinonia and Life Together in the New Testament." *Concordia Journal* 38, no. 1 (2012): 23–32.

Kolesnikov, Nikolai. *Khristianin, Zhayesh Li Ty, Kak Dolzhno Postupat' v Dome Bozhiyem? (Christian, Do You Know How to Behave in the House of God?)* Blagaya vest'. Vol. 1, 2, 3 vols. Moscow: Blagaya vest', 2001.

Kolesnikov, Nikolai. "Pospeshym k Sovershenstvu (Let Us Hasten to Perfection)," no. 2 (1979): 34–39.

———. "Tserkovnyie Svyashchennodeystviya Evangel'skikh Khristian-Baptistov (Church Sacred Acts of Evangelical Christians-Baptists)." *Russkiy Baptist* (blog). 17 January 2022. http://rusbaptist.stunda.org/svdejstv.htm.

Kolomiytsev, Aleksey. *Pridite, Poklonimsya! (Come, Let Us Worship!)* Slovo blagodati. Kharkiv: Slovo blagodati, 2018.

———. "'Tsel' i Zhacheniye Vodnogo Kreshcheniya (The Purpose and Significance of Water Baptism)." *Slovo Blagodati* (blog). 2014. https://www.slovo.org/ru/resursyi/blog/tsel-i-znachenie-vodnogo-kreshchenia.

Koval'chuk, Ivan. "Shcho Bibliya Kazhe pro Gospodnyu Vecheryu (What the Bible Says about the Lord's Supper)." 23 December 2021. https://ehb.lviv.ua/resursy/statti/30-shcho-bibliia-kazhe-pro-hospodniu-vecheriu.

Kratkaya Evreyskaya Entsyklopediya (*Concise Hebrew Encyclopedia*), vol. 7, col. 587–588. Jerusalem: Keter, 1994.

Kratkoye Veroucheniye Khristian Yevangel'skogo Veroispovedaniya, Priyemlyushchikh Vodnoye Kreshcheniye Po Vere (Imenuyemukh Inogda Baptistami) (*The Concise Exposition of Beliefs of Evangelical Christians Who Accept Water Baptism by Faith [and Are Sometimes Called Baptists]*). Sevastopol': P. A. Kovalyov, 1909.

Kucheryavyy, Andrei. "Obzor Ucheniya o Vechere Gospodnei u Evangel'skikh Khristian-Baptistov (1867–1945) (An Overview of the Doctrine of the Lord's Supper among Evangelical Christians-Baptists [1867–1945])." *Bogomysliye*, no. 16 (2015): 151–67.

Lagrange, Père Marie-Joseph. *L'Evangile de Jésus Christ: Avec La Synopse Évangélique*. Paris: Lethielleux Editions, 2017.

Lalleman, Pieter J., Peter J .Morden, and Anthony R. Cross, eds. *Grounded in Grace: Essays to Honour Ian M. Randall*. Eugene: Wipf and Stock Publishers, 2020.

Leith, John H. *Creeds of the Churches: A Reader in Christian Doctrine from the Bible to the Present*. Louisville: John Knox Press, 1982. https://archive.org/details/creedsofchurches03edunse_f0o7.

Leonard, Bill J. "Salvation and Sawdust: The Rise and Fall of a Baptist Conversion Liturgy." *Baptist History and Heritage* 45, no. 3 (2010): 6–23.

Lillie, Betty Jane. "Koinonia in the New Testament: Integral Dynamic of the Christian Life." *Proceedings* 28 (2008): 55–66.

Lohse, Eduard. *Die Ordination im Spätjudentum und im Neuen Testament*. Berlin: Evangelische Verlagsanstalt Berlin, 1951.

Luchenko, Xenia. "The Digitalization of Worship Practices during the Coronavirus Pandemic in the Context of the Mediatization of Orthodoxy." *State, Religion and Church* 39, no. 1 (2021).

Lumpkin, William Latane. *Baptist Confessions of Faith*. Valley Forge: Judson Press, 1959.

Luther, Martin. *The Large Catechism of Martin Luther*. Translated by Henry Eyster Jacobs. Philadelphia: United Lutheran Publication Society, 1911.

Lyakhu, Viktor. "Bogosluzheniye Kak Sozertsaniye i Uyedinionnaya Molitva (Worship as Contemplation and Secluded Prayer)." In *Tserkov' Vchera, Segodnya i Zavtra (The Church Yesterday, Today, and Tomorrow)*. Cherkassy: Kollokvium, 2014.

MacCulloch, J. A. "Hand." In *Encyclopedia of Religion and Ethic*, VI:492–99. New York: T&T Clark, 1913.

MacDonald, William. *Believer's Bible Commentary*. Nashville: Thomas Nelson, 2016.

Malkov, Piotr Yurievich. "'Ne v Sud ili vo Osuzhdeniye...': svyatyie Ottsy o Dostoynom i Nedostoynom Prichashchenii ('Not into judgment or Condemnation:' The holy Fathers on Worthy and Unworthy Participation in the Communion"). *Vestnik Pravoslavnogo Svyato-Tikhonovskogo*

Gumanitarnogo Universiteta. Seriya 1: Bogosloviye, Filosofiya, Religiovedeniye 24 (2008).

Mamardashvili, Merab, and Aleksandr Piatigorsky. *Simvol i Soznanie: Metaphizicheskiye Rassuzhdeniya o Soznanii, Simvolike i Iazyke (Symbol and Consciousness: Metaphysical Discussions on Consciousness, Symbolism, and Language)*. Moscow: Shkola "Yazyki russkoi kul'tury," 1997.

Manson, Thomas W. "Entry into Membership of the Early Church." *The Journal of Theological Studies* 48, no. 189/190 (1947): 25–33.

Marion, Jean-Luc. "Métaphysique et Phénoménologie: Une Relève Pour La Théologie." In *Le Visible et Le Révéle*, 75–97. Paris: Cerf, 2005.

Marshall, I. Howard. *Last Supper and Lord's Supper*. Vancouver: Regent College Publishing, 1980.

———. *The Pastoral Epistles, The Blackwell Companion to Paul*. Oxford: Wiley-Blackwell, 2011.

Matviyiv, Volodymyr. *Svyashchennodiyi Pastora (The Pastor's Sacred Acts)*. Luts'k: Khrystyyans'ke zhyttya, 2004.

McClendon, James, Jr., *Ethics: Systematic Theology*. Vol. 1. Nashville: Abingdon Press, 2011.

———. *Doctrine: Systematic Theology*. Vol. 2. Nashville: Abingdon Press, 1994.

———. *Witness: Systematic Theology*. Vol. 3. Nashville: Abingdon Press, 2010.

McDonald, William P. "Re-Membering the Body: *The Lord's Supper and Ecclesial Unity in the Free Church Traditions* by Scott W. Bullard, and: *Eucharist and Ecumenism: The Eucharist across the Ages and Traditions* by Owen F. Cummings, and: *God the Spirit: Introducing Pneumatology in Wesleyan and Ecumenical Perspective* by Beth Felker Jones, and: *A Service of Love: Papal Primacy, the Eucharist, and Church Unity* by Paul McPartlan (Review)." *Journal of Ecumenical Studies* 50, no. 3 (2015): 500–502.

McDonnell, Kilian, and George T. Montague. *Christian Initiation and Baptism in the Holy Spirit: Evidence from the First Eight Centuries*. Collegeville: Liturgical Press, 1991.

McGlothlin, William Joseph. *Baptist Confessions of Faith*. American Baptist Publication Society, 1911.

———. "The Laying on of Hands: A Forgotten Chapter in Baptist History." In *Publications of the Kentucky Baptist Historical Society* no. 2, 35–50, edited by W. J. McGlothlin. Louisville: Baptist Book Concern, 1911.

McKinion, Steve. *Life and Practice in the Early Church: A Documentary Reader*. New York: NYU Press, 2001.

McKnight, Scot. *Jesus and His Death: Historiography, the Historical Jesus, and Atonement Theory*. Waco: Baylor University Press, 2005.

Meier, John P. "'Presbyteros' in the Pastoral Epistles." *The Catholic Biblical Quarterly* 35, no. 3 (1973): 323–45.

Michael, Larry J. *Spurgeon on Leadership: Key Insights for Christian Leaders from the Prince of Preachers*. Grand Rapids: Kregel Academic, 2010.
Miller, I.Ya. "O Rukopolozhenii (On the Laying on of Hands)." *Baptist Ukraïny*, no. 8 (1928): 21–23.
Miller, Samuel H. "Reducing the Reality of the Lord's Supper," *Foundations* 1, no. 4 (31 December 1958): 24–29.
Minyakov, D. V. "O Vechere Gospodney (On the Lord's Supper)." *Vestnik Istiny*, no. 1 (1983): 8–10.
Mohyla, Petro (Peter Mogila). *The Orthodox Confession of the Catholic and Apostolic Eastern Church*, translated and edited by Julian Joseph Overbeck. London: Thomas Baker, 1898.
Moltmann, Jurgen. *The Coming of God: Christian Eschatology*. London: SCM Press, 1996.
Moody, Christopher Bryan. "American Baptismal Sacramentalism?" PhD Diss., Southwestern Baptist Theological Seminary, 2006.
Muller, Richard Alfred. *Post-Reformation Reformed Dogmatics: The Rise and Development of Reformed Orthodoxy: Ca. 1520 to ca. 1725*. 4 vols. Grand Rapids: Baker, 2006.
Myshtsyn, V. N. *Ustroystvo Khristianskoy Tserkvi v Pervyye Dva Veka (Internal Structures of the Christian Church in the First Two Centuries)*. Sergiev Posad, 1909.
N.A. "Kto Mozhet Pristupit' k Sv. Vechere? (Who Can Partake of the Holy Supper?)." *Baptist*, no. 3 (1908): 10–11.
Nagirnyak, Aleksandr. "Khronika Dney Bedstviya (A Chronicle of the Times of Trouble)." *Mariupol'skaya Tsentral'naya Tserkov' Yevangel'skikh Khristian-Baptistov (Mariupol Central Church of Evangelical Christians-Baptists)*. 29 September 2022. http://www.domboga.com/index.php/novosti/161-khronika-dnej-bedstviya.
Nesterenko, Maksim. *Institutsyonal'noye pleneniye tserkvi (The Institutional Captivity of the Church)*. Kharkiv: Impress, 2017.
———. "Rossiyskiye Khristiane i Voyna v Ukraïne: Modeli Povedeniya v Kontekste Bibleyskikh Obrazov (Russian Christians and the War in Ukraine: Patterns of Behavior in the Context of Biblical Images)." *Bogomysliye*, no. 32 (2022): 216–43.
Nettles, Thomas. "Baptism as a Symbol of Christ's Saving Work." In *Understanding Four Views on Baptism*. Grand Rapids: Zondervan, 2009.
Newman, Elizabeth. "The Lord's Supper: Might Baptists Accept a Theory of Real Presence?" In *Baptist Sacramentalism*, 1:211–27. Studies in Baptist History and Thought. Carlisle: Paternoster Press, 2003.
Nikitin, Filipp. "Perepiska V.A. Pashkova s Protoiyereyem I.L. Yanyshevym (Correspondence between V.A. Pashkov and Archpriest I. L. Yanyshev)." *Bogomysliye*, no. 23 (2018): 120–45.

Nikolainen, A. T. "Yevkharistiya v Svete Issledovaniy Svyashchennogo Pisaniya Novogo Zaveta (The Eucharist in the Light of Studies of the New Testament Scriptures)." *Bogoslovskiye Trudy (Theological Works)*, no. 11(1973): 188–92.

Noordtzij, A. *Leviticus*. Grand Rapids: Zondervan, 1982.

O'Donnell, Matthew Brook. "Two Opposing Views on Baptism with/by the Holy Spirit and of l Corinthians 12:13: Can Grammatical Investigation Bring Clarity?" In *Baptism, The New Testament and the Church*, edited by Stanley E. Porter and Anthony R. Cross, 311–36. Sheffield: Sheffield Academic Press, 1999.

O'Loughlin, Thomas. *The Didache: A Window on the Earliest Christians*. Grand Rapids: Baker Academic, 2010.

Packer, James I., Anthony R. Cross, and Philip E. Thompson. *Baptist Sacramentalism*. Vol. 5. Eugene: Wipf and Stock Publishers, 2007.

Parratt, John. "An Early Baptist on the Laying on of Hands." *The Baptist Quarterly* 21, no. 7 (1966): 325–27.

———. "The Laying on of Hands in the New Testament: A Re-Examination in the Light of the Hebrew Terminology." *The Expository Times* 80, no. 7 (1969): 210–14. https://doi.org/10.1177/001452466908000705.

Parsons, Talcott. *The Structure of Social Action*. Glencot: The Freee Press, 1949.

Patterson, W. Morgan. "Lord's Supper in Baptist History." *Review & Expositor* 66, no. 1 (1969): 25–34.

Pavlov, Vasiliy. "Kratkoye Veroucheniye Baptistov (A Summary of Baptist Beliefs)." *Baptist*, no. 3 (1908): 1–2.

Payne, Ernest A. "Baptism in Recent Discussion." In *Christian Baptism: A Fresh Attempt to Understand the Rite in Terms of Scripture, History, and Theology* edited by A. Gilmore, 15–24. London: Lutterworth, 1959.

———. "Baptists and the Laying on of Hands." *Baptist Quarterly* 15, no. 5 (1954): 203–15.

———. "Baptists and Christian Initiation," *Baptist Quarterly* 26, no. 4 (1975): 147–57.

Pazina, Lyudmila Olegovna Pazina. *Tipy real'nosti i ih gnoseologicheskij status (The Types of Reality and Their Gnoseological Status)*. Rostov-on-Don: DGTU, 2012.

Pearson, Brook W. R. "Baptism and Initiation in the Cult of Isis and Sarapis." In *Baptism, the New Testament and the Church: Historical and Contemporary Studies in Honour of R. E. O. White*, edited by Stanley E. Porter and Anthony R. Cross, 42–62. Sheffield: Sheffield Academic Press, 1999.

Pedersen, Johannes. *Israel: Its Life and Culture*. Vol. 1. London: Oxford University Press, 1926.

Petersen, Anders Klostergaard. "Rituals of Purification, Rituals of Initiation: Phenomenological, Taxonomical and Culturally Evolutionary Reflections." In *Ablution, Initiation, and Baptism: Late Antiquity, Early Judaism, and Early Christianity*, edited by David Hellholm, Tor Vegge, Øyvind Norderval, and

Christer Hellholm, 3–40. Beiheft Zur Zeitschrift Für Die Neutestamentliche Wissenschaft Und Die Kunde Der Älteren Kirche 176. Berlin: Walter de Gruyter, 2011.
Peterson, David G. *Engaging with God: A Biblical Theology of Worship*. Grand Rapids: Eerdmans, 1992.
Pitre, Brant. *Jesus and the Last Supper*. Grand Rapids: Eerdmans, 2017.
Plato. *Phaedrus*. Translated by Robin Waterfield. Oxford World's Classics. London: Oxford University Press, 2002.
Poirier, John C. "Spirit-Gifted Callings in the Pauline Corpus Part I: The Laying on of Hands." *Journal of Biblical and Pneumatological Research* 1 (2009): 83–99.
"Polozheniye o Soyuze Yevangel'Skikh Khristian i Baptistov (The Regulations of the Union of Evangelical Christians and Baptists)." *Bratskiy Vestnik (Brotherly Herald)*, no. 1 (1945): 3–5.
Porter, Stanley E., and Anthony R. Cross. *Dimensions of Baptism: Biblical and Theological Studies*. Vol. 234. London: Bloomsbury Publishing, 2002.
Prat, Ferdinand. *Jésus Christ: Sa Vie, Sa Doctrine, Son Oeuvre*. Paris: G. Beauchesne et ses fils, 1933.
Prokhanov, Ivan. *Izlozheniye Yevangel'skoy Very Ili Veroucheniye Evangel'skikh Khristian (An Exposition of the Evangelical Faith or Doctrines of Evangelical Christians)*. St. Petersburg: Khrystyanyn, 1922.
Prokhorov, Aleksey. *Kipyashchiy Kotiol Iyeremiyi (Jeremiah's Boiling Cauldron)*. Moscow: Blagovestnik, 2014.
Prokhorov, Constantine. *Russian Baptists and Orthodoxy: 1960–1990: A Comparative Study of Theology; Liturgy; and Traditions*. Carlisle: Langham Academic, 2014.
Quarles, Charles L. "Ordinance or Sacrament: Is the Baptist View of the Ordinances Truly Biblical?" *Journal for Baptist Theology and Ministry* 1, no. 1 (2003): 47–57.
Rainbow, Jonathan H. "Confessor Baptism: The Baptismal Doctrine of the Early Anabaptists." *American Baptist Quarterly* 8, no. 4 (1989): 276–90.
Ratzinger, Joseph Cardinal. *Joseph Ratzinger Collected Works: Theology of the Liturgy*. San Francisco: Ignatius Press, 2016.
Rawlings, Harold G. *Basic Baptist Beliefs: An Exposition of Key Biblical Doctrines*. Springfield: 21st Century Press, 2005. https://books.google.com.ua/books?id=hUOwAAAACAAJ.
Repenko, Veronika. "Interaktivnost' i Immersivnost' v Media: Skhodstva i Razlichiya (Interactivity and Immersiveness in Media: Similarities and Differences)," in Mass-media Rossii i Zarubezhnykh Stran (Mass media in Russia and Abroad) (Moscow: Universitet Druzhby Narodov, 2020), 459–64.
Reshetnikov, Yuriy, and Sergii Sannikov. *Obzor Istorii Evangel'sko-Baptistskogo Bratstva d Ukraïne (A Survey of the History of Evangelical-Baptist Brotherhood in Ukraine)*. Odesa: Bogomysliye, 2000.

Robinson, H. Wheeler. "The Nature and Character of Christian Sacramental Theory and Practice." *Baptist Quarterly* 10, no. 8 (1941): 411–20.

———. "The Place of Baptism in Baptist Churches of Today." *Baptist Quarterly* 1, no. 5 (1923): 209–18.

Roberts, Alexander, James Donaldson, Allan Menzies, and Arthur Cleveland Coxe, eds. *The Apostolic Fathers, Justin Martyr, Irenaeus.* Vol. 1. of Ante-Nicene Fathers: *The Writings of the Fathers down to AD 325.* Christian Literature Publishing Co, 1885.

Rodes, Robert E., Jr.. "On Validity and Invalidity of Sacraments." *Theological Studies* 42, no. 4 (1981): 580–600.

Rogers, Cleon L. *The New Linguistic and Exegetical Key to the Greek New Testament.* Grand Rapids: Zondervan, 1998.

Romanyuk, Ivan. *Tserkovne Slyzhinnya (Church Ministry).* Rivne: Dyatlyk M, 2017.

Rowley, H. H. "The Meaning of Sacrifice in the OT." In *From Moses to Qumran.* London: Lutterworth Press, 1964.

Ruckstuhl, Eugen.. *Die Chronologie Des Letzten Mahles Und Des Leidens Jesu.* Köln: Benziger, 1963.

Rust, Eric Charles. "Theology of the Lord's Supper." *Review & Expositor* 66, no. 1 (1969): 35–44.

Sammons, Peter. *Reprobation and God's Sovereignty: Recovering a Biblical Doctrine.* Grand Rapids: Kregel Academic, 2022.

Sanders, Paul S. "John Wesley and Baptismal Regeneration." *Religion in Life* 23 (1954): 591.

Sannikov, Sergii, ed. *Istoriya Baptizma (The History of Baptist Movement).* Vol. 1. Odesa: Bogomisliye, 1996.

———. *Kreshcheniye Dukhom i Dary Dukhovnyye (Spirit Baptism and Spiritual Gifts.* Moscow: Bibleyskaya Liga, 2013.

———. *Znaki Prisutstviya: Vodnoye Kreshcheniye (The Signs of Presence: Water Baptism).* Vol. 1 of 3 vols. Kyiv: Dukh i Litera, 2019.

———. *Znaki Prisutstviya: Vecherya Gospodnya (The Signs of Presence: The Lord's Supper).* Vol. 2 of 3 vols. Kyiv: Dukh i Litera, 2023.

Sansom, Michael C. "Laying on of Hands in the Old Testament." *The Expository Times* 94, no. 11 (1983): 323–26.

Savinskiy, S. N. *Istoriya Evangel'skikh Khristian-Baptistov Ukraïny, Rossii, Belorussii, 1867–1917 (A History of Evangelical Christians-Baptists in Ukraine, Russia, and Belorussia, 1867–1917).* St. Petersburg: Bibliya Dlya Vsekh, 2001.

Sazonova, A. "Binarnyye Oppozitsii Kontsepta 'Arm' v Yazycheskom Sakral'nom Prostranstve (Binary Oppositions of the 'Arm' Concept in the Pagan Sacred Space [Based on the Modern German Language)." *Vestnik Irkutskogo Gosudarstvennogo Lingvisticheskogo Universiteta (The Irkutsk State Linguistic University Philological Review)* 22, no. 1 (2013): 123–30.

Schillebeeckx, Edward. *Christ the Sacrament of the Encounter with God*. New York: Sheed and Ward, 1963.

Schlonkin, Viktor. "Tainstva Yevangel'skikh Khristian-Baptistov (The Sacraments of Evangelical Christians-Baptists)." *Russkiy Baptist* (blog). 20 February 2021. http://www.rusbaptist.stunda.org/tainstva.htm.

Schmemann, Alexander. *The Eucharist: Sacrament of the Kingdom*. Translated by Paul Kachur. Crestwood: St. Vladimir's Seminary Press, 1987.

———. "Sobraniye Statey 1947–1983 (The Collection of Essays, 1947–1983)." In *"Mir Kak Tainstvo" (The World as Sacrament)*. Moscow: Russkiy Put', 2009.

Schneider, S. "Glaubensmangel in Korinth. Eine neue Deutung der 'Schwachen, Kranken, Schlafenden' in 1 Kor 11:30." *Filologia Neotestamentaria* 9 (1996): 3–19.

Schreiner, Thomas R. "Baptism in the Epistles: An Initiation Rite for Believers." In *Believer's Baptism: Sign of the New Covenant in Christ*, edited by Thomas R. Schreiner and Shawn Wright, 67–96. Nashville: B&H Academic, 2006.

Schweitzer, Albert. *The Quest of the Historical Jesus: A Critical Study of Its Progress from Reimarus to Wrede*. London: A & C Black, 1910.

Searle, Joshua T. *Theology after Christendom: Forming Prophets for a Post-Christian World*. Eugene: Wipf and Stock Publishers, 2018.

Shatrov, Piotr. "Deyaniya Svyatukh Apostolov(The Acts of the Apostles)." *Bratskiy Vestnik*, no. 4 (1984): 23–27.

Sheppy, Paul. "Penance." In *Baptist Sacramentalism 2*, vol. 25, edited by Anthony R. Cross and Philip Thompson, 117–34. Eugene: Wipf and Stock Publishers, 2009.

Sibanda, Jabulani. "Why Is the Doctrine and Experience of Holiness Important?" In *Africa Speaks: An Anthology of the Africa Nazarene Theology Conference 2003* edited by Linda Braaten, 112–16. Nairobi: Africa Nazarene Publications, 2003.

Sipko, Yu.K. "Kreshcheniye i Vecherya (Baptism and the Lord's Supper)." *Rossiyskiy Soyuz YeKhB (Russian Union of Evangelical Christians-Baptists)* (blog). 21 December 2021. https://baptist.org.ru/read/article/117005.

Smith, Gordon T., ed. *The Lord's Supper: Five Views*. Downers Grove: IVP Academic, 2010.

Smith, A.J. *The Making of the 1963 Baptist Faith and Message*. Eugene: Wipf and Stock Publishers, 2008.

Solovyov, Vladimir. *The Philosophical Principles of Integral Knowledge*. Translated by Valeria Z. Nollan. Grand Rapids: Wm. B. Eerdmans Publishing, 2008.

Songulashvili, Malkhaz. *Evangelical Christian Baptists of Georgia: The History and Transformation of a Free Church Tradition*. Waco: Baylor University Press, 2015.

Southern Baptist Convention. "The Baptist Faith and Message." Accessed 18 July 2025. http://www.sbc.net/bfm2000/bfm2000.asp.

Spadaro, Antonio. *Cybertheology: Thinking Christianity in the Era of the Internet*. New York: Fordham University Press, 2014.

Spurgeon, Charles H. *Baptismal Regeneration*. Minneapolis: Curiosmith, 2014.

———. *Till He Come*. Pasadena: Pilgrim Pub, 1971.
St. Athanasius Orthodox Academy, ed. *The Orthodox Study Bible*. Nashville: Thomas Nelson, 2008.
Stefanovich, Pavel. "Dobro Pozhalovat v Onlayn-Tserkov' (Welcome to the Online Church)." *Bogomysliye*, no. 27 (2020): 151–67.
Stein, Robert H. "Baptism and Becoming a Christian in the New Testament." *Southern Baptist Journal of Theology* 2, no. 1 (1998): 6–17.
Stott, John R. W. "The Evangelical Doctrine of Baptism." *Churchman* 112, no. 1 (1998): 47–59.
Strack, Hermann L., and Paul Billerbeck. *Kommentar Zum Neuen Testament Aus Talmud Und Midrasch: Das Evangelium Nach Matthäus*. Vol. 2. München: CH Beck, 1924.
Strauch, Alexander. *Biblical Eldership: Restoring the Eldership to Its Rightful Place in the Church*. Littleton: Lewis and Roth, 1997.
Sullivan, Francis A. "The Laying on of Hands in Christian Tradition." In *Spirit and Renewal: Essays in Honor of J. Rodman Williams*, edited by Mark Wilson, 42–54. Journal of Pentecostal Theology Supplement Series 5. Sheffield: Sheffield Academic Press, 1994.
Sutcliff, John. "The Ordinance of the Supper Considered: The Circular Letter from the Ministers and Messengers of the Several Baptist Churches of the Northamptonshire Association." *Baptist History Homepage* (blog). Accessed 18 July 2025. http://baptisthistoryhomepage.com/1803clbritish.html.
Thiselton, Anthony C. *The First Epistle to the Corinthians: A Commentary on the Greek Text*. Vol. 7. Grand Rapids: Eerdmans, 2000.
Thompson, D. M. *Baptism, Church and Society in Modern Britain: From the Evangelical Revival to Baptism, Eucharist and Ministry*. Studies in Christian History and Thought. Eugene: Wipf and Stock Publishers, 2007.
Thompson, Philip E. "Baptists and Liturgy – the Very Idea!" *Review & Expositor* 100, no. 3 (2003): 317–26. https://doi.org/10.1177/003463730310000302.
———. "Sacraments and Religious Liberty: From Critical Practice to Rejected Infringement." In *Baptist Sacramentalism*, edited by Philip E. Thompson and Anthony R. Cross, 36–54. Eugene: Wipf and Stock Publishers, 2006.
Thyophylact of Bulgaria. "Tolkovaniye Na Yevangeliye Ot Ioanna (An Interpretation of John's Gospel)." *Azbuka Very* (blog), 12 January 2024. https://azbyka.ru/otechnik/Feofilakt_Bolgarskij/tolkovanie-na-evangelie-ot-ioanna/3.
Tipei, John Fleter. "The Laying on of Hands in the New Testament." PhD Diss., University of Sheffield, 2000.
Tkachenko, Rostislav. "Bellum Justum or War for the Sake of Peace: The Christian Theory of Just War from Antiquity to the Present." *Bogomyslie* 32, no. 1 (2022): 105–54.
Trent, H. W. "Ourselves and the Ordinances." *Baptist Quarterly* 17, no. 1 (1957): 10–22.

Tuck, William Powell. *Our Baptist Tradition*. Macon: Smyth & Helwys Publishing, 1993.

Turlac, Oleg. "Yevkharistiya i Ekkleziologiya (The Eucharist and Ecclesiology)." *Put' Bogopoznaniya (Path to Theological Knowledge)*, no. 4 (1998): 125–47.

Turner, D. *A Modest Plea for Free Communion at the Lord's Table: Particularly Between the Baptists and Poedobaptists. In a Letter to a Friend* (J. Johnson, 1772).

Uchbova Rada, (Educational Council of the All-Ukrainian Union of Churches of Evangelical Christians-Baptists AUCECB). *Vyznannia Viry Yevangel's'kykh Khrystyian-Baptystiv Ta Praktyka Khrystyians'kogo Zhyttia i Slyzhinnia (The Confession of Faith of Evangelical Christians-Baptists and the Practice of Christian Life and Ministry)*. Kyiv: AUCECB, 2000.

Van Dam, Cornelis. *The Elder: Today's Ministry Rooted in All of Scripture*. Phillipsburg: P & R Publishing, 2009.

Van Roo, William A. *The Christian Sacrament*. Rome: Ed. Pontificia Univ. Gregoriana, 1992.

Vander Zee, Leonard J. *Christ, Baptism and the Lord's Supper: Recovering the Sacraments for Evangelical Worship*. Downers Grove: InterVarsity Press, 2004.

Vanhoozer, K. J. *Is There a Meaning in This Text?: The Bible, the Reader, and the Morality of Literary Knowledge*. Grand Rapids: Zondervan Academic, 2009.

Vedder, Henry Clay. *Balthasar Hubmaier, the Leader of the Anabaptists*. New York: G.P. Putnam's Sons, 1905.

"Veroucheniye Evangel'skikh Khristian-Baptistov (Beliefs of Evangelical Christians-Baptists)." *Bratskiy Vestnik*, no. 4 (1985): 30–49.

Veroucheniye Russkikh Evangel'skikh Khristian-Baptistov (The Beliefs of the Russian Evangelical Christians-Baptists). Rostov-on-Don: Izdaniye Russkikh Baptistov, 1906.

Vins, Yakov. *Nashy Baptistskiye Princypy (Our Baptist Principles)*. Harbin: L. M. Abramovich, 1924.

Vischer, Georg. "The Eucharist-Ritual and Reality: Towards a Meaningful Practice of the Lord's Supper." *Andover Newton Quarterly* 17, no. 3 (1977): 201–12.

Walker, Michael John. *Baptists at the Table: The Theology of the Lord's Supper Amongst English Baptists in the Nineteenth Century*. Didcot: Baptist Historical Society, 1992.

Wallace, Daniel B. *Greek Grammar beyond the Basics: An Exegetical Syntax of the New Testament*. Grand Rapids: Zondervan, 1996.

Waterworth, James, trans. *The Canons and Decrees of the Sacred and Oecumenical Council of Trent*. London: C. Dolman, 1848.

Whitaker, E. C. *Documents of the Baptismal Liturgy*. New ed. London: SPCK Publishing, 1970.

White, Reginald Ernest Oscar. *The Biblical Doctrine of Initiation: A Theology of Baptism and Evangelism*. Grand Rapids: Eerdmans, 1960.

Whitehouse, Michael Patrick. "Manus Impositio: The Initiatory Rite of Handlaying in the Churches of Early Western Christianity." PhD Diss., University of Notre Dame, 2008.
Winter, E. P. "The Lord's Supper. Admission and Exclusion among the Baptists of the Seventeenth Century." *Baptist Quarterly* 17, no. 6 (1958.): 267–81.
Witherington Ben, III. *Making a Meal of It: Rethinking the Theology of the Lord's Supper*. Waco: Baylor University Press, 2007.
Wright, Ben. *Slavoj Žižek: The Reality of the Virtual*. Documentary, 2004.
Yates, John C. "Role of the Holy Spirit in the Lord's Supper." *Churchman* 105, no. 4 (1991): 350–59.
Worgul, George S. "Root Metaphors and Sacramental Presence in a Postmodern Age." *Questions Liturgiques (1971)* 81, no. 3–4 (2000): 184–97.
World Council of Churches Commission on Faith. *Baptism, Eucharist and Ministry*. Vol. 111 of *Faith and Order*. Geneva: World Council of Churches, 1982.
Zaibel', Aleksandr. *Tserkov' Iisusa: Neuzheli Podvergnetsya Obolshcheniyu v Posledneye Vremya? (Jesus' Church: Will It Be Deceived in the End Times?)*. Moscow: Blagovestnik, 1994.
Zhabotinskiy, Yevgeniy. "Prosheniye Ivana Ryaboshapki (Ivan Ryaboshapka's Plea)." *Bogomysliye*, no. 19 (2016): 125–43.
Zhidkov, Mikhail. "Vodnoye Kreshcheniye i Vecherya Gospodnya (Water Baptism and the Lord's Supper)." *Bratskiy Vestnik*, no. 2 (1975): 52–60.
Zweck, Glen. "Why Did the Issue of Indulgences Trigger the Reformation?" In *Lord Jesus Christ, Will You Not Stay: Essays in Honor of Ronald Feuerhahn on the Occasion of His Sixty-Fifth Birthday*. St. Louis: Concordia Publishing House, 2002.

Langham Literature and its imprints are a ministry of Langham Partnership.

Langham Partnership is a global fellowship working in pursuit of the vision God entrusted to its founder John Stott –

> *to facilitate the growth of the church in maturity and Christ-likeness through raising the standards of biblical preaching and teaching.*

Our vision is to see churches in the Majority World equipped for mission and growing to maturity in Christ through the ministry of pastors and leaders who believe, teach and live by the word of God.

Our mission is to strengthen the ministry of the word of God through:
- nurturing national movements for biblical preaching
- fostering the creation and distribution of evangelical literature
- enhancing evangelical theological education

especially in countries where churches are under-resourced.

Our ministry

Langham Preaching partners with national leaders to nurture indigenous biblical preaching movements for pastors and lay preachers all around the world. With the support of a team of trainers from many countries, a multi-level programme of seminars provides practical training, and is followed by a programme for training local facilitators. Local preachers' groups and national and regional networks ensure continuity and ongoing development, seeking to build vigorous movements committed to Bible exposition.

Langham Literature provides Majority World preachers, scholars and seminary libraries with evangelical books and electronic resources through publishing and distribution, grants and discounts. The programme also fosters the creation of indigenous evangelical books in many languages, through writer's grants, strengthening local evangelical publishing houses, and investment in major regional literature projects, such as one volume Bible commentaries like *The Africa Bible Commentary* and *The South Asia Bible Commentary*.

Langham Scholars provides financial support for evangelical doctoral students from the Majority World so that, when they return home, they may train pastors and other Christian leaders with sound, biblical and theological teaching. This programme equips those who equip others. Langham Scholars also works in partnership with Majority World seminaries in strengthening evangelical theological education. A growing number of Langham Scholars study in high quality doctoral programmes in the Majority World itself. As well as teaching the next generation of pastors, graduated Langham Scholars exercise significant influence through their writing and leadership.

To learn more about Langham Partnership and the work we do visit **langham.org**

www.ingramcontent.com/pod-product-compliance
Lightning Source LLC
Chambersburg PA
CBHW071815230426
43670CB00013B/2464